This Volume is

1621

of a privately printed, limited edition

of

THIS WONDERFUL WORLD OF TROUT

This Wonderful World of Trout

Charles K. Fox

Art Work by Fred Everett and Ned Smith

FOXCREST

CARLISLE, PENNSYLVANIA

Library of Congress Catalog Card Number: 63-9745

Printed and bound in the United States of America
by THE TELEGRAPH PRESS, *established* 1831
Harrisburg, Pennsylvania

This
volume
is dedicated to
TROUT UNLIMITED
and its magnificent
objectives

ACKNOWLEDGMENTS

A MINOR portion of this book is quoted material. The author wishes to thank the editors of the following magazines for reprint permissions: Arnold Gingrich, *Esquire;* Art Tutt, *The Fisherman's Magazine;* Bill Rae, *Outdoor Life;* Joe Penfold, *Outdoor America;* George Forrest, *Pennsylvania Angler;* Dave Fisher, *The Pennsylvania Sportsman;* Ted Kesting, *Sports Afield* and Ken Peterson, *Trout Unlimited.*

The author also expresses gratitude to two outdoor men, and scholars, Dr. Henry M. Stebbins and Ernest G. Schwiebert, Jr., for editorial assistance and advice rendered.

And the author wishes to place a star in the crown of a girl named Gladferd, a fishing widow.

FOREWORD

GREAT ANGLERS are spawned and shaped on difficult rivers. Shy trout in the placid crystalline chalkstreams of England and France were the catalysts for our fly-fishing tradition. Such rivers were the inspiration for the 15th Century innovations of Dame Juliana Berners, the classic writings of Walton and Cotton, and the 19th Century dry-fly theories of Halford and Marryatt.

Like the chalkstream shrines of Europe, the lovely LeTort in southern Pennsylvania has silk-smooth currents and hyperselective trout as its challenging enigma. And like the chalkstreams, the LeTort has spawned its own circle of accomplished anglers. The LeTort regulars form a Round Table of great fishermen who practice their sport according to a strict code of chivalry. Charles K. Fox, the author of this volume and an angler of great reputation, is the acknowledged Dean of the LeTort. Vincent C. Marinaro, the celebrated angler-perfectionist who authored the classic *Modern Dry-Fly Code*, is the Merlin among the LeTort devotees. Ross Trimmer, the fly-fishing tobacco-chewing former police officer, is the undisputed court jester. There are others.

The love these acolytes have for their little river is almost incredible, and that love can be seen in every line of *This Wonderful World of Trout*. Men like Charlie Fox scorn the supermarket scramble for stocked fish, because they know the truck-dazed hatchery trout are shabby substitutes for real fishing.

And the wild stream-spawned brown trout of the LeTort have caused a modern innovation in our time. Their selective feeding to minuscule terrestrial insects was the contemporary catalyst that resulted in a whole series of flies as important to American anglers as the 19th Century development of dry-fly fishing in England and America. Modern anglers may not know the LeTort and its small circle of experts, but one day their trout-fishing heirs will rank the Fox-Marinaro collaboration on the LeTort with the Halford-Marryatt collaboration on the 19th Century currents of the Itchen and the Test. Their talents are already legend among those who have fished with them on their river.

This little volume is the testimony of a master angler, and the rich record of his river. Its pages echo a feeling for trout and trout water that tell much about its author. Charlie Fox is a priceless companion and friend, both on and off the stream, and one day anglers everywhere will know his hallowed place in the growing legend of LeTort Spring Run.

ERNEST G. SCHWIEBERT JR

Elm Ridge Road
Princeton, New Jersey

CONTENTS

PART I—FLY FISHING AND TROUT, REALITY

PART II—RISING TROUT, LEGEND

Fly Fishing and Trout—Reality

One fine May evening, obscured a bit now by the passage of the decades, the veil of mystery was stripped before my bugging eyes from what was then the mystic angling practice known as "dry fly fishing." As the Musconetcong River tugged at an oddity of those times, a pair of fishing waders, some surface feeding trout refused with disdain a cast of three time-tested wet flies. In desperation I finally disconnected them and attached to the leader's end a single fluffy creation (also on a snell) which a sporting goods dealer at Easton, across the Delaware, sold with persuasion. "Quill Gordon," he called it, "named after the Father of the floating fly in America."

I turned about and fished upstream. It drifted over trout number 1. There was a slurp, then a hooked fish. Here was a performance which was logical, fascinating, ever so thrilling and beautiful to behold; and, wonders of wonders, the use of the dry fly was not confined to the mythological angler. This pale, skinny, 7-inch brook trout was next to the grandest fish I ever landed, the premier being the 4-inch chub on my initial outing as a 5-year old.

At the same time the then-venerable REVIEW OF REVIEWS reported, "should a census of sports be taken, the angler might find himself in first place."

The die was cast. Henceforth it would be dry fly fishing for rising trout whenever and wherever possible by a dedicated member of the great clan.

The college year terminated and what transpired that summer back home in the limestone streams of the Cumberland Valley was the bewitching sort of thing which has its way of making angling a way of life.

Other things began to unfold, too, but the image was like the face in the fog compared with the conclusive Jersey incident. This sport, it was found, has two parts, the other half of angling not having to do with actual catching. Because it is difficult to observe habit, appraise habitat, decipher cycles,

[1]

measure carrying capacity, estimate balance between natural reproduction and rate of growth, ad infinitum, considerable time and observation is involved. And, too, it takes our most valuable commodity, time, to research the amazing and wonderful literature dealing with the most scientific sport of all, fly fishing. Then there are the matters of experimentation and correlation. The pages of the first section of this volume constitute reality in the life of an inveterate angler.

CHAPTER 1

History of Dry-Fly Tactics

History is a basic interest of *homo sapiens,* the thinker; and specialized history and tradition are of particular interest to the hobbyist. No sport has finer literature than angling, and that dealing with the dry fly features the work of those who expressed themselves extremely well. If a founder and anniversary date can be established, we turn to page 132 of *The Vademecum of Fly Fishing for Trout* by G. P. R. Pulman, 1851 edition:

"Let a dry fly be substituted for the wet one, the line switched a few times through the air to throw off its superabundant moisture, a judicious cast made just above the rising fish, and the fly allowed to float towards and over them, and the chances are ten to one that it is seized as readily as the living insect. This dry fly, we must remark, should be an imitation of the natural fly on which the fish are feeding."

In view of the facts that insects float and trout feed on the surface, it might seem strange that the wet fly preceded the dry by centuries; however, the deterrent was the matter of making the fly float. Once it was discovered that the imitation could be dried sufficiently in the air by "false casting," to insure buoyancy, the problem was solved. Francis Francis, reported in 1867 in his work, *A Book of Angling,* that the dry fly was greatly used in southern waters.

From the year 1880 to the present day there is documentary record by anglers of distinction which most certainly is definitive in nature and unique in the magnificence of expression. In the wake of the open book are names which have become a byword to anglers. These giants deserve to command respect but it should also be realized that the waters they fished were a vital developmental factor. Had there been no Marryatt and Halford in England, and no Gordon and LaBranche in America, there would have been other patron saints for the present-day vast array of disciples.

The cradle of the dry fly was the Hampshire district of England, the champions of it the members of the Fly Fisher's Club of London. The inefficiency of the wet fly on the free-rising brown trout of the fabulous chalk streams was most apparent. The efficiency of the dry-fly method won angling hearts.

[3]

George Selwyn Marryatt was a creative fly-tyer and master angler of the Itchen around Winchester. In the minds of some he is the greatest who ever drew breath. However, he produced no writings and was cut down at the age of 56. Years later another of the hierarchy of anglerdom, Skues, wrote that Marrayatt was "universally regarded as the prince of fly-fishers, fly-dressers and waterside naturalists." But he left his indelible mark by indirect means. The diadem was passed to a fishing companion, Frederic M. Halford, to proclaim the dictum—the effective Marryatt approach and fly patterns.

The first of Halford, the prophet's, books under the Marryatt influence, *Floating Flies and How to Dress Them*, 1880, formalized procedure and pattern. Great significance was attached to natural drift over the spot of the rise with a well tied imitation of the natural—form, size and color being all important.

Anglers funneled into the club quarters after trips to the Test, the Itchen and other chalk streams to compare notes, exchange ideas and to secure or fabricate flies closely relating to the insect of the moment. Actually their philosophy was to tie so "trout do not look for differences but rather for similarities." Deception had captivated their fancies. The great mind of the originator had brought into being the new approach; the followers made what they considered important changes, but the genius of the originators, Marryatt-Halford, remained.

Contributions stemmed from various club members: H. S. Hall, with the help of Marryatt, brought into being the eyed hook on light wire, and Major Turle a fine leader knot for it. The Hardy brothers improved reels. H. P. Hawksley and Nathan Durfie Coggeshall, an American-born Londoner who joined club ranks, added to the caliber of available fly lines and light rods. Dr. E. A. Barton, in a class with Brady of Civil War times, produced classic prints of rising trout and rise-forms from his negatives. The Frenchman, Elbie Bouglé, also a club member, refined reels and rods. Marryatt designed fly-tying equipment.

There developed an attitude that old-type, wet-fly fishing was both outmoded and injurious. This was based on more than sophistication. It was believed that a sunken fly indiscriminately cast quartering downstream scratched young trout and put down the larger, more shy fish, thus discouraging the cherished free-rising tendency; and, furthermore, it robbed its employer of the anticipation of the rise and the sight of the take. If there was a weakness it was the belief that finality had been achieved.

The rich flat water, so conducive to aquatic life, produced

[4]

great hatches which in turn stimulated surface-feeding activity. Rate of growth was great, carrying capacity tremendous. Natural reproduction was high in the gravel sections. However, there were demands in some waters which made advisable the planting of artificially propagated trout.

Restrictions were not a matter of governmental regulation. Private owners, inn keepers and clubs set the seasons and limits they decreed best under the existing conditions. Esteemed river keepers devoted their lives to the improvement and refinement of trout fishing, the most famous of these being William J. Lunn, 45 years at the Houghton Club on the Test, and Humphry Priddis, 33 years the keeper of fabulous Old Bardge at Winchester on the Itchen. Each stream section was, and still is, treated as an individual problem.

There was, however, one common problem: dense aquatic vegetation. The rich, flat alkaline environment produced confounding weed beds, mainly elodea, introduced by accident and called "the curse from America." To cope with the obnoxious and complicated situation, weed-cutting days were instigated and cutting took place thrice yearly. The crisp elodea was mowed with a blade like that of a crosscut saw, a rope attached to each end. When drawn back and forth downstream, it clipped the weed, which rolled to the surface and floated away. The operation was done in a patch pattern to produce the most interesting fishing possible. With everyone cutting the same day and with available manpower to remove the crop where it clogged the stream, the operation was brief, simple and effective.

The predominating and famous hatches of flies are: the blue-winged olive (b.w.o.), an ephemerid; pale watery dun, another drake; the Mayfly, similar to the American green drake; the Welshman's button, a caddis and the cinnamon sedge. The duns of these and other hatches emerge pretty well on schedule followed a day or so by the fall of the spinners. Day by day there is usually surface activity in one degree or another, a hatch and rise being the rule rather than the exception.

Not just anyone fished for trout just anywhere. It was a membership, invitation, clientele or ownership proposition; but anyone who generated sufficient enthusiasm to pay for the privilege could—and still can—find an inn or club to fit his pocketbook, or a kindred spirit to serve as host or benefactor. The common bond has always been interest, not caste.

As time progressed, more true-to-nature imitations were developed for specific hatches, finer silk-worm gut was drawn,

[5]

and improved split-bamboo rods came from across the Atlantic. Halford and the dry-fly school remained unchallenged for several decades. It was standard practice to proceed slowly upstream searching the surface with the eye, not a fly, for a good surface-feeding fish. When each worthy trout in turn was located, angling was a meticulous business; and, unfortunately, it was usually windy, a situation which popularized the sturdy rod. Deception is not simplicity, for involved are skill and craftsmanship. The great commercial fly-tyer with the amazing group of patrons was George Holland, who subsequently moved to streamside Winchester.

Talented club members contributed findings relative to entomology, imitation, equipment and technique, much of which has been recorded. Books and articles in the periodicals unfolded the developing picture. From the literary standpoint angling literature reached its zenith in this, the golden age of the dry-fly renaissance.

Across the Atlantic there fished a frail little man who angled for a different species of trout in a different type of environment. Theodore Gordon, a native of the state of New York, operated in a rustic setting where the stony fast-dropping streams were inhabited by brook trout. Like Marryatt he left no book or articles; however, there was correspondence—salvaged letters to and from Skues. Thus it was that the English dry fly found its way to America to be cast on the Beaverkill by Gordon. The father of the floating imitation in this country successfully applied his new craft to the slicks, glides and flats where the rises of brook trout occurred. But there was a second revelation: The hungry trout of the lean freestone waters would snatch at an isolated fly. Even when there was no rise of trout it was practical to fish with the dry fly. Gordon's fishing took him to other New York streams; and there is documentary evidence that he sought out and found some limestone water, namely Spring Creek and Big Spring in Pennsylvania.

It was estimated by Emlyn Gill that directly prior to the time he produced the first American work on the subject, *Practical Dry Fly Fishing*, 1912, there were less than 100 adherents in the United States and very few fishermen knew the meaning of the term dry fly. Gill, with two great assets, was well prepared to introduce formally this high form of angling to the wet-fly anglers of his country: He was the possessor of a keen and studious mind, being well read; and he, on occasion, fished with an extremely talented fellow, one George LaBranche. Gill had a

[6]

complaint—half a century ago: there was no available entomological data relative to American aquatic insects.

By comparing English reporting with his own stream observation it was evident that the hatches on the waters he fished were different and less frequent than those on the English chalk streams, yet he could catch trout on the dry fly when there was no rise. In fact he corresponded with the aging Halford about these matters. To him a fly was impressionistic and when there was nothing to imitate, exact imitation is academic. He visualized the water in graph-paper pattern and proceeded to float a fly in the likely places in each block starting with the closest and reaching out from there. Checkerboard casting was his answer to fishing the water well.

The first purist in this country, a dedicated angler who observed through the sharpest eyes you ever saw, the possessor of an analytical mind and coordinated reflexes, chose to wait until 1914 to produce a compendium of his trout fishing method. George M. L. LaBranche fished the great trout rivers of the East as well as some of the English chalk streams. Favorites were the Broadheads in Pennsylvania, the Neversink and Beaverkill in New York and the Itchen and Kennett in southern Britain. For good measure he fathered and popularized the fishing of the dry fly for Atlantic salmon.

Once and for all time he proved that dry-fly fishing was not simply a passing English fad as at this time was generally regarded in America to be the case. He bridged the fishing-procedure gap between two continents and two environments. The American approach as set forth in *The Dry Fly and Fast Water* was to fish the hatch when there is a rise of trout; but when this does not prevail, and it is most of the time, artificially create a hatch. Obviously trout have hiding places and feeding stations. Hunger and hatches bring them into the open. An undercut rock makes a perfect home and an adjacent line of drift a natural place from which to intercept food. Time and again he would float his favored iron-blue dun over the carefully calculated taking place so that it would appear to the quarry that a hatch is in progress and that it is time to move and partake of it. Involved were individual fish and repetitive flawless casting.

An American version of the Fly Fisher's Club of London came into existence and from it sprang refinement, knowledge and enthusiasm centering mainly around dry-fly fishing. Residents and nonresidents affiliated with the Angler's Club of New York,

[7]

and 101 Broad Street in the big city became an angler's mecca. The leading light was the late Edward R. Hewitt, the longtime fishing partner of LaBranche, who passed away in the fall of '61. Hewitt, the scientist, was an inventive genius who not only applied his vast store of technical knowledge to angling but planned things so there was ample time and opportunity to fish. Probably never in the history of anglerdom will there again be such renowned trout fishing teams as Halford and Marryatt, and Hewitt and LaBranche. Hewitt's definitive work on trout fishing in general, *Telling on the Trout*, was published in 1935.

During the course of the age of prosperity, the booming Twenties, American wet-fly fishermen investigated the potential of the floating fly in wholesale lot and the number of those who joined the dry-fly ranks continued to increase by leaps and bounds. The depression years, when there was much time and need for streamside recreation, proved to be no deterrent.

Drag, that unnatural movement of a dry fly on the surface, became recognized as the bugaboo. Because trout feed, for the most part, in a relatively narrow line of drift, casting was, and is, regarded as a target game—a game of inches.

Times differ, waters differ and physical change takes place. The forces of man and nature do not cooperate completely with the angler. Man tampered with nature's drainage system. Massive forestlands were literally scalped. Water temperatures increased during the summertime, springs diminished in volume and water tables receded. The environment for the native species of the East, the brook trout, was altered to the extent that owing to higher water temperatures the range diminished drastically, big waters suffering most. The fish culturist bridged the gap with a trout of a less precarious survival margin. Had it not been for the introduction of the brown trout, eastern trout fishing would have been reduced to mountain brooks. Thus, much was salvaged, but not at the expense of quality and opportunity. The importation is worthy in every respect—a grand dry-fly fish regarded by many as the finest.

Gradually there came a realization as comparison was made and experience mounted. Fishing is a relative matter. A veritable giant in one environment may be a pigmy in another; a big catch in one stream may be small elsewhere. Results are measured in terms of personal satisfaction. The big hope is to fish for pleasure and to catch it. Each succeeding generation in effect thinks: "Catching was never so good and fishing never before so poor." The angler understands too that he is dealing with a

[8]

complex creature in a complex environment where margin for existence is never broad. Obviously individual streams have individual personalities. The progress of the American trout fisherman was marked. He was catching up to his English cousin.

There existed a discrepancy between the aquatic insects featured in the English works and the hatches observed by Americans. As a result there developed a group of fishing entomologists who tied their own flies, Preston Jennings and Charles M. Wetzel leading the procession. Like these, others left a record between book covers: Bill Blades, the great Midwest fly-tyer; Art Flick, who holds forth on New York's Schoharie; Ed Leonard, Bus Grove and Vince Marinaro, Pennsylvanians; and Ernie Schwiebert, formerly of the Princeton University faculty. The transition period in America followed the amazing era in England by more than half a century.

To satisfy the demand for flies, a group of commercial tyers, all anglers of distinction, grew like Topsy. Some produced works on the subject, others were too busy to write or not inclined to do so. Flies by the hundreds of dozens were fabricated by Ray Bergman, Paul Young, Dan Bailey, Don Martinez, Rube Cross, Betty Gregg, Walt Dette, the Darbees, Roy Steenrod and Bob McCafferty.

A do-it-yourself school became massive. Once it become firmly established that brook, brown and rainbow trout could be attracted as well as deceived, great ingenuity was exerted at the fly-tying table as imagination ran rampant. Visibility of fly for both trout and angler became a consideration. The short level leader with dropper loops was supplanted by the long tapered leader. The old fly book gave way to the fly box and the contents of the American box included lures such as the English deceiver fishermen never dreamed.

Many a trout has been induced to rise to the bivisible, a palmer tie with a light front hackle; the spider, a fly of great hackle diameter with or without body and tail; the variant, a spider with a modest wing; the parachute fly, a sort of horizontal spider; the fan-wing patterns; the Wulff-type hair, tail and wing fly; those with clipped deer hair bodies; and fore and aft hackled flies. The amazing world of the attractor, the garish fish finder, has few limitations regarding style, color and material. But the deceiver-fly world remained much as the English had developed it, and of course there were American versions and modifications to match the hatch.

Fly-tying courses were made available, the most famous of

The Fan Wing Royal Coachman, like nothing in nature, is strictly an attractor pattern of dry fly.

which is the one established by Pennsylvania State College (now University) which since its conception has been conducted by the incomparable George Harvey, both on campus and at extension schools. Bill Blades taught thousands of veterans in hospitals. Classes for juveniles were and are conducted by dedicated anglers.

By the time the 20th century approached the midway mark it was difficult to foresee further development of any significance relative to flies tied to match the aquatic hatch. Many fishermen

[10]

became enthralled with the performance of the dry fly to the extent that they categorized the wet fly as secondary and something to be used only as a last resort. The frontier had been reduced; however, a lone vista beckoned.

Hot-weather warm-water trout fishing is the most exacting of all. It features shy well-conditioned fish. The aquatic hatches have pretty well spent their courses. Attractor fishing becomes touchy in that a high percentage of the rises are "one-timers" and result in last split-second refusal. With it all there is intermittent surface feeding, particularly in the placid places. Although the angler sees few if any insects in flight or on the water, he does observe rising trout. By necessity such activity is brought about by the presence of terrestrial insects which have found their way to the surface. There they are trapped in surface tension to float awash, all but imperceptible to the human eye. From the standpoint of the trout, however, their opaque bodies and wings and submerged legs are visible in the clear low water. The situation calls for a substitution of the flush-floating opaque imitation for the high-riding translucent standard fly. This brings to mind a statement of Theodore Gordon describing a specialized type of fly that was "tied neither to float nor to sink." That certainly fits the land-born insect and conceivably this could have been what he had in mind.

The personal is interjected at this stage, for the writer can give an eyewitness account by reason of location. There flows by the house a most exacting piece of water which has been attractive to prominent anglers. Ofter it has been expressed: "If they will take your imitations there, they will be taken anywhere." Here it is the rule, not the exception, to find some surface-feeding activity by stream-bred brown trout to misplaced land insects. Judged by eastern standards some of the free-risers are of large size. They can break your leader and your heart. The stream originates from strong limestone springs at which are located commercial watercress beds. The setting is rural rather than rustic as it follows its winding course with no suggestion of turbulence in a rich and buggy little valley. Frequently drifting trout can be seen inspecting a dry fly at a distance of several inches. Rejection is more common than acceptance. Those who fish here regularly do not tempt fish to their ruin, they educate them by their return—fastidious fellows, fastidious fish.

From the first hot days until the end of the season there is surface activity brought about by the presence of the various leaf hoppers, the jassids. July and August feature feeding to Japanese beetles and hoppers. Winged ants, a very special trout morsel, mark their periodic appearances in great quantity in the latter month. A certain number of houseflies and other members of the true-fly family find their way to the pellucid water. Each and every one of these is opaque and flush floating. In short, here is a place without peer for experimentation with imitations of the various terrestial insects, the oak worm and robber fly excluded.

The problems presented by the ultraselective surface feeders constitute a challenge to certain fishermen and this is their laboratory for experimentation with new ties to imitate the terrestrials. It might be said of the insects and the trout that they are as predictable as a man and as unpredictable as a woman.

Among those who periodically mark their appearance are: Vince Marinaro, author of *A Modern Dry-Fly Code;* Ernie Schwiebert, *Matching the Hatch;* Joe Brooks, *Complete Book of Fly Fishing;* Bus Grove, *Lure and Lore of Trout Fishing;* Sparse Miller, *Fishless Days;* Keith Schuyler, *Lures* and Don DuBois,

The brooktrout, the native species of the East, is the most beautiful freshwater fish. Due to deforestration and pollution the range had been drastically reduced.

[12]

The Fisherman's Handbook of Trout Flies. To be sure, there are other dedicated anglers and skilled fly-tyers who pay us— the LeTort and me—a visit. These particular members of the clan have become a firmly knit little angling society within the framework of the Fly Fisher's Club of Harrisburg. The irony of fate is that the bigger part of the stream has been knocked out, at least temporarily, by pollution; and it is along that part where the overnight accommodations are located.

From my ringside seat I saw Vince Marinaro study the jassids, then tie and test his imitations. From this meadow Joe Brooks first saw and fished this tie, then later proclaimed its merit to the dry-fly world. It was here that Vince developed his little cinnamon ant with the thorax horse-hair body tied without thread.

Then came the Marinaro and Schwiebert Japanese beetles, two versions of the jassid-style of tie. The wing is flat and opaque, and a V of hackle is trimmed from the bottom to produce something flush floating—'tied neither to sink nor to float.'

It seems everyone who fishes here has his own version of the hopper, yet no one is perfectly satisfied with it. They run the style gamut—Michigan hopper, fore and aft, clipped deer-hair body, hair wing, quill hopper, and so on. When an improved imitation of the grasshopper is fabricated, likely as not the initial testing will take place here.

Ernie Schwiebert has made an intense study of our most common and prolific insect, the ant. Every time he visits the meadow there are new ties in his box to be displayed to trout and anglers. LeTort findings will constitute supplementary material in his forthcoming book.

Experimentation with the imitation of terrestrial insects, here and other places, by individuals and groups, is now a part of the history of the dry-fly development, and it has been referred to as "the major break through"; but this effort must be cataloged as unfinished business.

Our dry-fly travelog of 110 years is the relatively brief background of a fabulous heritage. Future dry-fly fishing for trout is contingent upon the way in which man handles his growing domestic problem, the necessity for clean watre. Certainly it is agreed among all fresh-water anglers that streams and lakes are the cream of our America. Furthermore, moderation in dry-fly fishing doesn't work: Like the narcotic addict, the addicted one can't get along without it as the trout seasons seem to go faster than they come.

[13]

THE DRY-FLY TREASURE HOUSE

British

Floating Flies and How To Dress Them,
   Frederick M. Halford, 1880
Dry Fly Entomology, Frederick M. Halford, 1889
The Book of the Dry Fly, George A. B. Dewar, 1897
Fly Fishing, Sir Edward Grey, 1899
Angler at Large, William Caine
Dry-Fly Fishing for Trout and Grayling
   Red Quill, (James Englefield)
Fly-Fishing: Some New Arts and Mysteries,
   J. C. Mottram, 1914
Sunshine and the Dry Fly, J. W. Dunne
A History of Fly Fishing for Trout, John Waller Hills
Supplement to Dry Fly Fisherman's Entomology,
   Martin E. Mosley, 1921
The Way of a Trout with a Fly, G. M. E. Skues
The Fly Fisher and the Trout's Point of View,
   Col. E. West Harding, 1931
River Keeper, John Waller Hills, 1934
Sidelines, Sidelights and Reflections, G. M. E. Skues
Modern Trout Fly Dressing, Roger Woolley, 1939
A Summer on the Test, John Waller Hills, 1944
Trout Problems, H. D. Turning, 1948
Itchen Memories, G. M. E. Skues, 1951
Brown Trout and the Dry Fly, C. F. Walker
An Angler's Entomology, J. R. Harris

American

Practical Dry-Fly Fishing, Emlyn M. Gill, 1912
The Dry Fly and Fast Water,
   George M. L. LaBranche, 1914
Telling on the Trout, Edward Ringwood Hewitt, 1935
A Book of Trout Flies, Preston J. Jennings, 1935
Trout, Ray Bergman, 1938
Trout Streams, Paul R. Needham, 1938
Modern Fly Casting, John Alden Knight
Flies, J. Edson Leonard
Streamside Guide. Arthur B. Flick, 1947
Fishing Flies and Fly Tying, William F. Blades, 1949
The Fly and the Fish, John Atherton
A Modern Dry Fly Code, Vincent C. Marinaro, 1950
Lure and Lore of Trout Fishing,
   Dr. Alvin R. Grove, Jr., 1951
Fun with Trout, Fred Everett, 1951
Trout Flies, Charles M. Wetzel, 1953
Matching the Hatch, Ernest G. Schwiebert, Jr., 1955
Complete Book of Fly Fishing, Joe Brooks, 1958
The Fisherman's Handbook of Trout Flies,
   Donald DuBois, 1961

CHAPTER 2

Three Big Rounds

LIKE GOOD football teams, dry fly fishermen don't happen; they are made. They are permanently created in a decisive manner by a certain drama. The drama is mystifying yet convincing, mystifying because a blizzard of strange and beautiful insects appears from nowhere, convincing because trout surface feed so freely upon them.

As day is dying in the West a hoard of delicate flies mill about the overhead foliage in strong irregular flight—a nuptial dance, you notice. Little by little they approach the surface, the flight in general being upstream. Protruding from the end of the curved bodies are colorful egg masses. Suddenly a slurp attracts your attention and it is marked by a widening ring on the surface of the water. In quick succession there are more of those unusual watery glumps accompanied by rings.

You pick from the box an imitation to match the hatch. You cast it above the place where the mark on the water was particularly impressive. As the fly drifts toward the spot, anticipation runs rampant. There is that slurp, just as it was before; your fly disappears, and you lift the rod tip. The resistance it meets and yields to is electrifying. For fleeting moments there is a feeling of weight, a live throbbing weight; then a panic stricken trout bolts and the reel screams.

The activity continues until you can no longer see your fly; then it becomes too dark to see the rings but you still hear the rising fish. Whether or not you were able to capitalize on the opportunity is not the point. It is the potentiality of the situation which is intriguing. You leave the stream with a song in your heart and a resolution in mind:

"When Whippoorwills call,
   And evening is nigh,
 I'll hurry to my Blue Heaven."

Henceforth you are subject to a powerful desire to fish for rising trout with an imitation of the natural. It is difficult to express the nature of the hope and drive to a non-receptive mind—like trying to express the urge for motherhood to a pro wrestler—but suddenly your angling life has been placed in

[15]

constant overdrive. There must be more of this sort of thing. You must fish the hatch and the rise for the same reason that the bird watchers have to watch, the mountain climbers have to climb, the gardeners have to garden.

Suddenly it becomes a problem of being at the right place at the right time with the right fly. Knowledge is the key, so you determine to become an amateur entomologist and maybe a fly tyer, too.

You stick right with it in your campaign to intercept the hatches and work out effective deceivers. Gentle spring has a way of drifting unnoticed into summer, her exit not being heralded as is the case with her commencement. As summer sets in, the aquatic hatches are answering the last great curtain calls. But even as the dainty aquatics, with minor exception, call it a season, a new insect world is stirring.

The grasslands and the woodlands are becoming infested with what would become plagues if there were no song birds and carnivorous insects to balance quotas. Many of the terrestrials find their way to the streams where they are hopelessly trapped. They have no apparent destination and some among them ride with a tail wind. Nature has not endowed any with a fear of water, if indeed they are capable of distinguishing between land and waters. In their helter-skelter life and movements they land pellmell, top or bottom up, into a tenacious environment from which but few escape. They do not find their way to the surface in great waves as is the case with the aquatics, rather there is a steady dribble from the early hours of daylight throughout the long day. The trout sip these natural accidents in a dainty manner, yet so low and flush they ride that is is most difficult for the human eye to pick out any at all in the surface.

Trout still rise but now it is leisurely, dainty, daytime feeding. No longer is there the intensity of the evening feeding you have come to look for. Instead of the evening slurps and big rings to a high-riding, translucent, aquatic insect, it is a sip and a dainty rise form during the day to an invisible land insect. Now the water is low, clear and smooth, a sensitive situation.

Much of the stream traffic has washed out and you have things pretty much your own way as you enjoy your chance in a new kind of game with rising trout. You see a rise and you know another accident in nature has become trout fodder, but who could accurately estimate the size of the trout by the rise form? It is less dramatic but more subtle than matching the hatch

[16]

because the puzzle is, just exactly what must be imitated? what to imitate?

The good old summertime is hot; and as dog days approach, surface feeding is influenced by a new factor. Grasshoppers find their way to the surface, but unlike the others, they can kick their way out of the surface tension—if they are lucky. They constitute the favorite food of trout and bigger fish are more interested in them than is the case with *minutae*. The rise forms to the big kickers are different, too; trout slash at them, usually causing an eruption. The night air sparkles with fireflies as loquacious insects render a chorus which is a delight to the listener. This is the time for well-conditioned fish and inevitably they are both shy and prudent.

These are the three basic dry fly situations which encompass the trout season. The foundation of the sport is raising trout which first must be met by matching the hatch with a translucent high-riding imitation; then one copes with the dainty daytime feeders with an opaque flush-floating imitation of a terrestrial insect and, finally, artificial hopper fishing for the big slashers comes into its own. There is some overlapping, some variation in the degree of intensity and also some interesting side lines. There are infrequent hatches of odd aquatics which, like the seventeen year cicada, are cyclic; there are flies such as the Japanese beetle, limited by geographical bounds; and there are the unpredictables, such as the giant, mottled-wing, pink-body grasshopper. The unusual and the unexpected add spice. Each of the three basic situations deserves special attention and special consideration, for each is a game in itself.

Round No. 1—Matching The Hatch

The digestive process of trout operates at maximum efficiency when the water temperature is about 62°; hence below and above this point there is a proportionate diminishing of the amount of food consumed and feeding time involved.

When the nymphs of the aquatic insects leave the gravel, stones, silt or weeds, as the case may be, and emerge from their drab cases ("shucks") on the surface of the stream, the angler calls the butterfly-like subimagos, "duns." The warmer the weather, the more quickly they become airborne. The flight from the surface is laborious and uncertain. Once in the foliage or grass, they undergo the strange metamorphosis of shedding their skins and having their mouth parts sealed. They become more translucent, are vastly improved fliers and the only remaining function in life is reproduction.

[17]

DATA RELATIVE TO MAJOR HATCHES

Time[1]	Scientific Name	Fisherman's Name	Hook	Tail	Standard Patterns		
					Body	Hackle	Wing
Early	Iron fraudator	Quill Gordon	14	blue dun hackle wisps	peacock-eye quill	bronze-blue	wood duck
Early	Ephemerella subvaria	Hendrickson (female)	14	bronze-blue hackle wisps	light red fox fur	bronze-blue	wood duck
Early	Ephemerella subvaria	Red Quill (male)	14	bronze-blue hackle wisps	Rhode Island Red quill	bronze-blue	wood duck
Early	Brachycentrus fuliginosus	Grannom[2]	18[4]	grizzly hackle wisps	grey fox fur	grizzly & ginger intermingled	grizzly hackle points
Early	Leptophlebia cupida	Whirling Dun	12	ginger hackle wisps	muskrat & beaver dubbed	blue dum & ginger intermingled	bronze-blue hackle points
Variable	Baetis vagans	Olive Dun	22	olive hackle wisps	olive nylon dubbed	olive	none
Mid	Stenonema vicarium	March Brown	12	ginger hackle wisps	hare's ear dubbed	ginger	mallard
Mid	Stenonema fuscum	Ginger Quill	14	ginger hackle wisps	peacock quill	ginger	starling
Mid & Late	Ephemerella dorothea	Pale Evening Dun	18	cream hackle wisps	sulphur spun fur	honey	starling
Late	Ephemera guttulata	Green Drake	10	rabbit whiskers	clipped deer hair	honey	sulphur impalla[5]
Late	Ephemera simulans	Chocolate Drake	10[6]	cochy bondhu hackle wisps	cochy bondhu quill	cochy bondhu	wood duck
Late	Paraleptophlebia mollis	Blue Quill	16	blue dun hackle wisps	dyed blue peacock quill	blue dun	dark coot
Late	Isonychia bicolor	White-Gloved Howdy	12	pheasant tail fibers	brown seal	honey	white hackle points
Late	Hexagenia limbata[3]	Dark Green Drake	16[5]	none	none	honey skater fly	none
Late	Stenonema canadense	Light Cahill	14	ginger hackle wisps	light red fox fur	light ginger	wood duck

[1] In general the season for aquatic hatches is less than a three month period. It varies with latitude and altitude. Early, Mid and Late refer to the season of the hatches, not the fishing season.
[2] Grannom is a caddis; all others listed are Mayflies.
[3] Largest of the Mayflies and a placid-water insect.
[4] Adams.
[5] Honey Neversink Skater Fly is a highly effective imitation.
[6] Cochy Bondhu Quill.

Mating takes place in the air, usually after sundown, although the emergence may have been anytime. In the vernacular of the angler they are now "spinners." First evidence of a pending "fall of spinners" is a milling about at tree-top level. After copulation, egg masses protrude from the females and flight is upstream just over the water. The precious cargoes, the egg masses, are rendered to the stream; then the females drop spent to the surface. The males land both on the water and on land. The great family of "drakes" or "mayflies," the important group to the dry-fly fisherman, have wings which when at rest are in an upright position, whereas those of the caddes are tent-shaped and those of the stone fly lie flat on the back. In most cases the spinners offer greater opportunity but very early in the season the reverse is often the case. Unlike the drakes, the stone fly emerges by crawling out on rocks and debris and the caddis deposits the eggs by diving under the surface. Given the combination of a hatch of fly and clear water in the low 60s, there should be a heavy rise of trout.

The hatches are not as consistent in their timetables as the migration of birds, however their schedules are not subject to great annual deviation. A worthy policy is to make note of the occurrences of hatches and rises observed or heard of, with the expectation of repeat performances at the same place in future seasons upon which you can capitalize. The game of intercepting hatches in order to enjoy intense dry fly fishing is fascinating and rewarding. For everyone there is, "a time to plant, and a time to pluck up what is planted; . . . a time to seek and a time to lose; a time to keep, and a time to cast way . . ." And for the angler, there is a time to depart and a time to return.

Recently it has been claimed that emergence is contingent upon the number of sunshine hours to which the numph is exposed in late winter and early spring. This explains the fact why temperature and water condition could never be pinned down as the exact determining factors.

Early in the season the predonderance of aquatic insects we see are grey in color. As the weeks pass along the brown ones mark their appearance. The last of the hatches are of sulphur coloration or very pale.

Round No. 2—Flat Water And Dainty Feeders

Every hot-weather trout fisherman has been confronted with the flat water situation of dainty rise forms to an invisible food supply. Some of these trout, for practical purposes, are incessant feeders, and some not so constant but, nonetheless, dependable day after day. Summer has set in and the chief aquatic hatches are over, yet for hours on end throughout the day some activity continues.

It does not take long to discover that a #14 Light Cahill, or its like, is not the answer. The big attractors do not work either. Sooner or later, usually sooner, we are all convinced that the solution is diminuation—after all, one cannot see what they are taking; therefore it must be tiny. When our fluffy, well-tied 20's and 22's, from black to white are passed up, we are puzzled and chagrined. Maybe they are not feeding on the surface. Is it just under or could those rings be made by tails?

This was the sort of thing Vince Marinaro and I were faced with in the meadow along which I now live. We could not touch those 25 regular feeders. In spite of the delicate rings, we knew some of these were fine fish, for in certain light at some spots they could be seen, otherwise the entire group might have been passed off as energetic fingerlings.

For a week in July Vince put up at my little camp. When not fishing, he was either involved in conducting a series of water tests or tying more flies in an endeavor to produce something which would fool the regular feeders. In the late afternoons it was my custom to join him, replenish his diminishing larder, eat and fish. With me it was strictly a trial and error proposition to attempt to fool these fish; but Vince, the scientist, had other approaches.

He watched the surface with binoculars and he set up in front of the camp a cloth attached to a frame to strain a line of drift. What the mesh trapped was a revelation. In less than an hour at the waterline there collected a ribbon of small insects. They were practically all leaf hoppers but there was variation in size and color. This is what these trout had to be taking. The job now was to create an imitation.

About the fifth evening I was greeted by an enthusiastic and effervescing companion, "I have the fly. Show me a jassid-eater and I think I can hook him."

There were two outcomes. First, I pointed out an incessant surface-feeder with which I had a nodding acquaintance and which, as far as I was concerned, was an untouchable fish. The

A rising trout. That is the ultimate for which the ear is tuned, the eye is cocked and the fly is cast.

trout was taken by the new fly on the first perfect float. Second, Vince handed me three of his beautiful little imitations which he called "Jassids."

The previous evening I had played unsuccessfully with six regular feeders in an upper meadow and the best I had been able to do was raise one once in a while, none actually touching the fly. Here was the perfect testing ground for the newly created "Jassid."

Compared with results of the past, an extra ordinary twist of events occurred. Each fish was promptly hooked. It required no more than half an hour to deceive heretofore impossible trout. Notes disclose that the birth of the Jassid was 7/29/49.

The original pattern was tied on an 18 hook. The body material was orange tying silk. Ginger hackle was wound on palmer-style. A jungle cock eye was then tied in as a flat top. To make the fly float like the naturals, in the surface, Vince trimmed out a V of hackle from the underside. The result was a flush-floating opaque counterpart of nature.

In due time the Jassid was tied in various sizes and in different color combinations but always in the same form and style. My personal preference is for a roof of two jungle cock eyes, concave sides together, frozen flat against the body with a spot of lacquer. Over the years the most popular version has been black body and black hackle but various combinations have taken the dainty feeders here and elsewhere. I like an assorted supply on regular 18 hooks and another on short shank 20's.

The trout which make the dainty rings to *minutae* are in feeding positions not far under the surface of flat water. With a minimum of effort they tip and sip. Frequently they drift with the imitation, inspecting it at close range—three to six inches. If they were forced to work hard for such small food particles, it might be a case of diminishing returns.

A vast collection of this common terrestrial insect, made over a period of 75 years, can be inspected at the Pennsylvania Agricultural Department headquarters, South Office Building of the Capitol, Harrisburg, Pa.

But the leaf hopper is not the only insect which brings about this type of feeding. The most common land-born creature is the ant and, like the jassid, it prevails in various colorations and sizes. Wings develop for the annual nuptial flight but wingless ones too find their way to the surface of the water. After copulation, quantities land on the water, sometimes in such masses that the surface is coated, offering fierce competition to the imitation of the angler. Trout are particularly fond of them, due, according to Hewitt, to the acidic taste and according to Schwiebert, because they are available in good numbers at all times.

At other periods throughout the summer some wingless ones drop to the water, these being, for the most part, the large black carpenter ants, which colonize in dens of trees, under dead bark and in rotting logs. The best defense the wingless insects seem to be able to muster when they are besieged is to simply

[22]

drop out of sight; in fact some may drop when a bird lights nearby.

Fishing partner of yore, never to be forgotten, Bob McCafferty, tied flies on a commercial basis all winter long but not in the fishing season. The pattern he popularized, and which was in greatest demand, was a hard-body black ant with hackles in the middle—thorax-style tie. The fly was drifted or drawn submerged.

It was inevitable that the time would come when the black ant would be tied to float, just as the insect does for which it is named. Bob arrived at the conclusion that the terrestrials, as well as the stream-born clan, float unless they are temporarily sucked beneath the surface or have disintegrated into sodden pieces, the thinking of the patron saints, Izaak Walton and Charles Cotton, to the contrary.

It was also inevitable that it would be tied in midge size with cinnamon body and ginger hackle to imitate the little red ant in the same manner as the large black pattern simulates the carpenter ant, each in appropriate size. These flies really came into their own when some hackle was trimmed away in the shape of a V from the belly-part of the fly, thus insuring that they ride low—in the surface. Ultimately the floating partner of the submerged original became "the ant."

Ernie Schwiebert depends heavily, in the many trout waters he fishes, on his fur-body ants in thorax-style tie. Vince Marinaro has two interesting variations, also both thorax ties. In the case of the little cinnamon ant he uses no tying thread, just body material and hackle. The back-half of the body is built up by wrapping properly dyed nylon around the shank of the hook. The hackle is then tied and turned into the middle of the body. The fore part of the thorax is then built up and tied off. A more recent innovation is a body of porcupine quill, which is hollow, neatly wrapped to simulate the ant silhouette.

Either the jassid or ant, attached to a 6X or 7X tippet is the *piece de resistance* for the incessant risers. Together they open up a relatively new field; low, clear, smooth water—the flats— when things are at their toughest; but it is strictly a matter of fishing the rise, not the water.

Round No. 3—Hoppers And Brood Fish

As the season advances, a stream shuffle is underway. The brood fish are restless. One by one and little by little they are on the move, a slow upstream migration. The battle wagons are forsaking old hideouts such as the depth of big water and the overhead cover of brush piles and flat rocks and seeking new ones nearer the spawning grounds. There is something else other than a spawning urge in the air—and on the water, too. The greatest food of all for trout abounds—big, fat, protein-laden grasshoppers. Some are yellow bodied, some green and many of them have brown wings. All are grist for the mill of the trout which is at all inclined to surface feed.

This juicy morsel (no pun intended) is unique in the insect world in that once it finds itself on the water, it can kick its way through surface tension—unless it becomes entrapped in a spiked mouth. The trout take them two ways: natural drift or while kicking and twisting. The same is true of the imitation.

George Harvey, of the Pennsylvania State University, rightly has earned a fabulous reputation. To many, he is Mr. Trout. Put the question to this master angler, "What period of the trout season do you like best?" and he will answer it with the query, "How are you going to beat the hopper season?"

Sure, trout can be caught on a hook baited with a hopper but in effectiveness a good artificial has it licked by leagues. The fly can be cast and made to drift most anywhere and it is durable and available for the lifting from a box. I suppose we all have discovered that it is not fun to remove hoppers from the saw grass and nettles in 90° weather, particularly when waders are involved in which one stews in his own juice. The task of the fly tyer is to develop an imitation which gives a good impressionistic silhouette and rides right. There are various versions including: Joe's Michigan hopper, which is a palmer-tied fly with turkey wings and a red tail; the fore and aft hackle fly, also with turkey wings; George Phillip's clipped deer-hair body and bucktail wing; the pontoon hopper, a big quill in the middle flanked by two smaller quills, all realistically painted; a greased muddler minnow; and the Schwiebert Letort hopper with nylon dubbed body, no hackle, and hair and turkey wings.

All of the above will take fish but the last on the list may do it in the most decisive manner. Ernie and I used it to put a finale to the '60 Pennsylvania season which left us gabbing and gloating; and what is more, we tried the others, too, in order that a comparison could be made. Only big fish counted and they were all stream-bred. We ran the score of browns over 18 inches and brooks over 14 inches into the double column. What a day! What a fly!

It appears that there is a last resort practice with the hopper.

Let's assume that in one way or another a big hopper-eater has been located and he is known to be in business. With bated breath you drift your imitation over the spot. You know he is watching. But he does not move to accept it. A half dozen times you try him but there is no response. The next time the fly is in the window you give it a little kick-like twitch. Some where around half the time this is the clincher for a cautious one. The other half of the time, you give up, temporarily, that is. The next try, after a rest, is another adventure.

But before you leave, though, you realize that some of the fastidious fish have the habit of drifting with the fly. Possibly his taking place is upstream from the spot of the rise so carefully marked, therefore your gold brick has not even been seen, so you make some more casts accordingly. It ends up that you leave the spot unsuccessful but hopeful. You think to yourself, some of these educated fish are leader shy. Next time should I go down to 6X (.0047)?

To meet the hopper season head-on, the confirmed hopper angler starts with a small imitation, say a half-inch fly on a long shank 18 hook. As the hoppers develop, he steps up the size of the imitation. Towards the end he is fishing a fly at least an inch overall mounted on what is a big hook to some of us, a 14 or a 12.

The greatest surface feeding trout—by far—I have ever seen in operation was taking hoppers. He was hooked too, but not the first day. The rise form made by this fish, at least to hoppers, was downright vicious. A slashing noisy strike caused water to fly into the air. The first day Vince Marinaro and I found him he took 16 big hoppers but carefully avoided the imitation attached to a 2X leader. After a rest of an hour, he took two more for dessert before calling it quits. It was at a place now known as, "the 19th hole," the bench and fireplace near the parking lot in the turn around meadow.

The eruption this trout created as a hopper disappeared had Vince and me mumbling as we were en route home. Tomorrow we would try "Vesuvius" again but this time tipped out to 4X instead of 2.

"How big is he, Vince," I ventured.

"Better than two feet, 8 to 10 pounds, hog-backed and burly. Had a pretty good look."

The next day we threw in a big yellow-bellied hopper "as a feeler." Vesuvius was in business—same as before. I went about catching a half-dozen hoppers and stashed them in the Jap

[25]

beetle container. Vince sneaked into casting position and affixed to his long leader the current imitation, a hand-painted hollow-quill job. Then I crawled into position through the grass, turtle-style, about 30 feet above the taking place and made ready the camera.

A hopper was tossed into the water and it was picked up in the view finder as it drifted and kicked. As Vesuvius threw a water spout two feet high the shutter clicked. The film was advanced and Vince showed him the artificial. The leader was sufficiently long so that the fish was not lined on the necessary straight-upstream cast.

The first ten minutes of casting drew a blank; so I threw in another hopper. The reception was spectacular.

"This trout must be leader shy," Vince reflected. "Don't throw in another hopper till I put on a strand of 5X."

In due time the process was resumed. I tossed in a hopper, snapped another picture of the rise form and Vince started to cast. The film was advanced and I kept the camera pointing toward the spot with the angler in the background. There was the customary waterspout and the shutter clicked, only this time there was no live hopper involved.

The rod tip came up, and in a sort of state of awe Vince meekly announced, "Charlie, he's on."

Vesuvius did not bolt and jump; he didn't even move much. As far as he was concerned, depth was security; so he simply settled back into the bottom part of the stream bed depression which had become home.

The best way to wear down a sulker, pretty close in, is to lower the rod to the side and pull on the head. Every time the head is forced sideways, the current catches the body bulk and the fish must go to work. Vince harassed this trout for fare-thee-well with that low side pressure. The trout would no sooner readjust until it had to again put the same set of muscles to work.

In a weed-choked stream, such as this setup, it is necessary to stay below the fish in order to keep the leader free of the weed and to be in a position to literally make the trout back out of trouble. After the first hour of this strange encounter, the broad tail of the great fish began to show. No longer could he fight his way back into the special depression, being satisfied now with depth anywhere, thus the battleground kept shifting downstream. Finally the best effort of the fish was a tail-lowering wallow. It was time to draw him in.

[26]

I slumped low against the watercress, net in hand, by a little bay. Vince had Vesuvius coming—right towards the bay. I could see the hopper tight against the far side of the fish's face and that frail 5X leader extending between the jaws on the other side. It didn't look good, that leader crossing sharp teeth.

Suddenly there was a little snap and the line flew back in Vince's face. Vesuvius settled to the streambed in plain sight in a perfect attitude for recuperation.

That was the last we ever saw or heard of Vesuvius, the largest trout we ever saw lost and the most spectacular surface feeder we ever watched perform. That is, it was the last we ever heard of this fish unless it was the 10 lb. 2 oz. trout taken one mile upstream the next year.

The Decision

If trout fishing is to be considered a contest with a worthy adversary, then we should look for weaknesses, which in reality are opportunities. In appraising the opposition, Napoleon Bonaparte put it this way, "One should be thankful above all else for errors of the enemy." The challenge of a trout is the rise, which in effect is an advertisement: here is the location; feeding is in progress.

The one who claimed that, "opportunity knocks but once," was not a fisherman; neither was the one who said, "lightning never strikes twice in the same place." Such philosophies do not exemplify the attitude of the angler and they are inimical to his experiences with repetitive flashes. He dreams of past happenstance and the anticipation of re-occurrence leads him back to old haunts. Good fish have a way of taking the places of good fish and the insects have a way of reappearing season after season. Furthermore, a returned fish has a habit of continuing old practices.

The dedicated angler cherishes the three golden situations in the calendar of events which bring about rising trout to be met with a counterpart of nature. Each period extends over a substantial length of time; there is some overlapping and each in turn offers great reward. If one knows what to look for and what to do about it, then satisfaction is abundant. These situations are sure to arise and, furthermore, they can be sought and found.

A trilogy of phenomenon of Nature is the making of dry fly angling for trout and they take their forms in three action-packed rounds, like a good amateur boxing match. Problems are challenges.

[27]

Dr. Alvin R. "Bus" Grove, Jr., in his excellent work, *Lure And Lore Of Trout Fishing*, writes: "The trout are limited to available food, and available food fluctuates with season and stream section. Obviously the importance of each food changes as its relative abundance varies and as seasonal fluctuations occur."

The fact that things can be expected or anticipated, although they are not positive, makes each stream escapade an adventure. The only thing certain is the end of the season so that unmolested fish can take care of the important business of procreation. It is the stream-bred fish and the stocked holdovers which like best to have the flow of the current deliver to them the bounties provided by Nature. In our stream wanderings we should capitalize on rising trout—and rise they will.

FREE

Free of worry, free of care,
Free of dust-filled city air,
Free of crowded, noisy streets
Filled with traffic's blaring bleats—

Free to heed or free to talk,
Free to run or free to walk—
Free to listen to the breeze
Tell its secrets to the trees—

Free to go or free to stay
Free to lounge or free to play,
Free to wander far and wide,
Free to sit by campfire's side—

Free of all but keen delight,
When dawn ends this star-filled night,
Free I'll be another day
To stalk that trout that got away.

—*J. F. D.*

[28]

CHAPTER 3

Popillia Japonica

THERE ARE two kinds of angling control: the one is the rule; it is control of the angler; the other is rare, the control of trout. The golden days, which follow a deceptively short spring, feature shirt sleeve evenings, the song of the cicada, shy well-conditioned trout and Popillia Japonica. And with that soft name having the Oriental ring thoughts of wonderful fish come rushing back as though pages are unfolding in the book of an angler's memories. These are trout which were induced to surface feed.

Popillia Japonica, a beautiful misplaced land insect, was heralded as a scourge. Doleful voices predicted devastation and a fight to the finish between man and pest. The extermination of this accidentally introduced insect was as important to foliage as the presence of honey bees is essential for pollination of bloom; so it was said. There could hardly have been two more dour voices than those of my parents, Mother with her rose gardens and flower shows, Dad with his orchard and plantings of other deciduous trees as his sideline. Trouble was moving our way at the rate of 50 miles a year and there were only 100 miles to go. These were the first things I heard about the Japanese beetle.

That was toward the end of the second decade of the 20th Century. Those times presented a complication of a different nature, particularly for the generation in quest of its first job. In the days of The Great Depression, the amount of remuneration mattered but little; the thing which counted was whether or not one had a job. A college friend was one of the lucky ones, for him it happened that work and this insect meshed. Rich's governmental job was to inspect southbound cars and wagons in an effort to prevent the dreaded beetle from crossing the Mason-Dixon line near his home, Mercersburg, Pennsylvania.

His watch-dog team knew what it was looking for, because authorities had displayed pinned-up specimens, but during the course of the first summer not a one showed up on transported vegetables and plants, tourists' clothing or car upholstery. Back at Easton, Pennsylvania, where they were about to strike, he advised his fraternity brothers at Lafayette of the menace and his effort to keep America green.

[29]

The line against the invader was not held, for a few years later John could have picked them by the pint from the roses along the Richie house. But by this time man realized that he could live with Jap beetles and that destructiveness was limited to a short summer period and a relatively small variety of flora. At the top of the list are rose and grape leaves and certain weeds, then as dog days hold sway the concentrations shift to buttonwood and plum foliage, corn silk, milkweed blooms and several more weeds. Birds and praying mantis are not the only creatures which eat them, trout and bass do too, when they become available food.

There are those among us who are endowed with the gift of expression in a most intriguing and complete manner. Such a person is Vincent C. Marinaro. To angler, Vince, goes the credit for researching the records of the U. S. Department of Agriculture for the gripping story of the Japanese beetle invasion. The following is quoted from his literary fishing trip, the classic, *A Modern Dry Fly Code:* [1]

"What a rare thing it is to witness the advent of an entirely new insect on trout waters. I do not know of a single recorded instance of this nature in all of fly-fishing history. Not that the insect of which I am about to speak is new to the entomologists, but it is certainly new in fly-fishing practice and such an insect that would compel a Halford or Lunn to abandon anything else to study, to imitate, and to fish.

"Popillia Japonica is a very pretty name for a very pretty beetle, perhaps the handsomest of all the beetles—a strong composition of red-bronze, shiny green, and bronzy black, mild of manner and rather unobtrusive. No one without previous knowledge would suspect him of being one of the most terrifying and devastating colonizers of our time.

"Originally confined to the islands of Japan, these beetles found their way to the United States about the year 1916 when a few specimens were discovered and identified as Japanese beetles in a nursery near Riverton, New Jersey. These insects have some relatives in this country but they themselves had never before been seen or recognized here. Entomologists are convinced that they were introduced as larvae in the soil about the roots of nursery plants, possibly azalea or Japanese iris.

---

[1] Reprinted by permission of G. P. Putnam's Sons from A MODERN DRY-FLY CODE by Vincent C. Marinaro, copyright 1950 by Vincent C. Marinaro.

[30]

"After the first discovery, no more than a dozen-odd beetles could be found that year in the neighborhood of Riverton, and the area of infestation included a total area of less than one square mile. In 1917 and 1918 the spread was hardly noticeable and did not include more than a few square miles. In 1919 a forceful notice of the awful menace was served on the agriculturists when it was discovered that the beetles were alarmingly abundant in an area of some 48 square miles; in that same year it is likely that they crossed the Delaware River and reached the Pennsylvania side, where they were found for the first time in the following season. At the end of 1923 it was found that the territory infested by the beetles amounted to 2,442 square miles, covering wide areas in New Jersey and Pennsylvania, a truly astonishing increase.

"In 1916 only a few beetles could be collected, but in 1919 as many as 15,000 or 20,000 beetles could be collected by hand, by one person, in a single day. During the summer of 1923 beetles were to be found by many thousands in individual orchards on the foliage and the fruit of various trees. This condition obtained not only in a single orchard but in many orchards throughout the heavily infested territory. Here is an example of how abundant the beetles were during this season: early one morning, while it was cool and the adult beetles were more or less inactive, a large canvas was spread under each of 156 ten-year-old peach trees; the trees were shaken vigorously and the inactive beetles, instead of flying to other plants, as they would have done later in the day, dropped to the canvas and were collected. In a little over two hours 208 gallons of beetles, or 1 1/3 gallons of beetles to each tree, were collected. On examination twenty-four hours later it was found that, in spite of the removal of the beetles during the previous day, the trees were about as heavily infested as they had been the previous morning. Besides attacking the foliage, the insects feed on the fruit and are found clustered on apples and peaches in large numbers. As many as 278 beetles have been collected on a single apple.

"During the fall of 1923 larvae were found to be extremely numerous in some locations; for example, on one of the greens in a Pennsylvania golf course they were found to the number of 1,531 to the measured square yard. In pastures the infestation was found to be as high as 717 larvae to a square yard.

"The adult Japanese beetle is a beautiful and brightly-colored insect, varying in length from 5/16 to 7/16 inch and in width

[31]

from 3/16 to 9/32 inch. It is broadly oval in shape, moderately convex, and shining. The upper surface is somewhat flattened, without pubescence, hairs, or scales. The color is a bright, metallic green except for the greater part of the wing covers, which are coppery brown. The undersurface of the body is clothed with short, grayish hairs, and the legs are of a dark metallic, coppery-green color, varying in tint in different positions.

"The total life cycle of the Japanese beetle is one year, five-sixths of this time being spent in the soil as an egg, larva, or pupa. Having passed the winter in the soil at a usual depth of between 2 and 4 inches, the larvae become active late in March or early in April and feed actively until they change to the pre-pupal stage in May and June. The prepupal stage may last for ten days or as much as two or three weeks. The larva then transforms to a pupa and the adult emerges about two weeks later. In some cases the adults may remain in the pupal cells for several days before emerging but on the average the adults issue from the ground on the second or third day after transformation. In the area around Riverton, New Jersey, the first beetles to emerge were usually found between June 10 and June 20. The average emergence date for females in 1921 was June 20 and for males June 21. Although the first beetles were found June 10 on the heavier soils, it has been found that the beetles emerge from a week to ten days later on the soil of the sandy types. In 1922 the first beetle was found on June 11 and the average date of emergence was June 18.

"After emerging from the ground the beetles usually climb on various low-growing plants and if the weather is clear remain for a few hours without feeding until they are thoroughly hardened.

"During the morning the beetles concentrate on low-growing plants, such as smartweed and beans. As the heat increases during the day they become more active and disperse to the taller plants until early in the afternoon, when they are abundant on the tallest elms, oaks, and maples. After 3 p.m. their flight is toward the ground and the lower-growing plants.

"There is a general increase in the activity of the beetles during the day until 2 or 3 p.m.; after this time their activity decreases until dark when flight ceases."

Conditions vary, fish vary. The bass season did not open until August 1 in the tide-water section of the broad Susquehanna below the massive Conowingo dam. A summer Sunday is a day for the storage of water in the great pool above the hydroelectric plant. When the wheels are open and the turbines are grinding, this part of the river is a raging torrent but early this particular morning it was a broken chain of flats connected by trickles of water among a maze of protruding rocks. At such times, the fishermen who frequented the place would tell you, the scales are heavily weighted in the fish's favor. This was the odd time and space pattern with which I was faced.

A bright sun had just crested the hills and shone out of a blue sky as I sloshed toward the first little lake. For about an hour, maybe two, the placid surface of the pools was unbroken except for the splat and retrieve of the lure. There were no strikes.

Some little rings were then observed on the surface, rise forms which appeared to be made by baby bass and fall fish. Idly I pitched the lure to one within range, more as target practice than with expectation. There was a boil which would fill a wash tub followed by a heavy strike.

As I rolled the hook around the brushy jaw, preparatory to releasing the first captured smallmouth, there, deep in the mouth was an unswallowed Japanese beetle. I looked around. There were some beetles moving about. The human eye can pick up and follow the flight of an insect at a great distance. I focused on one which was crossing the river. He never made it, just dropped down and out of sight. Others were doing the same thing. Everything added up. A lot of beetles were finding their way to the water and the bass were sipping them from the unbroken surface.

Some good fast action followed, the kind I like best—top water feeding and surface fishing. It did not take long to realize that there was no way of telling what size fish made those insignificant rings and that it was beetles which set them off. As the day wore on and the insects warmed up, their flight became much stronger with the result that less dropped to the water.

Along about noontime a good bass, a keeper, came my way, and that means something 4 pounds or better in this country; so I headed for the bank and lunch. The weeds along the river's edge were alive with beetles—beetles by the bushels. With every step they whirred away. It was almost unbelievable. When that bass was finally cleaned, his belly was full of them; so was the gut.

This Conowingo Sunday beetle fishing was so interesting that for some seasons four of us made the 75-mile weekly pilgrimage

[33]

for it. What will happen back home, we speculated, when our trout streams get the beetles? We would have to wait to see if they fell to the surface of narrow streams. Would trout, like bass, take them if they could get them?

By 1940 beetles were in full bloom in the Cumberland Valley. But they needed some help in finding their way in quantity to the surface of small trout waters. The first thought expressed in this reporting was relative to control. Here is where control of trout enters the picture. No matter whether it be called the creation of a rise to natural insect or chumming, the fact remains, some trout take them and like them.

The first place I ever tossed any beetles on the water was at a nice line of drift on the Yellow Breeches Creek at my little farm. Three trout turned on them, two of the fish taking at least half a dozen each, the other only one. If you think I started to fish over these feeders and hooked each one in turn, you are only partly right. None were hooked. There wasn't a fly in the box which remotely resembled a beetle and apparently they wanted the like of it or nothing.

The next step, which incidentally took place the next evening, was to try a different follow-up deceiver. A ball of peacock herl was formed around a hook, then coated with muslin. That didn't deceive, for the trout would not have any part of that either. Maybe it needed three legs on each side. But time eliminated that possibility, too.

This wasn't like taking candy from a baby. Bass had proved themselves non-selective but trout are a more prudent fish. Finally one day a trout was fooled but a shooter might term the experiment "a dry run." Of all the things I could think of which looked like a Jap beetle, a coffee bean was the closest. After my three pets, which started it all, were chummed into activity, I tossed them some beans. They rose up in their medium-fast run and sucked them in. I know that one trout spit out his, for I saw it pop to the top; and no doubt the others, in disillusionment, did likewise.

The idea now was to affix a bean to a hook, something new in fly tying. With a three-cornered rat-tail file, a vertical groove was made on the under sides of some beans which were just the right size and shape. The wing and the top and bottom hackles were trimmed from wool-body #18 dry flies. These flies in turn were fastened into the grooves of the beans with waterproof cement. Now I felt I was really ready.

Time proved that some of the beetle eaters of the Breeches

would fall for the Java fraud. It was a frail imitation, for a hooked fish usually resulted in separation of bean and fly. The fact remained, however, that a few trout, some good ones among them, are on the lookout for Japanese beetles and no sixth sense is required on the part of the angler to locate willing feeders.

Attention was then turned to the small limestone streams— rich, fertile, productive water—where strong fleshy trout put up violent resistance and surface feed in hot weather. Some trout in the flat water of the serpentine bends were excited by a chain of the real thing, but unlike the fish of the Breeches, they would not touch the coffee bean imitation. Upset was the famous Marryatt quotation, "It's not so much the fly as the driver."

Historically the dressing of the fly is a progressive art. Progress was needed in the creation of a meticulous imitation of the foreign insect. Certainly it is possible to produce some impressionistic something which floats just right on the face of running water. By this time I was convinced that the way the fly nestled in the surface tension was as vital as the silhouette. Relief was needed for this unsuccessful slugging at a stream problem, so I turned to Vince for help. It was up to him to make history as I waited.

He was given the big pitch: "There is a hatch which can be carried in a pocket. It can be released at any time of day to float in any chosen line of drift. Its long duration is at a period when there are no duns and spinners. Some fine trout show to it."

"What are you talking about?" he interrupted, "panacea?"

"Reality," I corrected him. "But there is a catch. The imitation must be right. I know how to prime the pump, if you can match this." And he was handed a box containing a Jap beetle.

Since Vince pioneered the flat, opaque, flush-floating style of dry fly tie, it was no surprise when he produced an imitation of the beetle based on the theory that a trout is not able to perceive height or thickness of a land insect mired in the surface. His original beetle was a big six-legged jassid: hackle, black; legs, peacock herl; and flat wing, several jungle cock eyes.

With this fly we were in business, for it produced about 75% of the time. For the next few years it was the standard imitation of our group.

As of today, the fellows utilize three styles of tie. Strangely enough, one can never be sure which will work best or on what

[35]

trout none of the three will work at all. Some fish seem to see or appraise things differently than others.

One of the other two is a modified Schwiebert version: body, peacock herl; hackle, black and ginger intermingled; legs, none; wing, several flat black feathers from the dark neck ring of a ringneck pheasant, treated with clear nail polish. The other is a clipped-hair beetle made of antelope, which, because of its fine quality packs better than deer hair.

Admittedly, this extraordinary process of exhilaration motivated by the angler reaps a whirlwind. Some friends have looked on in amazement as they watch the unusual sequence. When we hold court on this technique, which is undefinable in the dictionary sort of way, it is recognized that new store trout are not takers, neither are the majority of wild trout, and of that number which have added beetles to the menu, not all can be deceived. To the chumming fraternity, the life of a beetle eater is too precious to blot out, even though we know that it in turn will wipe out smaller lives. That is how much we think of these special fish and the excitement they produce.

Deliverer of the Goods

AN OLD established idea is, big rod for big water and big fish, little rod for brooklets and small trout. This is based on the obvious. Distance is necessary to cover broad expanses and only a sturdy stick reaches far out—80 feet and more. Daintiness is required to drop a fly gently nearby and to appreciate the play of a small fish, and only the little rod gives the delicate close-range delivery and feel—Tom Thumb work. There are those who argue that they like the feel of an 8-inch trout on a miniature rod but they want something sturdy in order to boss a heavy fish. Such argument and logic are difficult to challenge, but here goes: I like little rods.

"So," you say, "Fox is one of those light tackle faddists. 'Pride goeth before destruction and a haughty spirit before a fall.'" Sure enough, that's the way it is, but . . .

The more fishing pressure to which trout are subject, the more wily and shy they become. To complicate matters further, as the season progresses, the water becomes lower, clearer and flatter. The paramount problem is to induce the quarry to accept the fly. The more invisible the leader tippet, the better the chance. That means the employment of the lightest leader which can be handled. Short thin rods with the super-sensitive tips protect fine leaders against breakage. Stout rods have less bounce to the ounce. So when the time comes when 3X and 4X leaders will no longer do an effective job, then add the 5X, the 6X and even the 7X strands. But such connections to the fly must have a cushioned background. To paraphrase an old adage, it is better to have hooked and lost than never to have hooked at all. But who says, "you always lose?"

Last year Ernie Schwiebert's best American trout was on 6X (diameter, .0047; pound test, 1.8) and a number 16 ant, a big Wyoming rainbow from Blacktail Spring Creek, Jackson Hole. He and I do our fishing together on July and August weekends over leader-shy flat-water trout. In the trunk of his car is an awesome battery of rods from which I have seen him select but two—a 6-foot midge, or, the same as I employ, one 7½ feet. At this stage of the game he utilizes mainly 7X tippets in order to fool more shy trout. He tells me the smaller of these two rods cushions his answer to the rise and to the bolting and the

[37]

bulldogging of a good fish to the degree that he feels relatively safe with 7X but it is touch and go with the slightly sturdier stick.

My effort is a bit more crude than his. Most of the time I tip out to 6X (.0047), sometimes adding a 7X strand for special situations and at other times cutting back to 5X or even 4X. Limp nylon is stronger than the old, Spanish, silk worm gut and certainly much more convenient, cheaper too. The fact that it is readily procurable in neat little containers and does not deteriorate is helpful and it makes the tying of your own leaders highly practical, which was not the case in the days of silk worm gut only.

Minor casting controls can be achieved by leader specification and it is only common logic to adopt a system for tying them. Since there are more diameters available than it is practical to incorporate into one leader, there is no reason to purchase and store each size. Mine are as listed, but they are tied by guess and approximation, not by exacting measurement. There is no claim that this is the only way it should be done or that this is the last word and the ultimate.

Designation	Diameter	Pound Test	Length of Strand
24 lb.	.0230 in.	24 lb.	1½ ft.
4/5	.0169	17	1½
6/5	.0150	14.3	1
8/5	.0126	10	½
0X	.0110	8.5	½
2X	.0094	5.8	1
4X	.0071	3.8	1
5X	.0059	2.9	1½
6X	.0047	1.8	1½

Thus the basic leader is about 10 feet, tapered out to 6X. Both wind and large flies which twist fine tippets are encountered evils which can be met by the removal of an end strand or two. On the other hand, an encounter with fastidious feeders, particularly those taking winged ants, can best be met with a good little tie attached to a strand of added 7X.

Definitely there is a relationship between the size of the fly and the diameter of the tippet. For example, a skater fly or imitation hopper attached to 4X may do a creditable job but it requires 6 or 7X to set up a tiny ant or jassid. The main thing is to meet sophisticated fish with refinement and the logical first consideration is the fly and the tippet to which it is attached. We are then going to have to protect the terminal tackle

[38]

with a shock absorber which is also capable of casting. Most of the fishing is going to be within a 50-foot range, some of it in very tight.

More and more of the clan are forsaking the leader loop and a knot on the end of the line for the undetachable nail-knot tie of the leader to the line.

A number of anglers, of which I happen to be one, are sold on the so-called "floating" nylon lines. The only trouble is that there are a few which have the exasperating habit of twisting. Torpedo-heads cast further and more easily, particularly when it is windy, but they splash when they hit the water and are difficult to control when specialized casting is attempted. Then too they are not reversible. The readily manageable double-taper is in effect two lines—reversible. Personal preference is the double-taper for trout and the torpedo-head as a part of the salmon and bass bugging outfits, which are one and the same. The nylon floaters are slightly lighter in weight than silk lines of the same designation, therefore one size heavier than the accepted normal should properly fit the rod.

The midge rod is not for the faddist; it is a wonderful little piece of fishing equipment which has its important place in our scheme of things. Those who use them love them. One ardent and skilled angler, Arnold Gingrich, publisher of *Esquire*, has 13 6-footers constructed by the same rodbuilder.

There are available some great little midge bamboos for which we have to thank Art Neumann of Wanigas, Wess Jordan of Orvis, the Paul Young family and the firms of William Mills and Sons and Payne. The Shakespeare Co. produced a custom-made glass model and Sylaflex has in production a so-called "progressive taper" which in reality is convex and concave engineering in fiber glass. No doubt there are other fine midge rods of which this angler has no knowledge.

The early American fly fisherman was under the influence of the spell cast by the writings of English cousins, the great trout-fishing pioneers. But England is different from America. Over there the wind blows much of the time, often in gale proportions. Little wonder that this is the cradle of the powerful rod and that its use had and still has sincere champions. G. E. M. Skues wrote much about his "wonderful little Leonard," 9 feet 5 ounce, secured through his friend, Eddie Mills of the famous New York firm. This served him admirably for the last 41 years of his fishing. When he grew too old to cast, at the age of 90, he tenderly presented it to his younger brother. Incidentally, his

[39]

catch on his last fishing day was a great one. It was in line with such tradition that American rods were built, bought and cast. Little by little experimentation was conducted by rod builders. Finally the powerful influence of two American anglers, Lee Wulff and Paul Young, "the fathers of the midge," provided the major impetus. By the standards of the present-day American angler, Skues "wonderful little rod" is quite a bit of rod for trout and for fine leaders too.

Crompton, the patron saint of the modern rod builders, broke away from progressive taper by setting the planeing molds to swell or restrict thickness in order to control action and add strength and backbone where needed most. He also invented a glueing machine. Lew Fierbend designed the Super Z ferrule. The first rods termed "dry fly rods" swelled from a limber tip into a stout midsection and thence into a husky butt—strictly tip action. The initial thought was to employ one rod for dry fly fishing and a different one, much whippier, for wet fly fishing.

One day the great French angler, Charles Ritz, broke his rod tip on his way to the stream. In order to fish, he had to improvise. A tip guide was affixed. Much to his amazement and delight the crippled rod cast beautifully but the action was different. Now it came far down into the rod. This was the start of the parabolic craze, now commonly called a "slow rod," whereas the tip-action rod is referred to as a "fast rod." Possibly no one can now be sure about the conception of the nomenclature but the facts remain, stiff tip-action rods work faster in false casting and they strike a fish more quickly but the slow rods extend the false casts more readily and more rapidly. That is why the parabolics are the favorites of those who stalk bonefish on the flats with the intent of dropping a fly in front of one in the shortest possible time. Fast rods, rightly or wrongly, enjoy the reputation of being the better for distance casting tournament style.

The flexing of a rod brings about tremendous contortions, first stretching the fibers or cells on one side as those on the other are compressed, then reversing the order. The great strength and flexibility must be on the outer portions, for the mid-part simply rides along. The real strength of bamboo, a grass, is due to the density of the outer cells. So far a complication with fiber glass is caused by defective strips. There must be inspection for and selection of perfect sticks and the discarding of defective ones. Don't be concerned about getting a bad one; you won't. If this loss can be overcome, the price will be effected accordingly. They are both great materials and make up into fine casting instruments. By comparison, it seems to me, that the action of bamboo settles and stops faster when the stresses cease and has more life than is the case with glass.

Possibly the day is coming when our scion will be amazed at the exacting hand labor and costs involved in splitting, planeing and glueing pieces of grass together to fabricate a solid six-strip, or five-strip, bamboo fly rod. Such operations put to shame the brazeing of the two tubes of a double barrel shotgun and even now its sun is setting in America.

The matter of backbone cannot be designated in measured terms. About all that can be said is that the rod has it or lacks it. Those who insist upon this quality and need it so desperately are the anglers of the meadow streams who operate from the banks. To the rear are reeds, high grass, low shrubs, and still worse, hot wires. A rod with insufficient backbone to keep a normal back cast above such obstructions along a trout stream in a rural environment is an abomination. Here, in my humble judgment, is where the 7½-footer tops the midge.

There is another type of rod, really a special-purpose gadget. It was introduced to the fly fishing world by Al McClane, who must be as great an angler as he is a fine writer. Here is a real dwarf, 3 to 4 feet in length, made from the tip section of an old rod on which is affixed a reel seat and grip.

At one stage I fished the Yellow Breeches Creek, along which I lived, almost eight evenings a week. This 37-mile stream once turned 19 grist mills. A few are still operational; many of the defunct ones still stand. Each had a dam. At that time, in most instances, some water ran through the races; and in the bowls of the mill where the turbines are located was a deep pool pretty well blocked by a low stone archway. It was always possible to wade into casting position but to shoot a fly well into the tunnel under the mill was a problem. Needed was a sturdy short rod and a short leader so an extremely tight bow in the line could be cast through the aperture at the right angle.

A stubby little fly rod was made from the tip of an old bamboo bait casting rod. A little antique reel which carried about 60 feet of a home-spliced torpedo-head line was taped to the grip. With this oddity a fly could be driven further back into the dark recess than it was possible to do with anything which resembled the standard rod. There was a deterrent though. When a fly from a high cast cracked against the stone wall, it was time to reel up and replace it.

Much to my surprise the dungeons produced mostly newly-stocked trout. The fish trucks had access to the pools below the mill dams. Apparently a number of the new plants would drift downstream, then run up the tail race and settle in the hole under the mill. Funny thing, too, these were the prime places for ailing fish—sort of trout hospitals. After the novelty wore off, I gave up on the tunnel fishing with the Tom Thumb equipment.

Self portrait by the late Fred Everett, who had an abundance of "fun with trout."

[42]

The friction of a fast shooting line on the guides, particularly the tip guide is great. Once the guides are cut, they in turn wear out a line—a vicious circle. In this day of torpedo-head lines and double-hauls to make them work faster and shoot further, the pressure on the guides is intense. Lefty Kreh, the great ambidextrous caster, has settled on carboloid ring guides and a carboloid tip guide. Joe Brooks sticks with the snake guides but at the end of each fishing season, if his has an end, he returns his rods to the home plant for new sets of guides.

The fly reel has three functions. Obviously it is a storage place for the line. It should be used in the give-and-take battle when a fish is hooked, particularly a good one. And less obviously it is a shock absorber working in conjunction with the rod. Unless the click is soft with a minimum of inertia, those 5, 6, and 7X tippets are in trouble when a fish bolts. It is desirable that there is just enough tension to prevent over-lapping of the line on the drum as an active trout "runs the reel."

It is possible with the midge rod to throw a big trout off balance immediately after it has taken the fly. Often it is possible to quickly turn the head of a good fish near an obstruction so that the panic-stricken bolt is away from trouble.

There is a variation in rods and variation in reels. Since the margin of error between maintaining attachment and leader breakage is not broad, we need the most efficient equipment we can afford and locate. With care and with no misuse a rod and a reel will last a long time, so the long-term investment is not great. Secure, enjoy and employ the finest you can latch onto, but remember there are always compensating factors. Give a little here to gain a little there in this interesting percentage game. The choice of the balanced fly fishing outfit (not fly casting outfit) is a matter of individuality—not a job for a second party.

The main points I want to make are these. As time marches on, trout will not become less difficult to deceive and neither will fishing pressure diminish. The sophisticated angler will meet the challenge with a refinement of technique and tackle. The complete angler will think in terms of the competent outfit, not the least of which is that last strand of monofilament. When rod-tip leader protection is built into a stick which has an overall length in excess of 7½ feet, backbone disappears and the rod is a spineless thing, one which cannot hold up the back cast. On the other hand, a thin rod of short length will protect fine tippets and can possess the desired backbone to maintain steepled casts.

[43]

Therein lies the secret of the short lithe rod—a marvelous trout-catching implement in conjunction with leaders tipped out to 6 and 7 X. The common conception of the midge fly rod is one 6 feet in length, however, I like to think of them as a class: something between 5½ and 7½ feet long, and thin. Why not call them the 6 and 7X leader protectors. Here is the answer to prudent trout. Here is the match-maker's happy marriage.

Illustrious Lee Wulff uses midges for salmon as well as for trout. Yes, sir, the little rod will do the job:

> Under the transparent finish
> On four of those glistening sides,
> The great builders of bamboo midges
> This doggerel should inscribe:
>
> Be not afraid of any trout
> No matter what its size;
> When battle beckons, call on me,
> And I will tranquilize.

CHAPTER 5

Postgraduate Fly Casting

EVEN BEYOND childhood we are enthralled by the story of Aladdin and his magic lamp with the powerful genie incased therein, ready to heed the bidding of the master. Fantastic? Of course. But in the realm of reality there are forces in one form or another ready to respond to man's command. Cases in point are firearms, baseballs, pianos and typewriters. Mastery is a combination of desire, application, knowledge and native ability; but unlike Aladdin's lamp, no monopoly is involved. Is there any implement or instrument when placed in controlled animation which is more responsive and more versatile than the fly rod? We can think of none. The reasons why fly-rod wizardry is the counterpart of the giant in the bottle are herein related.

Just because one is of the opinion that fly casting cannot be mastered in an hour or a day, he should not stand so far off, or so close by, to be unable to see its unique advantages. The cold truth of the matter is that this is the only manner in which some fish can be taken. These are the shy ones, made so by fishing pressure, which have arrived at the stage where they can be deceived only by a direct imitation of the natural, presented in a perfectly normal manner and attached to a well nigh invisible connection. Involved is a feather-weight fly in conjunction with a gossamer leader made to drift or swim just so. The balanced tackle delivers the fly and the lithe rod protects the leader. Fly casting is a fascinating game of inches and it is a game in which the controls exercised by the caster are remarkable, even as they become second nature to him.

The statement that, "a vital part of fly fishing is fly casting." is not even debatable. One would expect to see on the streams, lakes and ponds, casters in approximate numbers who are good, bad and indifferent; but amazingly there are mighty few of each of the two extremes and a vast army of the mediocre. It must be that Mr. Average Angler is so involved with habits, environment, approach and equipment that he postpones the day when he makes a science out of delivery. Probably a stylist, such as Ted Williams, starts his serious effort at the other end of the line, then faces problems in a methodical take-them-as-they-come approach. It has been noted that this is the psychology of

[45]

the trap shooter turned angler. Isn't it foolish, though, not to make an honest attempt to cast up to the ceiling of one's ability, particularly if there exists a genuine love of the sport in its entirety?

It is basic, of course, that the line fits the rod and the leader fits the line. Strangely enough, a new line often creates a problem. Many of them have too long a level section in front of the taper. Two feet of it before one sees and feels the taper is fine, for this casts well and lands lightly. If the cast has a tendency to bog down and neither shoot nor straighten, either it is too light for the rod or there is excess level line out front. It is not wise to permit a conservative instinct to rule out the barber treatment. On the other hand, if it bogs down too much, particularly on the back cast, it is too heavy for the rod.

Assuming that the tackle is balanced, we set forth on our campaign of competent casting. Like the styles of the top-flight bowlers we watch perform on TV, the styles of the casters vary. It is not fair to state that there is one correct form only—one right way and everything else is wrong.

Among the great early tournament casters in this country were two who were also dedicated and skilled fly fishermen: the late Art Neu in the East and Frank Steel in the Midwest. It was the practice of each to instruct many others and to promote angling. Neu, in his exhibitions and films, would gracefully false cast a comfortable amount of line anchoring it against the rod grip with two fingers of the casting hand. With the other hand he would point to the casting wrist to demonstrate the importance of the rolling wrist action, a circular motion with the hand, as the arm from the shoulder to the wrist moved but little. On the other hand, Steel taught his proteges to practically lock the wrist and utilize the elbow as the fulcrum. Neu cast with his palm toward the direction in which the fly is to land; Steel with his knuckles in that position. They were both superb performers on stream or platform. Is it fair to say that one was right and the other wrong? Either could have made you eat such words.

Among the top-flight fly fishermen with whom I hobnob, Ernie Schwiebert exemplifies the Midwestern school, for as a boy he was coached by Steel; and Joe Brooks is one of the free wrist clan. In writing of the truly great casters, one stands above all others in one respect. The colorful, effervescing Lefty Kreh is just as ambidextrous as the slugging Mickey Mantle. In spite of his nickname, he can curve cast, double haul, et al from either side.

[46]

Like Schwiebert, he was well schooled. One day Joe Brooks and Tom McNally made him go with them to a sporting goods store where they bought him a fly rod. That was the starting point for the making of a wizard. Like his teachers, he is at home on a trout stream, a salmon river or a bonefish flat; but the fact remains, he is the foremost living authority on wet flies, nymphs, dry flies and bugs for big river bass. Jack Knight is a classicist and a student of the fly rod and the author of a definitive book on the subject.

Certain fundamentals, which have their way of hiding, must be understood. When one false casts as though he is using the butt section only, the line travels back and forth in a wide bow; but when the pressure is applied as though it were to the tip section only, the bow of the line and leader tightens. This is controlled by the casting hand. When the hand and arm move with circular motion, the bow is wide. When there is no circular motion, the bow is tight. When more than the normal amount of line for that particular cast is shot, the line and leader curve to the side of the casting hand; but when the shooting line is checked short, the curve is in the other direction. The greater the velocity of the line as it travels through the air while being false cast, the more power to the cast and the greater the amount of line which can be shot. Casting upstream, with the result that the current carries the line and leader toward the rod, presents a pickup problem which is non-existent with downstream casting. False casting is a necessity when casting upstream but not necessary when wet fly fishing down current. And most important of all, all phases of casting—the pickup, the back cast and the forward cast—are examples of gradually-accelerated motion: a little persuasion which builds as power is applied. It is a blend of movement, a smooth progressive application of power. On the pickup for the backcast, one slides the line from the water.

Armed with the above knowledge, the caster can exercise amazing controls in order to make the fly land at the desired spot then drift in a perfectly natural manner. He can cast from either side of the body with the same hand. He can effect a curve to the right or a curve to the left. He can utilize an open bow or a tight bow of the line and leader. He can speed the flight of the line as it travels back and forth through air. He can make the fly and leader kick back before they land on the water. It is because of these controls that problems can be solved, and problems there are. As Shakespeare said of Cleopatra, "Time cannot stale nor custom wither infinite variety."

[47]

The manner in which the rod is grasped determines whether the wrist or the elbow is to be the fulcrum. With the thumb to the side, the wrist is free to roll; with the thumb backing the grip, the fulcrum drops to the elbow. In either instance the balanced tackle does most of the work and the fact remains that it is wonderful to behold a good performer put it into operation. Be it wrist or elbow, it is poetry in motion. There is a grace and an at-homeness which gives the impression that the equipment is an extension of the caster's body.

The talented George Harvey, fly tying and casting instructor at Pennsylvania State University, tells us that within ten minutes he can have one of his boys or gals who never cast before operating in a creditable manner. That means that after a few tries, the line is being picked up with the required gradually-accelerated force, the back cast is not low, and there is the little pause between back cast and forward cast. In ten short minutes the feel, the timing and the progressive application of power become known and governable factors.

With the express intent to fish the water well let's you and I, a couple of right handers, go fishing. We will try to solve the problems as we meet them and see if we can't refine technique.

We step into the water on the left side looking up with the intention of casting up and to the right. At the same time we peel some line from the reel and set the rod in motion—back and forth. Right now the purpose is to get the desired amount of line in the air before we permit the fly to drop to the water; thereafter false casting, casting in the air, is multipurpose.

The fly drops on the water and immediately the current begins to carry the line, leader and fly toward the rod. Like the multitude of casts to come, it must be picked from the water for the next cast. If our upstream fly fishing is to amount to anything, we are going to have to get that fly off the water and into the air easily and cleanly—and frequently.

A neat trick accomplishes the desired result in admirable fashion. Instead of throwing the rod tip back over the shoulder to start the back cast and at the same time lift the fly from the water, we draw the tip back slightly then flip it forward. This sends a roll right down the line and into the leader. Just as this roll picks up the fly in a general upstream direction, the back cast for the next series of false casts starts. Because we were standing on the left side of the stream and casting quartering up and to the right, we made the roll pickup from the right side— the midstream side. Had we been on the other side of the stream, casting quartering up and to the left, we would have made our roll pickup backhanded—again from the midstream side. In either instance the fly is beyond the line so there can be no common meeting point with the result of a fouled fly on leader or line.

In order to lengthen the line and swish off excess water from both line and dry fly so both will float, we cast in the air several times. In our upstream fishing this false casting is going to be three quarters of our casting effort, so naturally we want to do it just right. We are faced with a matter of timing. Before the back cast reaches the end of its rearward journey, the forward cast is started. Then before the fly reaches the end of its forward journey, the back cast is started. We are lazily casting in the air with the rod slightly lower than the vertical and we are applying but little force to the butt section to maintain an open bow. The path of the line, leader and fly is a figure 8 on its side above the water.

Now the fly and line are sufficiently dry and the line has been lengthened in the air, so we are ready for the last back cast of the series. This one however, is a little different from the others. A bit more force is put into the cast and the fly is permitted to go back just a little further than the other false casts but we keep it high. Our forward cast which follows is also a little more decisive than the false casts which preceded. The fly is aimed at a point three or four feet above the water. As it arrives at that point we release the remaining loose line from the non-casting hand. The line, leader and fly settle to the surface and we are pleased how gently the fly puts down. That little shoot at the end has its way of softening delivery.

Thus we have accomplished the standard stream repertoire—the initial cast, the false casts, the pitch, then the pickup. Now we are going to look for problems and meet the situation with the right delivery.

Number 1, The Kick Back Cast: Twenty feet across stream, tight against the grassy bank, a good trout rose. The only available casting position for this fish is straight across. The goal is to make the fly drift naturally over the site of the rise. The hazards are two fold: tangling with the grass across the way and a dragging fly over the fish. The equipment is put into motion with its short timing with the rod in a near vertical position. The last back cast is a bit more decisive than the others and a little more time is allowed for the line and leader to straighten out. The last forward cast, too, is more decisive than the false casts. The pitch is aimed well-above and beyond the opposite bank. The excess line is shot and we stop the rod tip in a high position. The pitch is made. Suddenly all becomes taut and there is a slight jolt from the excessive pressure of the forward cast. The line jerks back and lands straight on the water but the leader lights in a series of curves or kinks. The fly does not land on the grass but has been jerked back and gently flutters to the surface.

The first pitch was a conservative feeler cast and it is three feet short of the mark. About a yard of line is stripped from the reel and another three feet or so is drawn back through the guides and we start the procedure again. This time the kickback drops the fly just right. It drifts naturally along the grass over the spot of the rise. Although the leader is 10 feet in length, the fly is about half that distance from the juncture of the line and leader. Between the fly and the line is a nice snaky leader which slowly straightens as the midstream current pulls the floating line. The series was perfect. There is good reason for anticipation to be at a high peak. Will he take?

The brown trout, transplanted to America from Europe, has been the salvation of Eastern, big-water, trout fishing. Today this is the most sought-after member of the speckled tribe by the majority of the members of the fly-fishing clan.

[50]

We arrive at a spot where there is an interesting brush pile across the way; and what is more interesting, a trout rises directly above it, in tight. There is only one possible way to drift a fly into him and that is from above. Thirty-five feet beyond the brush pile we ease into position. This time the cast must be a downstream kickback cast; and there is no room for the conservative feeler, for we can't have drag over the fish.

After the false casts, the final forward cast propels the fly high over the brushpile but it comes to an abrupt jolting halt then kicks back a good eight feet. The line, leader and fly settle to the water. The fly looks like the head of a long hair snake gradually straightening as it moves naturally toward the hot spot. We notice as it drifts to within inches of the brush, there is a backwater effect which almost stops its progress. Slowly the circling current moves it parallel to the obstruction. We have done our part; it's up to the fish now. If he does not take the first drift, we'll let the fly glide by the spot along the brush then gently skitter it out of there preparatory to the next try.

Number 2. Curve Cast To Rod Side: Upstream to the right is a protruding rock with a backwater in the front of it, a good-looking spot to drift a fly. There is a wet blotch on the rock. We wonder, could anything other than the rise of a trout have done that? Unless we cast a loop in the line and leader, the midstream channel will quickly set up drag and draw the fly out of there.

From our position thirty feet below, we lengthen the line by false casting and hold an extra 6 feet of loose line. The rod is operating almost parallel to the surface of the stream. Because the forward cast is a lazy butt-section cast we aim the fly to the right and well above the rock and over-shoot the extra line. The fly drops off to the right and short of the point of aim but right where we want it and the line and leader is in a big curve to the right. The fly has time to drift toward the rock before the faster midstream channel bows the line the other way.

Number 3. Curve Cast To Free Hand Side: The very next problem is the reverse of the last. This time we are on the right side of the stream as we look up; the taking place is above us to the left with the main channel intervening. The hook in the line and leader should be the other way now. The fly is a small one, offering little air resistance. We go into the familiar line-lengthening false casting but this time we make a tight bow by tip-section casting and the rod is well off the vertical. We find that when the elbow is propped against the hip, it is easier to put the tip section to work and at the same time hold the butt

[51]

rigid. There is nothing lazy about the last back cast and final pitch in this series. As the line shoots through the fingers we snub it short. The cast could have handled additional shoot. Line and leader hesitate above the surface, then momentum carries the fly and leader to the left. On the water it looks like a shepherd's crook, just what we want.

The cast was good enough but it drew no response. Trout have not been rising, so we decide to remove the small deceiver fly and substitute in its place a big spider, an attractor. Such a large fly offers so much air resistance that it will not turn over properly but there is an alternate approach to the problem. Now we false cast back-handed in the big-bow butt-casting manner, the point of aim being well above and beyond the desired destination of the fly. As the line goes out on the final forward cast, we shoot a little more than the cast will handle. Even before the line and leader drop to the water we see the big curve which cannot straighten. The fly lands to our side of the point of aim and that is where we want it. There will be a long float before the pull of the current reverses the bow in the line.

Number 4. The Angle Change: Our position is on the left bank as we look upstream. Tight against the grass on our side a fish rises but the high overhanging grass between us and the trout presents a problem. This time we sneak within 15 feet of the surface feeder. The fly must light closer to the bank than the intervening tufts of arching grass. Boldly we false cast above the grass in the decisive, tip-section, tight-bow manner. A small amount of line is shot on the final cast and even as it shoots through the guides we stop the rod tip high and immediately shove the tip almost to the surface of the water. The line drops on the water at right angle to the rod and the fly gently settles above the taking place. The fly is closer to the bank than any part of the leader and line and all are free of the grass.

Number 5. The Under Cover Cast: There is a good-looking place beneath the boughs of that tree. We are going to try to shoot the small fly back in that dark recess. Again the cast is sidearm and we must keep that bow in the line and leader as tight as possible, and, of course, that means cast as though we are making nothing but the rod tip do the work. The elbow is propped against the hip and more power is employed than is normally the case. This one is a challenge, for we do not want to tangle with the foliage. If the line were a dull color, it would be a little more difficult to see it in the air and judge the dis-

[52]

tance accurately than it is with our bright-colored line. The forward false casts carry the fly low and almost to the overhanging branches. Just as the line straightens out from our last peppy forward cast, we shoot the excess. It goes back under there six feet and there was only a yard of clearance.

Number 6. Mending: The water in the tail of the pool is shallow and slow flowing just before it spills between some rocks and forms the riffle below. A fish is in a favorite feeding position in the shallow tail of the pool in front of these rocks, for anything which drops into the pool is carried along to become grist for the mill. At best the float of our fly is going to be a short one. To the side and directly opposite the taking place is casting room, so we ease in and hunker down. The kickback cast places the fly above the fish and the slow flow starts. The rod tip is pointed at the fly and the arm is extended. Just before the current at the rocks pulls the line and drags the fly, we make a gentle upstream roll with the rod tip—just enough to pick up the line and place it upstream but too weak to pull the leader and fly. The natural drift continues right to the fish as floating time is increased. From the right side looking upstream, we would use a backhand roll, whereas it is a forehand roll from the left bank.

Number 7. The Roll Cast: Now we are hemmed in. There is no room for a back cast but prospects appear to be good if we can get the fly straight out. We peel some line from the reel then grasp the line below the lowest guide. The rod tip is drawn back until it is over head with the line hanging down. A down stroke of the rod makes the line and leader roll out in front of us and shoots the loose line but it is not nearly far enough. As fly and line ride out front, we strip off more line. Again we draw it toward us by elevating the rod tip until the line hangs under the rod. Again we roll it out with that down stroke, gradually accelerating the motion as power is applied to the butt section. This we continue until the length of line is sufficient to float the fly in the desired line of drift. The swoosh of the roll removes excess water from line and fly so both float, however, this cannot be continued indefinitely without both becoming waterlogged.

Now for the fun of it, let's reel in, start over and be fancy. The fly is held by the hook bend between the thumb and fore finger of the free hand and it will not be released until we think it is time to drop it on the water where we would like it to land. Some line is stripped off with the free fingers of the left hand, then we roll upstream, but still hold the fly. Some more line is stripped off and the loose line is anchored in the palm of the hand with the free fingers. Again the rod tip is elevated for the next roll but this time the roll is made from the opposite side of the body. All the while we are hanging onto that fly and rolling first upstream, then down. The process continues until what appears to be the right amount of line has been put in operation. The final roll before the fly is released is upstream from the downstream side.

Number 8. The Roll In The Air: We are faced with the situation where there is room for a limited backcast. The regular roll cast might work but that extra room in back invites a better delivery, in a sense an application of the roll. The weak back cast just lifts the fly from the water so that it lazily sails by us and slightly to the rear. The rod tip moves to the vertical. Just before the fly drops, the butt of the rod is pushed forward and the tip down in the customary gradually-accelerated motion. The result is a roll in the air instead of a roll on the water. The line and leader straighten out front and there is sufficient power to shoot the extra line. This is followed by false casts of the same motion before we again administer the final down-stroke delivery.

Number 9. The Spey Cast: There is a place straight across stream where the fly should land but the trees behind us make a backcast prohibitive. We have been fishing for some hours with the result that false casting is required to make the line and fly float. The rod employed is a wonderful little midge and we do not want to abuse it by roll casting a heavy sinking line. Feet are solidly planted, each an equal distance from the shore-line as we face midstream—body and head. False casts are made up and downstream so line leader and fly travel back and forth parallel to the foliage. The final delivery is a long swoosh from an extended backcast with the rod tip traveling in a semi-circle with tip finally pointing to midstream. Line, leader and fly in a great exaggerated semicircle follow the course of the rod tip. The power shoots the extra line and extends it straight across stream. A recent generation of anglers named this the Spey cast.

Number 10. The Galway Cast: Our situation is such that we are going to need distance to reach the desired spot across the way yet there are some trees behind us. Here and there is room for healthy back casts but these are of limited dimensions. Unless the fly travels through a hole in the foliage, we are in for trouble. In order to be sure to hit the opening, we are going to face the hazard so we can direct the forward cast into a hole. Just as the cast enters the opening we reverse our body position so we face the stream. Thus what would have been a backcast is transformed into a forward cast. Although the line, leader and fly travels back and forth, all are forward casts as we turn with each pitch.

Number 11. Distance Casting: Long casts are contingent upon proper timing and some practice is necessary to condition reflexes. The rod packs resources of energy. The right moves, each in gradually-accelerated tempo and blended together in a smooth manner bring forth the built-in energy. The backcast must be right and just because it is behind us does not mean that we cannot turn our heads to watch it.

We are not going to make the mistake of attempting to lift from the water and toss into the air more line than can be readily handled, rather we operate with a comfortable amount and depend upon shoot. The faster the line travels back and forth in the air and the more butt-section rod action we can put into play, the greater the power which is generated.

The start of the first back cast is exacting. With the line and leader taut and the casting arm extended forward we start the gradually-accelerated back cast. This outward stretch make a steepled cast possible. When the back cast is well in progress we shoot a yard or two of line. Just as the line and leader straighten out, we start our gradually-accelerated, butt-section forward cast and aim it high. When the fly is far on its way and line momentum has built up, we release the shoot. Before another back cast is attempted, considerable line must be retrieved —hand twist for the wet fly cast downstream and the bone fish peel-back in little jerks when casting a wet or dry upstream. The resistance of the current against the line makes downstream casting much the easier of the two.

This is the basic distance cast, however the tournament boys have developed a refinement which adds distance and is applicable to fishing, in their parlance, the left-hand haul. As the line begins to straighten out on the back cast, the hand holding the line drifts up toward the butt guide. Coordinated with the forward, butt-section cast, the line is pulled downward from which point it is not released until the outgoing line and leader are far on their way. When incorporated into a series of hauls while false casting, the velocity of the line traveling through the air is built up to the point where an abnormal amount of line can be shot.

[55]

Another method of distance casting is more simple than the left-hand haul and highly effective in wet fly fishing. The backcast is a lazy affair with the fly passing by the rod side, low and not fast. When it reaches a point where it is about to drop, we throw in a strong vertical roll. As the line and leader straighten out front we apply a strong, stapled, vertical, accelerated-motion backcast, and shoot some line. The forward cast which follows in this series of three is a strong butt-action cast. There has been a fast build up of progressive speed and the line is traveling back and forth fast so that the shoot of the remaining loose line will be great.

There is but one other control to be pulled from our bag of tricks and it is applicable to wet fly fishing only. This has escaped all but a very select few. No false casting is involved and it is a joy to use when casting quartering downstream from the left stream side. When the cast is fished out and the fly is well downstream, it is picked up back handed in the customary gradually-accelerated force and without a pause and in a wide semi-circular manner, the rod tip describes an overhead arc only to be pushed straight out in the direction the fly, leader and line are to travel. Considerable force has been generated and the loose line shoots out straight and true. The arm, the rod and the line and leader are all extended for a fast wet fly retrieve which can hold the fly just under the surface—great stuff on a salmon river.

The big difference between this and the normal cast is that the line travels in a plane horizontal to the water in a continuous semicircle, whereas the usual is vertical to the water and the motion is back and forth. This delivery, which Hewitt called "the lariat cast," is a fine way to buck the teeth of a wind. It is easiest and most comfortably accomplished when the feet are planted so we face downstream. This is most useful on big rivers.

Tradition decrees that the sound made by the narrow single-action reel in response to an outgoing hooked fish is a scream. We'll let that nomenclature pass unchallenged with the simple reflection that a "screaming reel" is next to the most wonderful sound on earth, the premier being the watery glumps made by surface feeding fish.

Drag and its disastrous effect have been lambasted from pillar to post, but the very fact that trout are strongly inclined to pass up a dragging fly and at times even go off their feed by the mere sight of one, is the circumstance which presents us with

[56]

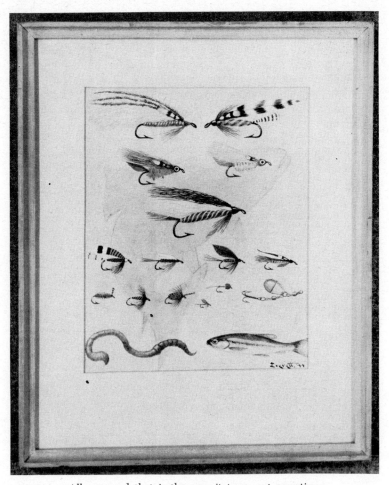

All wet, and that is the way it turns out sometimes.

our most interesting challenge. The fly fisherman meets the problem of drag with control. He develops accuracy, the ability to curve his casts or place slack in the leader and he can range out when he so chooses.

There are fish in hard-fished waters which cannot be touched by a fly attached to a heavy leader point, yet these same trout will accept the same fly connected to an ultra-light strand of leader (.0047—.0041). Then too there are leader-shy fish which must be shown the fly before the leader moves into view. The fly rod is the only casting instrument which will successfully

[57]

protect light terminal tackle and present the deceiver or attractor first. This means but one thing: There are some fish which can be taken by fly fishing only. If you, like the vast majority of anglers, depend upon waters subject to considerable fishing pressure, this is of considerable significance. To that add the joy of fly casting, the pleasure of playing fish on the fly rod and the satisfaction and the challenge of problem fishing. This matter of fishing the water well is a wonderful game. It is interesting to look forward to fishing situations which invite the various fly-casting applications.

CHAPTER 6

A Most Versatile Fly

IN HIS EFFORT to accelerate the slow grinding wheels of trout fishing refinement, Edward R. Hewitt developed styles of tie, one of which is extra special. The origin of the spider dry fly seems already to be a part of lost history but such is not the case with a Hewitt deviation. The brain child of the great angler had no tail, no body—just wide hackle—tied on an abnormally small hook. The catch is that it has to be tied just so.

The introduction of it to the fly fishing fraternity was via a remote channel. One day back in the mid '30's, while sitting in the office of a doctor, I was idly paging through a magazine, not the hunting-and-fishing type but a plushy paper dealing mostly with horses, yachts, skiing and golf, none of which happened to be down my alley. Imagine the surprise and pleasure when I encountered a beautifully illustrated piece entitled Butterfly Fishing, by Edward Ringwood Hewitt.

The author described a new type of surface trout fishing which he had developed. Before the article was concluded I was interrupted but after the doctor had executed his function I went right back into the office to finish the intriguing reading.

Nothing would do but to call for help. My SOS was answered by an assortment of "Neversink Skater Flies" from the creator of them. They appeared to be simplicity itself—just two hackles, concave sides together, wound around a short-shank, light-wire, #16 hook.

According to the article the idea was to jerk and drag them across the surface over the known or suspected position of a good trout in an attempt "to jump him."

After becoming the recipient of the modest supply, the first place they saw action was at the Fisherman's Paradise on Spring Creek. This might or might not be a good testing ground. There were big fish there but they were handfed on ground fish and red meat after dark each evening of the relatively short open season, the natural food of this rich stream being but a supplementary diet.

Right smack in the middle of the day, when things were quiet, I tried one on and pinched off the tip of the barb. The fly offered considerable air resistance and fluttered to the surface after the long fine leader had already settled. If ever a fresh fly rode on the tips of its toes, this was it. When the rod tip was given a little jerk upward, the fly tilted and slithered into a skating dance. It looked interesting and certainly was different, a thing lifelike and animated.

There was a brush pile across the way and right below it a gouge in the bottom created by a V dam. Everyone who ever fished the place knew there was a school of good trout out there. The spider again drifted to the surface and I became involved in a new game of making a dry fly dance to my own rhythm. The second skip in the retrieve was met by an explosion. My reaction was not good; it was spontaneous. The untouched fly sailed back over my head.

"Certainly appeared that he liked it," came a voice from the bridge. It was Dr. Dick Hoffman.

Everything went about the same way on the next pitch, only this time a surging fish snapped off the fly so fast that the jolt was probably never even felt.

"Settle down, boy," says Dick. I shook my head and tied on another.

A skater fly does not cast as decisively as a small wet or dry. Due to air resistance it lags behind, calling for different timing in casting. I hadn't made more than several false casts when a poor back cast made this fly tick the rod. The well tempered hook of the precious skater fly was broken. In disgust I snapped it off the tippet and let it drift to the ground. Things were not going according to script and it was all my fault.

The first thing I knew, Dick was bending over beside me picking up the fly. "Let me see that thing," he demanded, and he took it back to the bridge.

When skater number three nestled to the surface, I said to myself, "easy does it, from here on out."

Easy did it well. Two good fish were quickly hooked played and returned. Then I jumped a battle wagon—once, twice and a third time, but he wouldn't come back again.

I gave him the prescribed treatment, a rest. Five minutes later when casting was resumed, the fish was in business again. This time I hooked him and after tiring a little from fighting out in the open, he bulldogged his way into the brush pile, and with him went skater fly number 3.

"Dick!" I said. "Half my good flies are gone; I'm going to move to a safer place."

The two of us walked upstream to the backwater of a dam.

In good light and with the aid of Pollaroid glasses—something new at that time—we could barely discern the forms of fish in a suspended position about two feet under the surface.

"They're looking for surface food," advises Dick. "Show them that big fly."

These trout liked what they saw—at least to a degree. Everyone we could watch would take a turn at the skating fly, some creating a wake or breaking the surface, but I wasn't doing very well in getting the hook into them. Dick and I, nevertheless, were impressed. He was going to tie some of these flies.

By the end of the day I had one fly left, having broken one and left four in hooked fish. On the otherside of the ledger, about ten trout had been caught and released, a few ticked and dozens raised which would not take.

The thing now was to get some more flies. I still had a sample and so did Dick.

A courtesy report was made to Mr. Hewitt and back came the following reply:

"This method of fishing has now been tried all over the angling world and it is very often by far the most successful way to get a big trout. I had a most interesting time with it on a Scotch loch belonging to the Duke of Athol. I caught large trout from three to five pounds right in the middle of the day when none of these large fish had been taken for months by any fishing methods.

"Skater fishing has been most successful in the Rockies for large fish; and last year my friend, Jack Atherton, got 32 large landlock salmon during his trip in Maine when there were no other large fish taken during his stay.

"The technique of this fishing is most difficult and the tackle must be just right. The fact that you raised the large trout at Bellefonte with the skater but did not hook all or most of them, shows that you have only partly mastered the technique, because such fish should always be hooked if you work the fly as it should be worked. No doubt you get too excited and move the fly too fast, away from the fish when he breaks water. When a large trout once shows interest in a skater fly, he can nearly always be hooked. Very often he must be rested quite a long time as we do in Atlantic salmon fishing. Often they come two or three times for the fly but not more unless rested for five to ten minutes.

"If you don't hook the trout on the spiders, you are striking much too fast. Do just as Arthur Wood does in Scotland. When

[61]

he sees a fish break, he says, 'and now I've got this one,' and then he strikes. He gets about all of them too. Big fish move much slower than small ones and they also let go of the fly much slower. You can hardly ever loose one if you don't strike at all. One will carry the fly in its mouth several feet under water."

The words of wisdom from Mr. Hewitt, along with the Spring Creek results, prompted more spider testing. The next episode was entirely different in nature. I was still down to one skater fly, a light-honey one; but more were ordered from a commercial fly tier, and then, too, there was Dick Hoffman. This was in the days before I tied my own but I had no doubt that the supply would be promptly replenished. The remaining skater fly was tucked away in the box. One early June evening as I worked over a selective Penns Creek riser to green drake spinners, one "special imitation" after another was refused as every so often the good fish would gulp another natural. A blank was drawn by George Phillips' hair wing and rabbit-whisker tail imitation. Hass Lose's cork bodied spent wing suffered the same fate. So did Howard Shilling's wingless spider with the unique clipped hackle body. I had no intention of running away from that fish. It was the sort of thing for which the trip had been made; I wanted him. There was only one other possibility left; out came the honey skater fly.

The wading in Penns Creek can accurately be termed Hellish, so instead of moving into an upstream position in order to properly skate the fly over the fish, I elected to stay put and show a natural drift of the skater fly to the cantankerous one. Down it drifted, cocked as prettily as you please. There was a deliberate and majestic head-and-tail rise and the fly disappeared in a slurp. When I lifted the rod tip, he was there.

After the fish was landed, there was still enough time and light to try for more. I sloshed the fly in the water to wash it, blew on it violently, then pitched it over what appeared to be another good-size feeder.

It was a case of two casts, two fish. Before darkness descended, a third fine brown had taken the natural drifting skater. In all three instances there was no fooling around; they liked it—or its impression. The evening ended and I still had one skater fly—and a new use for the tie.

Bob McCafferty came to me with a request, "Give me the fly to take apart; I can't understand how they are tied. Mine flange out at the hackle tips instead of coming together."

Before it was over, he had the last fly. After the tying silk was cut, the hackle unwound and it appeared just as we expected—two hackles, dull sides together. "I don't get it," Bob observed. "I tied mine the way this is tied but they don't look same. Can't understand how he makes all hackle ends on the perimeter come together."

I sent an S.O.S. to Dick Hoffman. His reaction was, "mine look like thistles, ends all over the place. When you try to skate them, those odd ends pierce the surface and dunk the fly."

Quickly I contacted Mr. Hewitt. He did not advise how to tie them but he did put me in touch with his man on the Neversink, "who would furnish some." In due time, back came some flies, mostly honeys, and I was in business again.

That is the way things stood for a few years. I was ordering skater flies, not only for myself, but for capable fly tiers and various other anglers. There was a fly tying trick involved which defied imagination, to which we all agreed. Skater flies were popular within the group but we fished them two ways, natural drift and in jerks, and sometimes both ways on one cast. Beyond all shadow of doubt they proved their value as a deceiver imitation of the green drake; at times they served their worth as a natural drifting attractor, and there were times when the skated fly jumped big trout. The one weakness was that the hackles readily mat and the fly becomes sodden. We tried greasing the leader so the fly could be lifted directly from the surface in the pickup without submerging, and this was a refinement. A long fine leader made them settle ever so delicately.

Twice by accident I experienced the same thing. When I give up, the habit is to pitch out the last cast then reel in until the jointure of the line and leader approaches the tip guide. In both these instances good fish had been raised to the skating fly but apparently had lost interest and would not come back. On the underwater retrieve, following this last cast, a breathing, pulsating, wet skater fly was smeared in a businesslike manner. That was the conception of a last resort practice, a skater fly fished wet.

Vince Marinaro is a great champion of direct imitation and I have heard him refer to skater flies as, "those confounded spiders," nevertheless he has given them a fair trial. One day when we were fishing together he advised, "I want to show you something."

In the box he handed me was a nest of assorted spiders—true

[63]

Neversink skater flies. Not only were they shaped just right—hackle tips together, broad part of fly at hook shank—but there were colors and combinations of colors we had never tried. Beside the established honey were all black, slate, bronze-blue and ginger faced with grizzly and black faced with green. I looked from them to him.

"The solution is so simple; that is why we missed it. The first thing everybody does is to wax the tying silk. Use slick nylon and don't use wax; that is the simple secret." In those days everyone used waxed silk. "Tie in the hackle"; he continued, "advance the tying thread; wrap the hackle; then with the nails of fore finger and thumb, jam everything toward the bend. Keep doing this until the two hackles are on, shiny sides out. It's the back hackle which takes the beating, so use more turns with the back one than with the front one."

The following spring, elderly Mr. Hewitt made the trip to Harrisburg with Sparse Grey Hackle Miller to attend the annual dinner of The Fly Fisher's Club. As I stood by, Vince showed those two patriarchs a small box loaded with assorted Neversink skaters.

There was a quizzical look as the question was put, "Where did you get them?"

"I tied them," answered Vince, whereupon the old gentleman smiled, nodded his head and patted Vince on the shoulder, and Sparse winked at me.

The cat was out of the bag but it was just about this time that the practice of waxing tying silk became passé.

Since that time, there has been considerable experimentation with color and size. Local popular favorites are: honey, black, slate, and ginger faced with grizzly in size ranges from the diameter of a nickle to the diameter of a silver dollar. Both Sparse Miller and Ernie Schwiebert showed up later with some tied of hair.

In September of '61 three local stalwarts put up at Livingston, Montana, to sample the fishing Joe Brooks had raved about. Tommy Thomas, Norm Lightner and Bill Wald practically revolutionized mid-day blue-bird-weather fishing with their skating of the Hewitt deviation. It was a note from Joe which divulged this information, later verified by the trio.

CHAPTER 7

Enter Ernie Schwiebert

A YOUNG GIANT is striding across the trout horizon just as though it were planned that way. A fishing father placed his boy who had just become a teenager in the capable hands of Bill Blades, the great Midwestern fly tier, so the youth would learn to fabricate his own imitations of the natural. Then with loving care the boy was turned over to the great fishing expert and champion tournament caster, Frank Steel, so he would come to handle equipment properly and fish the water well. From thence it was the great trout and salmon streams of our continent and beyond.

Later as a student of architecture at Ohio State University he attained *Cum Laude*. Versatile athletic experience has its bearing on the physical skills of casting. Even as an undergraduate he was writing what was destined to become an angling classic, Matching The Hatch, now being reprinted.

Since those days, there have been a lot more casts on a lot more waters. As a teaching fellow at work on his doctorate in architecture at Princeton University, he enjoys a fisherman's holiday of which he makes the most. Somehow in his whirlwind life he finds time to produce angling articles for the periodicals and he is one of the most articulate angler-speakers of the age. Those who read his work and hear him talk marvel at his knowledge, experiences, enthusiasm, power of observation, and thrill at his command of the English language. This is Ernest G. Schwiebert, Jr.

Here is a relatively young man. At this critical time of a faltering conservation in a new era of meglopolis, striptowns and water problems the trout angler is in need of expert advice and recreational champions. Planning and architecture is the Schwiebert vocation, the science of angling his avocation. He projected into the second annual convention of Trout Unlimited a crystal ball talk which every trout angling father of a son should have heard.

There is something about the understanding of a common interest and affection which molds together kindred spirits. A trout stream has a way of doing this to its regulars in about as complete a manner as possible. The feeling for cherished waters can be strong. Rudyard Kipling sounded a warning:

[65]

Go softly by that river side
Or when you would depart,
You'll find its every winding tied
And knotted round your heart.

It was at such a riverside as Kipling wrote that the paths of Ernie and me first crossed. Ross Trimmer, the dean of the LeTort regulars, appeared one evening with a stranger. "This young fellow asked me if I know Vince Marinaro and if I could lead him to Fox's meadow, on a limestone stream with a strange name" and his hearty laugh carried up and down the water course. "If the trout are not coming up, we'll make 'em come up," he added.

Well, they were not rising much and Japanese beetles were in full bloom, so Ross busied himself with the collection of a few dozen of the pretty insects. Ernie explained that he was fascinated by the Marinaro book, "The Code," and he was not only anxious to meet its author, but he also wanted to have a look at some of the waters about which Vince wrote. It developed that his dad, Dr. Schwiebert, is a governmental official active in the administration of scientific research. Since Ernie was temporarily located with his parents near Baltimore, he decided to jump in the car and make the run to investigate Vince's trout streams of the Cumberland Valley.

The first stop was Big Spring near Newville. As he drove along the road which parallels the stream he saw a dry fly fisherman in action who appeared to know what it is all about, so he parked and went over to talk with him. The initial contact was a good one. The tobacco-chewing ex-State policeman is a dedicated and avid angler, commercial fly tier, and a personality if ever there was one.

Ross returned with a grin on his face and immediately took charge. "Now I gilly while you fish." That was Ernie's indoctrination to what can be called, "the creation of a natural hatch and a rise of some real trout." You see, Ross knew just where to chum.

It required but little time for the visitor to acquaint himself with the sophistication of the quarry. The challenge of the beetle eaters as well as the dainty feeders to minutae was the sort of thing which stirred his angling blood.

That night back at the motel he tied some special ammunition for the ensuing day.

The next evening, after breaking away from the office, I confronted him in the meadow and asked for a report. He was beaming from ear to ear. "The problems are wonderful; this is my kind of trouting."

In answer to the query, "How did you do," he admitted that he wasn't exactly sure, "but there had been a few bolting fish somewhere over 16 inches which took me to the cleaners." They seem to have made a deep impression, but I pressed to find out what didn't steal his flies. "Landed three around 18 inches and returned about a dozen others, some on imitation beetles and hoppers, some on ants and jassids."

This fellow caught on fast. These are the accepted four big patterns for late July. And 15 trout, including some good ones, is a whopping day on the LeTort.

"What size tippet?" I asked, to which he responded ".0047" (6x). I admitted to myself, the one who wrote Matching The Hatch knows the score.

After dark on the bench at the "19th hole" the group had a high old time of it. Ernie was one of the boys—and fast.

"Come on up again next weekend to end the season," we urged. "On the 31st there will be a little closing-out picnic— after fishing, that is."

"I'll be back," he assured us, "if I'm not called to active duty."

It so happened that there was scheduled a meeting of the Board of the Fish Commissioners for that date and it so happens too that we knew that Dr. Albert Hazzard, the fisheries specialist, had recommended an extension of the trout season upon which his board would act. Arrangements were made that as soon as the meeting adjourned, Bob Glover, the P. R. man in the office, would call the house to advise of the outcome.

My wife got the message and called over to the nearest fisherman: "September 15th." This in turn was relayed up and down the line and you could hear it travel. Probably never before or since has there been so much noisy jubilation along trout water. The intermittent yelling continued until dark.

The picnic was a celebration instead of a wake and as happy as any was the foreigner to the stream.

"If they don't call me up, I'll be back next weekend," we again heard.

He operated with three-day, Pennsylvania, non-resident licenses. Well, Air Force active duty didn't catch up with Ernie and before it was all over that season he purchased seven of those three-day licenses, thinking probably each one would be the last.

The rainbow trout, native of the Pacific Coast streams, has been re-distributed to most trout watersheds. The hatchery strain is a migrant; a hooked fish is a good jumper.

We made it our business to learn more about this remarkable young man. Little by little the pieces were put together and they sure did fit. Most of the information about him was drawn from his dad, who now and then utilizes the meadow as an appropriate meeting place for a father-and-son reunion.

The last such meeting produced one of the most dramatic angling incidents it has been my fortune to witness. The LeTort grows them big and some of the well-conditioned stream-bred trout are inclined to surface feed. It was a Friday evening and the Schwieberts were due to arrive on the scene the next day. Partly because I like Ernie and partly because I cherish the stream, it is good to see it put on a show for him.

I threw a handful of beetles in the rushing water below a temporary pipe in the stream. Just where the water drops off and widens out, there was a majestic rise of a great battle wagon. Altogether four of the beetles were engulfed by that impressive maw. Thinks I, here is the one to reserve for Ernie.

Upon his arrival he was advised that there was a big beetle eater waiting for him upstream—not far up. He was to go up and get into him.

[68]

"I'll work my way up," he advised.

I knew what that meant. If he found any coming up on the way, it might take a long time to get there. To him a rise of a trout is the signal for a duel. It seems impossible for him to desert the spot until the contest has been resolved one way or another. At any rate, I slipped up to test the fish. I showed him one, and only one beetle. He was in business.

In answer to my yell, "Come on up," I drew a blank. Half an hour passed and I could see Ernie's hat above the grass at the bend below and every so often a rod tip and wet leader flashing in the sunshine.

There was a temporary dirt-fill road impacted around and over the pipe, not 30 feet from the feeding station of the great fish. All of a sudden there was a commotion down the road. Along came a scraper, followed by several big tractors making their way toward this temporary stream crossing. As the big "cats" crossed the fill, the ground gave to the weight of the front wheels, then sort of waved back into an approximation of the old form. Along with the commotion some mud was created by the tumbling of loose ground over the banks. In about five minutes some more beetles were drifted to the trout but he was through, no doubt glued to the bottom of the most secluded part of the pool. He didn't show anymore that day either.

The morrow being Sunday, there should be no such interference. Possibly he would again be back in his feeding position, only this time I would try to prevail upon Ernie to start there.

The fellows gathered in the meadow. Along with five of the local fishermen and the two Schwieberts was Don DuBois of Arlington, Virginia, author of *The Fisherman's Handbook of Trout Flies*. The seven of us sneaked up on the temporary roadway in such a position that we looked right down into the pool with the sun at our backs. Ernie worked his way into casting position below. He had the 6-foot midge rod and the leader was tapered out to the now customary 7X.

"How big did you say this trout is?" he inquired.

The answer was to throw some beetles on the water. They floated their way into a chain. The first had no more than arrived at the spot until the trout tipped up. The well spiked open mouth broke the surface and a beetle disappeared. Before the trout sank out of sight he turned just enough to display a very board side and a grand array of big spots.

The simultaneous "oohs!" and the "aahs!" answered the question.

"I couldn't see the fish," commented Ernie, "only the rise form, but judging from what was heard, I better take off the 7X." To this all concurred, probably believing that it was reckless to use 6X on such a fish.

The imitation beetle landed just right and drifted naturally—and undisturbed—over the spot. Four such deliveries followed and there was nothing doing.

"More beetles," says Ernie in a sort of whisper. "Maybe he's scared out."

But he wasn't. Beautifully he eased up and sipped one more.

Ernie switched to his LeTort hopper. The cast and the float, as usual, were precisely right.

The battlewagon moved under it, inspecting the fraud at very close range as he drifted with it, then convinced that here was grist for the mill, the mouth slowly opened and the fly disappeared. The little rod jumped into a throbbing arc as the line was lifted from the water. The gallery issued the cry, "He's on!"

Sometimes big trout settle back; sometimes they bolt, but this one did neither. There was a wild jump right at the taking place and it seemed that the fish did not have time to settle in the water until he was out again in another sparkling shower of flying water. There was no breakage. But this time the fly lost its hold. It wasn't the fault of the angler. Well, that's the way it goes sometimes; and that's the way it should be—sometimes.

Ross takes delight in steering Ernie into tough situations. Now and then a great surface feeder is encountered which seems immune to the best angler's wares. The thought often expressed is that leg movement of the struggling insect is the equalizer of events. If such is the case, they are safe, for sure.

Late one season there was a fine free riser which spurned the best efforts of each angler in turn who took a crack at him. This one fed for hours on end each afternoon on what we assumed to be leaf hoppers (jassids); but show him some beetles, and he took them too. After about three weeks of such feeding at the same place, Ross named the fish, "The trout without a mouth."

When Ernie came around, Ross adroitly maneuvered him to the spot. "Think I saw something come up out there under the willow. Sure enough. Look!"

Ernie was like a pointer drawing on a running bird. He eased into casting position, then watched before he made his pitch. Ross left with the words, "I'll look for another around the bend."

I happened to be up there. When he sidled up to me, he was a study in restraint.

"What's new?" I asked, suspecting something.

"Ernie's here. I put him on the trout without a mouth. After he has fooled around with it for about half an hour, let's go down and offer some no-good advice."

"That's hitting below the belt," I admonished.

When we finally rounded the bend, the fisherman was in the process of changing flies. We were greeted with the words, "You sure have one here that looks them over."

"Oh, Ernie," I replied, "forget that fish. There is a better one coming up around the bend."

"This is an interesting trout," was his reaction. "You can't run away from something like this." And he was busy casting again, engrossed in his favorite sport of fishing over a prudent surface feeder.

Suddenly there was that trained hand-and-eye reaction and that finger-tip skill in setting a hook. The trout without a mouth was hooked, played, landed and released.

I looked at Ross. He spat a speculative tobacco stream. "Well I'll be damned," he whispered.

"What fly, Ernie," I asked.

"Undersize Jap beetle," he replied.

"Six X?" I ventured.

"No. 7."

One year circumstances dictated that the trout season in his case would come to a finish one week before the official closing time. For his final fling in the failing light I showed him a group of eight good dusk risers located near the house. These fish having watched numerous imitations drift overhead and having been rudely jolted on occasion, were no pushovers. The attractions of the setup were two fold: the trout were located in a small area so that a minimum of moving about was required on the part of the angler and they were feeding in a silvery sheen which made rise forms visible in the afterglow.

Ernie's idea was to start with the lowest in line, working his way up, to see how many could be taken before darkness called it a season. One of each of the four big patterns of the moment was put aside in a handy box—a 22 cinnamon ant, a 20 black jassid, an 18 partridge caddis and a 14 hopper. He is a believer in pattern. Aren't we all? Because of time limitation,

[71]

no one fly would be shown any trout more than six times.

What transpired in the ensuing thirty minutes would confound established conception and explode theory. No trout accepted the first pattern shown it. That means that there was as much time consumed in changing flies as there was in casting them. It ended up that each trout in turn was taken and two on each of the four patterns. Here was a clear-cut case of individual preference. Most of us would have stuck with one fly and figured that we had fished well had we caught two trout.

As the first stars twinkled in a velvet firmament the weak beam of his fountain-pen flashlight provided sufficient illumination to display the satisfied smile of an appreciative angler. "Like Lee Wulff says," he mutters to himself or maybe to trout number eight which he was carefully releasing, "'too valuable to be used only once.'"

Just prior to the opening of another trout season there is a gathering of the clan under the banner of The Fly Fishers Club of Harrisburg. For the last two events we have employed his services as a speaker in the full knowledge that there is no finer in the Land. We certainly look forward to the Schwiebert fishing and non-fishing visits, now particularly in view of the fact that this master of his time is one of the old alumni of the stream who frequently reappears.

CHAPTER 8

Advice and Device

NORMALLY MUTUAL understanding fosters conversation but there are times when the subject is so uninteresting that talk dwindles. Two dedicated anglers who team up together and who thoroughly enjoy the company of one another have their own way of breaking platitude and starting up a fresh conversation directed into the chosen channel. One will break the silence by asking, "Do you know what?" to which the other, with a fish-eye stare, will respond, "No, what?" No matter which one poses the initial query, the stock positive reply is, "I love trout fishing." One of these is Dr. Donald DuBois, author of *The Fisherman's Handbook of Trout Flies*, the other one is Ben Schley, Chief Fish Culturist of the Fish and Wildlife Service. Don, a psychologist and inventor, is a real stickler for exactitude as applied to his work or his play. When he employed the "You-know-what?" routine on me, I retaliated by prying into his favorite subject. "All angling problems can be solved," I ventured. "It is just a matter of conscientious application. What do you propose to do to refine and standardize equipment?" That did it, he took the bait. Thereafter followed a problem-and-solution lecture as I listened.

The Problem:

"Very often, soon after a new pattern goes into the fly box, its name cannot be recalled. No easy way to recover the name has existed. Since using pattern names is part of the fun of fly fishing, this limits pleasure. It also limits communication, for unless the fly in question is a common one, the answer to the usual question, 'What were you using?' is apt to be something like 'Well, it was a sort of a dark fly,' which certainly doesn't convey much information. The inability to use names for new patterns also tends to make us stick to a few old familiar ones that we *can* name. Thus, we miss the fun of experimentation.

"Many flies of the same name have little or nothing in common. Since all the trout can react to is the actual makeup of a fly, the fact that we call different flies by the same name makes no impact on him. Yet we are always acting as if the *name* is

[73]

all that counts. This creates confusion and again limits communication.

"To understand trout flies you must know about the materials they are made of. But this information is scattered here and there and writers are always assuming that the reader knows things he doesn't."

The Solution:

"A system that makes it possible to easily identify fly patterns.

"Different patterns of the same name should be given individual identification.

"Materials should be described and terms explained."

The Problem:

"The size of flies is important to trout. But it is the size of the *parts* of a fly that influences trout—not the hook size. Unfortunately, part size varies greatly from fly to fly tied on the same size hook. So, when (as is our custom) we use hook size to designate overall size, we are not being very accurate.

"Making absolute judgments, such as those required in estimating hook size, is something humans do very poorly. Therefore, hook size, as well as shank length, is often judged erroneously."

The Solution:

"A scale for fly parts based on the measurement of top-quality flies. This allows the tier to tie the same size fly again and again. It permits the buyer to select what he wants.

"A scale for hook size and shank length, so these can be measured by relative, rather than absolute, judgment."

The Problem:

"Hackles must go on edgewise to make a proper dry fly. But, many hackles tend to twist and go on flat. The control exerted by the hackle pliers is so far from the hook shank that this twisting cannot be prevented.

"When two hackles are put on together, they tend to separate and one of them developes slack."

The Solution:

"A device that exerts control over the hackles so that they cannot twist or separate."

The Problem:

"To match the hatch the fisherman must first get one of the insects the trout are feeding on. This is very difficult without a net. And nets are clumsy and the fisherman may feel a little silly carrying one. Also, standard insect nets have handles that are too short to effectively reach spinners."

The Solution:
"A pocket net which attaches to the rod, the rod acting as a long handle."

The Problem:
"A leader should be fairly straight to work properly. But, every time a leader comes out of its package, or from its container, or off the reel, it is kinked."

The Solution:
"A device that takes advantage of the fact that stroking a nylon leader with rubber will remove the kinks."

The Problem:
"One often carries leaders of different tapers and lengths. But it is not always easy to tell what a given leader is by looking at it. Also, the ends of a leader tend to spring out of the normally open-ended envelope in which they are carried."

The Solution:
"Envelopes with write-on surfaces so their contents can be indicated. If the write-on surfaces are of different colors, the leaders that go in them can be color coded by dipping their butt ends in enamel of the same color as the envelope.

"The envelopes should swing out of the leader wallet one at a time so the leaders in which you are not interested cannot spring out of their envelopes."

The Problem:
"In tying leaders, in repairing broken leaders and in tying on tippets you need to know the diameter of the strands being used. If you don't you can't make the proper taper for a new leader or rebuild a broken one. Also, if you jump more than about two thousandths in the diameters, the strands won't hold together. Unfortunately, even the strands that are in labeled containers are often labeled inaccurately. For all these reasons a micrometer is needed, since estimates by eye are not accurate enough. However, standard micrometers are expensive and not something to be taken on the stream.

The Solution:
"An inexpensive micrometer of simple design made especially to measure leader material."

[75]

The Problem:

"The ring or guide used to hold the fly during carrying holds the fly so close to the rod that dry fly hackles are often mashed and a shooting line frequently loops around it. The two decrease effectiveness."

The Solution:

"A holder that keeps the fly away from the rod and folds flat when not in use."

The Problem:

"It is difficult to remember how much body material is required for different size hooks."

The Solution:

"A calculator which, when you set the hook size and shank length of your hook on it, tells the length of body material required."

The Problem:

"With the development of new materials of differing density for fly lines, the old size designations lost their meaning. A new weight system was developed. But to use it the fisherman has to take his line to the drug store to get it weighed in grains."

The Solution:

"A simple lever scale calibrated for fly lines."

So what has Don done and what is he doing? In his great enthusiasm he continues to produce the solutions and they are tangible in form and they are procurable too. Anyone interested can take advantage of his effort to overcome specific problems.

First there was the book, *The Fisherman's Handbook of Trout Flies*, which standardizes pattern and nomenclature. Following the book are available devices, which, in a most positive way, solve other problems—the gauge, the hackle wrapper, the pocket net, the leader straightener, the micrometer, the fly holder, the calculator, the leader case and the line scale.

Even as this is being written, he is busily engaged in the development of a series of fast-water imitations of terrestrial insects. Looking in from without on his side-line activities, one cannot help but wonder, what will it be next? It is going to be possible, though, for me to keep abreast of his thinking and new innovations because when he comes up to fish from Arlington, Virginia, his brain can be picked by another simple device, the honest declaration, "I love trout fishing."

CHAPTER 9

Wet-Fly Development And Practice

THE HISTORY of fly fishing for trout is the story of dedicated people who glory in an outdoor challenge. It is the story of a cunning quarry which thrives in a beautiful environment where margin for existence is narrow. It is the transition of refinement and skill into tradition. It is an instance of masters of the pen talking to each other and to us across the centuries. The remarkable literature of fly fishing for trout is a study of how earlier anglers anticipated us and how those who followed improved upon them, always advancing, refining and improving the sport.

Streams have their way of developing anglers and techniques. England, the cradle from whence all this developed, has tumbling, acidic, mountain streams in the northern part, and placid, alkaline meadow streams in the south, with brown trout the native species of both. These two backgrounds are very different in most respects, so it is not surprising that each supplemented the other and the combination gave to the American angler a solid angling foundation upon which he could build. The saga of the sport of fly fishing for trout in the two great English-speaking lands is fabulous and unmatchable in recorded development by any other avocation or recreation. The stream of English angling literature runs clear and clean from the approximate date of the discovery of America until the present day.

It was an authoress who set the stage for color and tone. We learn from Dame Juliana Berners in *Treatis On Fyshynge With An Angle*, first published in 1496, that wet fly fishing for trout was then in full bloom.

The seventeenth century, a golden angling age, produced four giants: Barker, Venables, Cotton and Walton—two Cromwellians and two Royalists. In regard to them, and also including Frank, John Waller Hills, in his *History of Fly Fishing For Trout*, wrote:

"All five resembled each other in being practical fishermen, but otherwise were as different as men could possibly be. They approached their tasks from different points of view and with widely different temperaments and equipment. Indeed this company of five, who had so deep an influence on the history of fly fishing, are the most diversified crew that ever embarked on the same boat: you could hardly imagine a collection of such opposites; had they all met together, which thank heaven they never did, there is no subject on which they could have agreed except fishing, and there would have been broken heads over that."

(J)ohn (D)ennys in *Secrets of Angling*, a poem, made the first notation in angling literature relative to fly casting, a whole cane rod, net and creel in his volume, which was published in 1613.

Gervase Markham in *Discourse of The General Art of Fishing with The Angle, Or Otherwise* recommended that the fly be drawn or moved through the water—1614.

Thomas Barker, author of *The Art of Angling*, was the first to write about the reel, to describe how to make a fly and to employ a single hair leader—1651.

Robert Venables in *The Experienced Angler* was the first to advocate upstream fishing and gave considerable detail about fly tying directions—1662.

Samuel Pepys wrote in his diary, 18 March, 1667, "This day Mr. Caeser told me a pretty experiment of his angling with a minikin, a gutt-string varnished over, which keeps it from swelling, and is beyond any hair for strength and smallness. The secret I take mightily."

Charles Cotton, *The Compleat Angler*, Part II, wrote: "To fish fine and far off is the first and principle rule for trout angling," and he recommended fishing down wind—1676.

James Chetham in his *Angler's Vade Mecum* first wrote about fishing for individual fish—1681.

Izaak Walton, master of simplicity and dialog, is thought of as the patron saint of fly fishermen but in reality he was basically a bait fisherman. His writing has endured because of literary quality, not because of applicable angling information. Indeed it is now accurately questioned if Walton was the original writer. This pious person adopted as his spiritual son, Charles Cotton, a playboy man-of-the-world type, but one of fly fishing's greatest pioneers. Possibly no book other than the Bible is better known than *The Compleat Angler*. Cotton, the author of *Part II*, is the one who placed fly fishing on a high sporting plane.

Seventeeth century rods were either single- or double-handed and extremely long, as would be suspected where dapping is a standard practice. The many sections were spliced together, some being of one wood, others a combination of woods. A common tip was whalebone. Some butts were hollow. The line was twisted horsehair or silk and horsehair mixed; and of great significance, they were tapered, the end being a single, double or triple hair. Barker wrote that you can handle on a single hair the largest trout that swims if you have "sea-room" and "a single hair will outfish three twisted hairs five to one." Un-eyed hooks were available on the market and some improvised by making their own hooks from needles. The basic fly list of 12 imitations of the natural handed down from Dame Juliana Berners was expanded and appropriately modified. Innovations of the seventeenth century were fancy attractors and impressionistic ties. Barker apparently pioneered the reel, but the common practice was to affix the line to the rod tip. It was the belief that the fly should land in the water before the line.

There followed an orderly but slow procession of advances which individually had minor significance but collectively amounted to considerable. Rods became shorter, silk lines were manufactured, everyone employed a reel. There was a century of perfecting implements, which set the stage for mental achievement and the development of new techniques.

Alfred Ronalds was a great artist-angler-entomologist and the first of a long line of those who have, in such a vital manner, connected trout with natural food—the insect world, and the imitation thereof. *The Fly Fisher's Entomology*, first edition 1836, was a scientific work of great beauty. The art and the reproductions are superb and Ronalds himself handpainted the earlier editions. The standard he set is high; the work is museum-piece quality and it is thought provoking for all trout anglers who follow his time. He sought direct imitation in a day before it had been discovered how to make an artificial fly float on the surface. Among the insects he thought should be imitated were some land forms.

W. C. Stewart, author of *The Practical Angler*, published in 1857, championed upstream fishing in a day when most casting was a downstream operation. His effort caused a controversy, but his argument was strong! "The advantages of upstream fishing are that you are unseen by the trout whom you approach from behind: you are more likely to hook your fish, for when you strike you pull the hook into him instead of out of his mouth: you do not spoil unfished water in playing a heavy fish: and you imitate the motion of the natural insect. With

[79]

these advantages you can kill trout in the lowest and clearest water."

He turned about and went from a long line thrown downstream to a short one tossed upstream. Just as we have discovered the lineing of a fish to be fatal, he learned this about overcasting more than 100 years ago.

Stewart preceded a period which featured the most amazing refinement and voluminous literary effort ever enjoyed by any sport: the creed, the techniques and the teachings of the dry-fly school which fished in the remarkable chalk streams of southern Britain. This was a golden era even though it was an intolerant one. All interest, all activity, all writing for several decades had to do with the dry fly, tied as a direct imitation of the natural and basically to simulate the *ephemeroptera* which hatch on the flat streams of Hampshire. The fly fishermen were so enthralled by and obsessed with the new method designed to deceive rising brown trout that fishing a fly under the surface was spurned. In due time the practice of dry fly fishing spread to the tumbling streams to the north and finally its employment found its way to America.

Then a chalk stream fisherman deviated and the dry fly school was challenged. The challenger was a man of keen intellect, a skilled fly tyer, a resourceful angler and a talented writer. A fisherman of the Itchen and a member of the Fly Fisher's Club of London, G. E. M. Skues, had observed something else in the behavior pattern of feeding trout. He was fascinated by the rise to the about-to-emerge insect as the drifting or swimming nymph approached or arrived at the surface. Imitations were tied accordingly and presented in classic dry-fly fashion—upstream cast, downstream natural drift to feeding fish. Technically this was not dry-fly fishing because the fly was not floating, but the effect was the same.

Skues attached to his leader what he regarded to be the imitation of the moment and it mattered not to his conscience whether judgment dictated a floating or sunken counterpart of nature. He wrote much and he wrote wonderfully about dry-fly fishing, so it is not strange that he entitled his book on wet-fly fishing, *Minor Tactics*, which was published in 1910. The influence of this angler was far reaching and he left his everlasting mark on the sport.

The trout fishermen of America were pretty well concentrated on the fine trout streams of New York State with a spillover into New England, Pennsylvania and New Jersey. It was wet-fly

[80]

fishing for brook trout in fast-falling, rocky, mountain streams. Although dry-fly fishing had reached a dizzy pinnacle in southern Britain, the practice of it was destined to follow the turn of the century across the Atlantic, with but the mildest kind of popularity until after the conclusion of the First World War.

Times have changed, streams have changed and we fish for two exotic species along with the native brook trout. Possibly the beginning angler does not realize it, but trout too have changed, both in personality and address. We all got our start by bungling casts and fumbling with knots, but one never learns it all. Frontiers have a way of being pushed into biology, chemistry, physics, geography and fly tying. "The great schoolmaster is the trout himself." One who is learning is a beginner; thus a paradox of angling is that we are forever beginners.

One's first fly fishing is generally wet-fly fishing, but as sure as beards will grow on youthful faces, wet-fly fishermen will give the dry fly a try. That is the way of a stream and the way of a trout with an angler. In the vast majority of cases he will like it so well that he will adopt the psychology, when there is a hatch and a rise, fish dry; when dry fly fishing is hopeless, fish wet. He impatiently looks forward to, and impatiently awaits, the presence of insects on the water and a rise of trout thereto, but he resigns himself to the role of victim of the whims of Nature, taking advantage of the opportunities when they present themselves, making the most of adverse conditions. Francis Francis, for many years the editor of the English periodical, *The Field,* put it thus, "Some fishing is better than others, but there is no such thing as bad fishing."

Compared to dry-fly fishing, wet-fly fishing is blind and to a degree lacks the anticipation of the acceptance of the fly. Someone has said of the latter, "The golden rule is that there is no golden rule." But as we make this fly fishing journey, let us carry our knowledge as far as possible.

Since the days of Barker, Venables and Cotton, one technique has been practiced more frequently and has accounted for more fish than all others put together: wading downstream, casting down and across. This is not only the simplest and easiest form of fly fishing; it is often the most effective. There is a rhythm: back cast, forward cast, hand-twist retrieve the line pickup, re-cast, shoot the line, then move down a step or two, and repeat. In no other way can so much water be covered; in no other way can a fly be shown to so many fish. Wading, casting and hooking are reduced to their elementary efforts.

[81]

This is an attractor form of fishing, for the traditional assembly of a wet fly bears but scant resemblance to aquatic larva and minnow life; water life does not swim down, across and around; and feathers, fur and tinsel create their own light flashes.

This type of fishing is better for certain situations and certain people. The judicious approach is to fit the fly to the condition of the water: for big, heavy, cloudy water utilize a large fly on a stout leader; and low, clear, thin water calls for a small fly on a light tippet. Appropriate compensation is in order for anything in between. We can run the attractor wet-fly gamut from the minnow-type streamer fly and hair fly, through the standard wets, to the midge. The leader tippet is chosen with an eye to fly size, water condition, and size of fish. Rod-tip action to effect swimming motion is a trial-and-error game. More often than not, a trout in pursuit of the fly catches up with it as the line straightens out below, with the result that many fish are at first "ticked" and not hooked.

Memories of happenings back in my boyhood baliwick are so precious that when the time appears to be ripe, an attempt is made to bring about a repetition of history. The several biggest trout I have managed to catch, and the several biggest catches I have managed to make were during or after rains to swinging streamers or bucktails. So I keep in readiness a rainy-day and rising-water outfit to be placed in operation when the big trout leave overhead cover and go on the prowl. Neither rod, line, leader or fly approach the midge variety. The hope is to "roll a big one," and significance is attached to the places where the fly should make its swings.

A closely allied game is working after dark with a big night wet fly, only this time the fly is a large juicy-body affair, fished ever so slowly in the riffle at the head of a great pool or holding flat. It is a mechanical proposition, standing quietly and casting into the blackness hoping for a big forager, a trout shy of the light, to come upon the fly, a fly which at first blush appears to have no business in trout water. Old brown trout become nocturnal, and as cunning and shy as they are, they are not immune to the wares of the wet-fly fisherman.

The mud and mulch areas along a trout stream harbor a dainty little insect which hatches in great quantity, mainly at dusk. These *diptera* are minute and difficult to imitate. Feeding to this is a regular event in a trout's day, which is a regulated affair. Just as sure as a trout outglamours a carp, we, on occasion, are going to be faced with this type of feeding activity.

Called for is a midge fly with a short body and a collar around the neck—no tail, wings or hackle. To give it the best possible motion in the water the leader tippet must be extremely light and the fly should be activated with high rod-tip motion. The danger of the fly being snatched from the leader on the strike can be appreciably diminished by casting downstream with a short line and striking from the reel—no hand-twist retrieve, no sudden jerk, everything soft and absorbing.

Another downstream wet-fly approach, is very much a one-fly practice, the pattern being the hard-body ginger or black ant with the hackles tied in the mid-part—thorax-style tie. In relatively slow flat water, trout like this fly when tied to a fine leader point as it is drawn slowly and steadily away from a hiding place. This makes for target casting. It is at its best when the surface is broken by a gentle drizzle.

Judging from their writings, Stewart and Skues would have looked upon these downstream practices with a jaundiced eye, but how better can a neophyte embark on a fly-fishing career than to catch some fish as he learns to cast? This is the way to do both.

A nymph is a wet fly representing the natural in its final aquatic form, thus it is strictly a deceiver fly. The insect in pupa form rises or swims to the surface where it must struggle through the surface film before the adult can emerge from the nymphal shuck. The artificial enjoys one of its two big innings when trout are intercepting the hatching insect before it rides atop the surface tension.

Upstream nymph fishing is a most demanding game, exacting from its practitioners concentration, observation and skill to a greater degree than any other manner of fly fishing. Lord Grey of Fallodon, in his classic, *Fly Fishing*, London 1899, describes it thus: "You loose touch with your flies, a rise comes, you see it too late and miss the fish. Or else you see nothing and do not even know a fish has risen. It is a far greater difficulty than the inexperienced imagine: the power of knowing when a fish has risen is the hall-mark of proficiency. Many never attain it: and I fancy none do unless they are bred to it."

One tightens connection at the slightest provocation—a bulge in the water, a flash, an odd movement of the line or leader. A good upstream nymph fisherman seems to know just when a fish has taken, but he might not be able to tell you how he knows. When a heavy fly and a sinking line are involved, angling problems intensify, but the potential for action may increase.

[83]

The other big inning for the nymph is brought about by the combination of drought and heat wave and it may be the only possible way to take fish when such conditions prevail. When the stream shrinks and the water warms, trout become uncomfortable and seek relief. Warm water holds less oxygen than cold, and trout is a fish which requires a high percentage, relatively speaking, of dissolved oxygen in the water it inhales. When a stream becomes sluggish, certain areas must be deserted. It is at such a time when there is a movement to spring holes, the mouths of cooler feeder streams, broken runs and the falls pools, all of which contain more oxygen. Feeding is but scanty, but feed they will. A well directed nymph attached to a fine strand of leader is often accepted.

There is an irregular marriage between wet and dry fly, which falls in the category of secret weapon. With a dry fly attached to the end of the leader and a nymph dangling from four inches of excess tippet at a barrel knot, the cast is fished in accepted dry-fly manner. The angler concentrates his attention on fishing dry, forgetting about the nymph until such time as the floating fly is given some unnatural movement. My fishing companion of old, Fred Everett, regarded this double-barrel practice as "the painless approach to good nymphing." I am sure it was his brain child. How would the English chalk-stream fishermen of the '80's and '90's have appraised this procedure?

The day of the long whippy rod, the light line, and the eyeless fly is long gone; but when we read the floods of words of yesteryear, we recognize that here is a sport which is deeply rooted in the past. Our fishing books and articles of today have a most reputable ancestry.

"The final master in the school of trout fishing is the trout itself." In considering it in the angler's sense, not the biological aspect, the fly fisher recognizes that the variety and types are great. The quarry is met under an infinite number of circumstances and the unexpected sets angling apart from other sports. We lump all together and call it fly fishing for trout, but the world of trout angling offers scope for numerous approaches. A look at the contents of the fly box reflects the mental outlook of the individual and divulges his fishing personality, but it is amazing how those contents have a way of changing with the passage of the seasons. This wonderful world of trout fishing has been everchanging; and, like those before us, we wonder how there can be further refinement; but so long as there are anglers, that will be the case.

[84]

CHAPTER 10

How They Think

I MAY HAVE a few years on Vince Marinaro but what seems now to be the day before yesterday he had a wife and husky family on me. Since then, though, the gap has closed a little. It was our custom to get together frequently—on the streams in the spring, summer, and fall, then during the winter the bachelor spent delightful evenings in the family man's home. During the days of the out-season Vince was working on a trout book, which was ultimately published under the title of *The Modern Dry Fly Code.* I would induce him to read new sections of the manuscript as midnight oil produced them. Too, I kept reminding him that he is unduly modest, but such advice did no good, or harm. (It ended up that the "Code" was cited by the Yale Library as the finest from the literary standpoint of any outdoor book published in America in the last 50 years. This was his only attempt at writing for public consumption). One evening, however, we got off the subject.

There was agreement between us that there were too few dedicated trout anglers who were a part of the inner sanctum of the average sportsman's club. We further agreed that the regular club meetings lacked glamour and that the routine business sessions encompassing committee reports and "rez-zolutin" were often a bit hard to digest. The outcrop was that we decided to initiate a new and different kind of thing for the local angler, so different in fact that it would be the exact opposite of the standard fish and game association. It may sound like a joke but we were serious: the "newly organized" Fly Fishers' Club of Harrisburg would have no officers, no constitution and by-laws, no dues, no business and no membership drives. Simply we would follow our noses and invite anglers to get together.

There developed a highly constructive weekly luncheon meeting at which a paper or talk was delivered. This continued for some years until it became impossible to obtain a private dining room in the busy convention-ridden and political-infested capital city. The inevitable, of course, was an annual banquet, which featured highly regarded and colorful public speakers. The first was a combination of Edward R. Hewitt and Sparse

[85]

Grey Hackle Miller. Subsequent speakers were Charlie Wetzel, Bus Grove, Fred Everett, George Harvey, Art Flick, Ernie Hille, Vince Marinaro, Joe Brooks, Ernie Schwiebert and Herb Moore. Incidentally, the club is now basically the Pennsylvania Chapter of Trout Unlimited. The one meeting, however, was a question-and-answer panel proposition.

By way of identification, the participants were: Dr. Alvin R. Grove, Jr., author of *Lure and Lore of Trout Fishing* and then Prexy of the Pennsylvania Outdoor Writers Assn.; George Harvey, considered by many to be "the greatest trout fisherman" and for many years the fly tying, casting and fishing instructor at Pennsylvania State University; Ernest Hille, one of the nation's major distributors of fly tying material; and Charles M. Wetzel, author of *Trout Flies* and *Practical Fly Fishing*, "the modern American Halford."

The questions put to the panel and the answers, condensed, are as follows:

Q. What water temperatures produce the best fly-fishing?

A. *Grove:* Between 55 and 65. *Harvey:* 55-60. *Wetzel:* For wet-fly fishing, 55-65; dry-fly, 55-70. *Hille:* From 55-60, because that's when the natural fly hatches occur, causing fish to feed.

Q. What is your choice fishing period of the twenty-four hours?

A. *Grove:* Generally, in the middle of the day in the first part of the season; later in the day as the season progresses. *Harvey:* All twenty-four hours, but from May 15 to extreme hot weather, from 10 a.m. to 3 p.m., then 6 in the evening to early the next morning. *Hille:* Until noon early in the season, mid-day to dusk in the middle of the season, late evening to dawn in the latter part of the season.

Q. If you were limited to three wet flies, what would be the patterns and the sizes?

A. *Grove:* Dark Sedge, black or brown, numbers 8 to 16; Ant, 6 to 18; Skue's-type nymph (grey-yellow), number 18. *Harvey:* A black fly with mottled turkey wings (the Harvey Special); a night fly in sizes 4 to 2/0; and a hard-bodied black ant. *Wetzel:* Black ant 10 to 14; Green Caddis, number 12; and Red Quill, number 8 to 12. *Hille:* Hare's Ear and Coachman, yellow.

Q. If you were limited to three dry flies, what would be your choices?

A. *Grove:* Blue Quill, number 16; Light Cahill or Sulphur, number 14; Adams, number 12. *Harvey:* Adams, number 14 (best all-round fly); Sulphur or Cahill, number 16; Ginger

Furnace Variant. *Hille:* Hendrickson, number 14 to 18; any neutral subdued color; Golden Quill. *Wetzel:* White May Fly, 10 and 12; Ginger Quill (dun and spinner), 10 and 12; Green Drake, 6 or 8.

Q. Do you, at times, cast a dry fly downstream, even when it could be cast readily from a spot below the point of interest?

A. Yes, by entire panel.

Q. Do you, at times, cast a wet fly upstream?

A. Yes, by entire panel.

Q. In fishing the wet fly, do you prefer a natural drift, a slight movement and slow draw, or lots of life and a fast traveling fly?

A. *Grove:* Start with natural drift but change to meet conditions. *Hille:* Fish to the trout anyway at all. *Harvey:* Adjust to conditions. *Wetzel:* Natural drift entirely.

Q. Do you alter the size and pattern of your wet fly to conform to varied water stages, temperatures, and water transparencies?

A. *Grove:* I believe presentation and approach are more important than the type of fly. *Harvey:* I don't change sizes very much. *Wetzel:* Use the same sizes throughout. *Hille:* Generally use larger sizes in darker waters.

Q. Do you believe that very large trout can be caught with flies?

A. *Grove:* Yes. The difficulty is finding the big trout working. *Harvey* and *Wetzel:* Yes. *Hille:* Yes, especially when fishing after midnight. All agreed that live bait takes larger fish day in and day out.

Q. What is the largest trout you have ever seen taken on a dry fly?

A. *Grove* and *Harvey:* 25 inches. *Wetzel:* 19- and 20-inchers. *Hille:* 22½ inches.

Q. What is the largest trout you have ever seen taken on a midge wet fly, size 18 or smaller?

A. *Grove* and *Wetzel:* 20 inches. *Harvey:* Have seen George Phillips take a 24-inch trout on Spring Creek. *Hille:* Have never used the fly.

Q. Do you fish at night with large wet flies for big trout? If so, how do you operate?

A. *Grove:* Yes. Use bigger fly, shorter line, and heavier tackle, and sometimes a cast of three flies. *Harvey:* Like night fishing the best. Can get away from the crowds. Use big flies, sizes 4 to 2/0, diagonally downstream. Fish as slowly as you can and then cut that in half. *Wetzel:* Don't fish at night.

Hille: In the riffles and along the shore lines.

Q. What three aquatic hatch imitations do you consider the most important?

A. *Grove:* Blue Quill, Pale Watery Dun, and Green Drake. *Harvey:* Hendrickson, Pale Sulphurs, and Green Drake. The latter because I have more streams in which to follow the hatch (3½ weeks). *Wetzel:* Red Quill, Ginger Quill Dun, White May Fly. *Hille:* Don't pay any attention to the hatches. When fish are gorging on large natural hatch, present something entirely unlike the natural.

Q. Do you prefer heavy, medium, or sparse hatch?

A. All agreed on medium to sparse hatch, but like to watch the activity of trout rising to large hatch.

Q. What style tie of dry fly do you prefer?

A. *Grove:* Quill body, heavy hackles, and spent-wings. *Harvey:* Spent-wing with heavy dressing (hackle). *Wetzel:* Roll-wing. *Hille:* Upright divided-wing and quill body.

Q. Do you fish the water with a large attractor dry fly when the trout are not surface feeding? And if so, what is the nature of your fish-finder?

A. *Grove:* No. Fish wet in limestone water. In freestone water I use any fly. *Harvey:* Not in limestone water, but in freestone water I use a big ginger hackle fly with peacock herl body. *Wetzel:* Sometimes a Hewitt Neversink Skater Fly. *Hille:* When there is no surface feeding, I sit it out.

Q. What week of the season do you anticipate the most interesting fishing of the year?

A. *Grove:* After the green drake hatch. *Harvey:* Last two weeks of the season (end of July in Pennsylvania at that time). *Wetzel:* May 20 to 30—Green Drake. *Hille:* When laurel is in bloom in freestone country.

Q. Do you attach great significance to any of the terrestrial insects and, if so, which ones?

A. *Grove:* Ants and the little brown and black beetles. *Harvey:* 'Hopper season is hard to beat. Ants and green oak worms are important. *Wetzel:* Same as Harvey. *Hille:* Don't pay any attention to them.

Q. Which species of trout offers greatest sport?

A. *Wetzel:* Rainbow. *The others:* Brown trout.

CHAPTER 11

A Big Trout

DON MARTIN was light hearted and easy going but when it came to hunting and fishing he was all business—no joking. His report and appraisal of things having to do with wildlife were very accurate. A "150-pound buck" was not described as a 200-pounder, "20 flushes of grouse" were 20 flushes, "returned trout" were not those that got away. What he had to say about size and number was about as accurate as the electronic tabulators which followed his time. So one day when he soberly advised, "I know where the biggest trout in Pennsylvania is located," you could safely bet your pet fly rod that it was big— plenty big.

The annual custom of a little group of us, Don included, was to pursue the green drake hatch on upstate streams, first picking it up on lower Spring or Spruce Creek, moving upstream with the peak for a few evenings, then shifting to Penns, where the same pursuit took place, and finally fishing out the season for *guttalata* on Honey Creek. But this year (1945) Don was not going.

"How come?" we asked.

He shrugged his shoulders. "That big brown, he's worth all the others put together." So Don stayed home.

Upon my return from green draking, late one Sunday night, or more precisely, early one Monday morning, there was a penciled note on the pillow, which read: "Call Don no matter what time you return." Signed, "Mother." By virtue of the fact that Don and his wife, Gladys, operated a gas station and restaurant at Fort Hunter, up the Susquehanna River from Harrisburg, they were night owls and morning sleepers by habit.

In answer to my call at the horrible hour he said, "Don't mind me I'm celebrating. Come on up and see a trout."

We were five miles apart. I was tired and sleepy and the bed looked good. "How big?" I pressed him.

"See for yourself," he answered. "Tomorrow morning it goes to the taxidermist," and he hung up.

When I entered the restaurant, he simply nodded and his wife winked. Without speaking, let alone chortling, he walked over to the big ice box, withdrew the fish and slapped it in front of us on the counter. His attitude was like that of the cat which has just swallowed the canary.

The thing looked more like a salmon than a trout. "Don!" I gasped.

Without speaking a word he handed me a spring scale. It was hard to hold that heavy weight steady. The quivering dial hovered around the 15½-16 mark.

The Pennsylvania record trout from the unrestricted waters of the Commonwealth was a 15½ pound brown caught by fishing partner of old, Don Martin, at Big Spring.

[90]

Then Gladys took charge. "Sit down, you two. I'll tell you both the last part of the story; then Don can go back from there.

"He came staggering in about ten this evening, drunk and crusty. Sneaked in the back door so the customers wouldn't see him. There was a splotch of dried black blood around that gash on his very high forehead and blood spots down the front of his shirt. Looked like he had gone through the meat grinder and I don't know if he smelled more like a Billy goat or a brewery. And he was hugging his fish. All he could say was, 'Here we are Gladie, here we are.' I sent him to the showers. Now, Don, you give Charlie a blow by blow description; start at the beginning."

His eyes were glued to the great prostrate form before us. To sort of break the spell I offered, "Would you like a beer?"

That set him off. "Hell no! Couldn't look another in the face. Had more today than the two of us together drink during a summer. On the way home I stopped at Johnny King's Fish Bar in Carlisle and as fast as they came into the place they pushed beer at me."

"Stopped at Carlisle," I reflected. "That means Big Spring or the LeTort."

"The head of Big Spring. Above the Blue Hole, where I first saw him. Only made two casts," and again his gaze rested on the fish.

"Go on," prompted Gladys.

Don held his head. "I got a headache," and he blinked at the trout—sort of in disbelief. "A 12-inch brookie came out at the first pitch but did not snap. Naturally I showed my lure to him again and this time I saw the big Bozo moving toward it."

When dry flies did not seem in order, Don had unbounded faith in a black Strawman nymph behind a 4/0 Colorado spinner. He fished it like a nymph instead of a spinner and talked about "rolling" it. When he said, "my lure," I know it was his standard under-water combination.

"I was afraid," he continued, "that the brook trout would get there first. Bozo came up close; his mouth opened, and I saw the lure disappear. When I lifted the rod tip, he had it all right. 'Nough to scare anybody. Gladdie," he hesitated, "I need a drink of water."

His good wife was up to the occasion. Upon her return with it, there was an effervescing Alka Seltzer tablet in the bottom, but if Don noticed it, he offered no comment.

"All that brute did at first was to settle back. I could see his mouth open and close a few times, like he was chewing, then his gills flanged out. It seemed like a long time but I guess it wasn't. Finally he shook his head, swapped ends, and bolted for the Blue Hole."

"Right where you wanted him," I interrupted.

"Heavens no!" It was his habit to nimbly jump in exclamation from one extreme to the other. "Some guy stuck a pole to anchor a boat to at the head of it."

"How much leader, Don?"

"By luck 3x. Right before I tied on the lure I took off the 5x and the 4x tippets. But if that fish ever decided to dive into the weeds or go round the pole, there never was a trout leader tied that would have done you any good."

As he took a series of slow swallows his eyes ran up and down the length of the trout. "Hasn't he got big spots?" he observed. "And that adipose fin is like a hunk of leather." After a suppressed burp he apologized, "Must have been something I drank. Now let's see, where were we?"

"He's headin' for the Blue Hole."

"Yeah," said Don. "He makes it too. Then he turns around and comes back, back on the right side of the pole, almost to my feet. He must have seen me, for he turns again for the Blue Hole, only this time he went faster and farther. Must have been scared. He got below that damn pole. All the fly line was out and maybe 25 feet of backing. This is the only trout that ever had me into the backing.

"I considered working my way down to him but then decided to stay put and try to ease him away from the pole. Upstream he comes again and that was the last chance at the pole.

"After that he just kept going up and down the channel, like in a bowling alley; but every time he went downstream after that second run, I'd give him the butt and got him turned. Couldn't make it into the backing anymore. All the time I was afraid he would dive into the weeds off to the side. Don't know how long this kept up but finally he could hardly swim anymore. The big tail was sticking out of water most of the time."

Don had another drink. "Good stuff," he observed, and he took a long breath. "Brought him up close" he continues, "and he rolled over on his side. Slowly I eased down to sort of meet him until he was between me and the moss and I got the net ready. One look at the fish with the net under him was enough. You can't put a quart of water in a pint bottle. I threw the net up on the bank and out of the way." Don paused; his brow knit. "That reminds me, it's there yet.

"The fish was still on its side, so I stepped in closer to pinch him against the moss. Never moved; guess he couldn't. After winning the battle I didn't want to lose the war. Do you know what?" He patted the fish.

"No, what?" I asked.

"I simply laid my rod on top of the moss, reached down with both hands and brought them up right under him. I hunkered over and got him against my chest. If the water didn't run down the inside of the waders, something else happened. Thought to myself, if the fish starts to wiggle, I'm going out of here like a fullback through a hole," a throw back to his old cheerleading days at the University of Pennsylvania.

"Why didn't you slip him down the inside of your waders where you would have him for sure?" asked an innocent-looking wife.

Don ignored the remark. "Slowly and gently *we* walked right back to the car as the line pulled off the reel. Everything went fine except I banged my head on the corner of the trunk lid."

"Was anyone else around?"

"Not a soul. Didn't even see a car pass all the time the fish was hooked."

"When did you get to the Fish Bar?" Gladys was inquisitive.

Don rubbed his bald spot but stopped short when he hit the sore place. "Hadn't thought about that. Must have been between four and five. There were about a half a dozen there when I arrived. Johnny King called the newspaper, then he started to call fishing friends. As fast as they came in, they wanted to buy me a beer. At one time there must have been a half dozen full mugs on the bar in front of me. I kept swallowing."

"Repulsive," proclaimed Gladys.

"Now Gladdie," conjures Don, "you wouldn't want me to insult anyone?"

"How about supper?" asks Gladys.

Don shook his head, "No supper."

"You mean beer for supper," she suggests, but Don did not seem to hear her.

"The photographer finally got there and took a picture for the *Sentinel.*"

"Horrors!" explodes his wife. "You mean you let them take a picture of you looking like you did?"

"You don't understand, Gladdie," he stammered. "The picture was of the fish."

[93]

"And you were only holding it" she adds, but Don did not seem to hear that one either.

I thought it was time for a fisherman to get another fisherman off the hook, so I ventured, "Tomorrow the big Bozo goes to Merle Crawford."

Don drew a box from a pocket and pushed it my way. "Look it," he said "See what almost happened."

There was the #12 black Strawman nymph and the little 4/0 Colorado spinner to which was attached a few inches of the successful tippet.

The hook was opened a little. "Almost, Don," I reflected. "Another couple ounces of pull at the critical time and Bozo would have made a miniature harpoon out of your Fuller brush."

"Don't ridicule that lure," he shot back. "When trout aren't coming up, it is the most wicked thing ever devised."

"Provided you fish it right," I added.

Don almost smiled. "Roll it," he answered. "Think of all the regular wet and dry stuff this fish has seen in his day; then he inhales this."

I wasn't going to whip a dead horse by reviving our old hardware argument, besides the evidence was now overwhelming.

A patch of shoulder skin was sent to Fred Everett of the New York Conservation Department for a scale reading. In due time his report revealed that the fish was in its ninth year and the growth the first six years had been *extremely* great.

The taxidermist did a superb job, the skin being hand-painted after it was stretched over a mold which was the exact form of the fish. Three extra molds, which could be painted,—sans skin— were also made.

For some years the great trout hung in the restaurant at Fort Hunter, a popular stopover for hunters and fishermen going to and coming from Northern Tier camps. One of the painted forms is in the office of the Executive Director of the Penna. Fish Commission and another in the Carlisle Fish Bar.

To this day it is the largest trout ever reported to the Pennsylvania Fish Commission from the unrestricted waters of the Commonwealth.

Now let me tell you something. I know where there is another Bozo. Wonder if this one would like the looks of a #12 black Strawman nymph and a 4/0 Colorado spinner. Maybe a feller better find out. Maybe a 100% fly fisherman should be like Ivory soap—99 44/100% pure. Maybe that is pure enough.

[94]

CHAPTER 12

Re-creation and Recreation

TWO EVENTS took place in 1883 which marked that year as the turning point for a faltering conservation. Although the current meaning of the word had not yet been coined, it was its greatest year, the starting time for benefits reaped by the modern angler and hunter. One innovation was spectacular in nature, the other obscure. Doubtless these changes ultimately would have been attempted, but it appears that it might have been a case of too little and too late for the welfare of waters and lands and certain species of wildlife. The fact that two far-sighted and capable men were ahead of their time, or just in time, is the difference between verdant plains and dust bowls, the improvement or passing of certain outdoor sports, and the perpetuation or extinction of certain species.

A clear conception of the situation as it then existed is necessary to understand the timeliness of events. The period of deterioration was interrupted by the Civil War. A two-headed monster waxed fat on exploitation as it crossed mountains and plains. One head gorged itself on the vegetation while the other gobbled up the creatures of nature. Part of the trail was ashen grey, part the brown of erosion, and part blood red.

In the wake of the axe there was a tinder box, a forest floor littered with dry limbs. The most valuable wood was white pine—straight-grained, free of knots, easily worked and exceedingly valuable for building purposes. Although the wood of hemlock was not as good, being brittle and coarse-grained, the thick bark was rich in tannic acid, exactly what was needed at the tanneries. Sometimes when a prostrate hemlock was stripped of its bark, the trunk was left to rot.

Primeval forest stands of these two conifers were so dense that every square rod yielded one or more trees. Trunks grew straight and tall, bare of branches almost to the top. Some single trees furnished five logs, sixteen feet in length, and from twenty to forty inches in diameter. This was the form in which they were floated down the watersheds to the mill towns. In the year 1883 the Williamsport boom in the West Branch of the Susquehanna River harbored about two million logs from which three hundred million feet of lumber was sawed.

A second lumbering wave concentrated on the scattered hardwoods. This forest product was used in the manufacture of furniture and farm implements, the construction of vehicles and for railroad ties and mine props. If an immature tree would yield a small log or a railroad tie, down it came. Whereas the pine logs were floated from the woods to the mills, in the case of the deciduous trees, the mills came to the woods.

The plowman mined his rectangular plots for their fertility knowing that when they played out there was virgin soil for the taking, to the west. When the range was over grazed, new herds could be established on grass lands in the direction of the setting sun.

The population shifted with the plucking of the fruits of the land; America was on the move—westward. Wealth beckoned beyond. At first, transportation was negotiated in the "prairie schooner," the sturdy wagon made at the jump-off point along the Conestoga River in Penn's Woods. With it went an amazing shooting iron fabricated in the same Lancaster County, an accurate muzzle-loading rifle which had its barrel bored with lands and groves to make the bullet spin, thus giving it great accuracy. This was the long-range game getter which made it possible to live off the land. Sam Colt's pistol with the revolving cylinder served a more personal purpose.

Finally there was woven westward a network of steel to speed the movement. Young men went West as the Great Northern Railway offered, "greatly reduced Colonist rates," one-way tickets.

Such a ready market for meat and hides developed that commercial hunting was prosperous. Under this pressure great herds disappeared like snow in springtime until there was nothing but dregs in the bottom of the wildlife barrel. Life was soon to pass from the last heath hen, and the passenger pigeon would fly no more. Buffalo, antelope, deer and other species were at their nadir. So were trout in all but the coastal streams of the Pacific.

Raging forest fires persisted. When the ashes were washed away, often the mountain showed its bare bones. The good earth lost its ability to absorb rainfall then slowly deliver it to the under-ground water channels from whence to outcrop at springs. No longer could the ground hold the water like a sponge for the time of need. Instead, the water rushed down the bleak hills into the streams and carried with it, in the form of silt, the finest top soil. In some spots nothing but rock remained upon which no living thing was ever again to grow. Fire, which burned fertility from the soil, continued to follow the lumberjack and the bullwhacker. Washed gullies appeared. Floods became more devastating, droughts more acute. The great blotter had been set back a millenium.

Beautiful rivers which had flowed clear and cool in a constant manner became muddied with silt, at times raging torrents spilling over the banks and at other times they were abnormally low and warm. The native trout east of the rockies, the brook trout, became the frail step-child of a new civilization. Its range was greatly reduced by an increase in the summer water temperature, the vital oxygen supply becoming insufficient at 75°. One sizable stream after another, in low water periods, slipped over the brink, not by much, but any at all was too much. Thus, brooktrout water by necessity became small water —brooks and rivulets that managed to keep cool enough to insure at all times a sufficient supply of the vital gas. Dedicated trout anglers were writing and talking about the "vanishing native."

As a result of this common characteristic, waste, a weak warning was sounded; but it was a case of a voice crying in the wilderness. President Rutherford B. Hayes had appointed as his Secretary of the Interior a Civil War hero. Gen. Carl Schurz, a political refugee from Germany, had cast his lot with Abraham Lincoln and his new Republican Party. As a youth he had learned in Germany to evaluate the relationship between land use and water supplies. In his capacity as a member of the cabinet he unsuccessfully attempted to instigate a Federal forest service.

So the matter rested in 1883, strictly out of control. The greatest wealth any nation on earth had ever seen approached the point of no return, a squandered birthright. Needed was knowledge and activity. American history has been marked by the development of capable leadership at critical times. It has been marked too by unsung deeds which have a way of disappearing from knowledge with time. The little pioneer takes his place with the great leader, if not in notoriety, in results obtained. Two men were alarmed and each in his own way set out to engineer a turning point, a reclamation for his special interest.

It was early in the year 1883 when a young man, a little bespectacled fellow, rode the iron horse into the Bad Lands of North Dakota, where he expected to hunt, rough it, explore

[97]

and botanize. What he knew about the "West" came from reading, however he was familiar with the changing watersheds of his native New York. Although the trip was enjoyable and successful, he did not like what he saw. Everyone regarded game as a commercial resource, whereas he looked upon it as a recreational resource. It was obvious to young Teddy Roosevelt that without control and protection, buffalo herds, bands of antelope and other resources were facing the twilight zone. It was just a question of time until the great forests of the Pacific North West would go the way of those of New England and the Middle Atlantic States with the resultant deterioration of the streams. Too many were either ignorant or selfish to the core.

Twenty-four-year-old Roosevelt returned home a dedicated man, and the owner of a North Dakota ranch. He would do all in his power to preserve the American heritage he cherished. Help was needed and there would have to be organization; so his initial move was to ban together kindred spirits, including men of influence in what he named, the Boone and Crockett Club. So it was that at precisely the time when leadership was so desperately needed, a self-appointed one, farsighted and vocal, took charge.

New York benefited first, for he became the Governor of the Empire State. In due time, as President of the United States, he took his campaign to all the people. The inaugural message delivered December 2, 1901 expressed the following fundamental ideas: forestry is the perpetuation of the forests by use, with controlled cutting to protect watersheds; there must be government-owned areas with wildlife refuges therein; market hunting must cease; preservation must be interjected into State government.

Thus the first real American conservation movement was launched. The all-time low had been set; henceforth the pendulum would swing in the other direction. The stage was set for watershed improvement.

This was the era of the golden age of trout fishing in England and Europe. Frederick M. Halford and George Selwyn Marriatt had successfully promoted the use of the dry fly and the method of its fabrication. Their disciples spread from southern Britain to the continent. Trout fishing history was not only being made, but was being recorded and expressed in a manner finer than that of any other sport. It was all based on the fishing for brown trout, an unknown species in the new world.

The year 1883 was to be of special significance to the angler.

[98]

When the angler counts his blessings, he thinks of the trout calendar, which shows many weeks and long evenings.

Fred Mather, who later was destined to work under Governor Teddy Roosevelt for the Empire State, had been fascinated by a major difference between the trout of the Continent and the Eastern brook trout of the United States and Canada. The oxygen requirement of the foreign brown was not as high as that of the native brook, which meant it could thrive in warmer water. Conceivably it could fill a void by repopulating waters which could no longer sustain the native. Furthermore, it must

[99]

be a great fish, as witness the literature, the lore and the enthusiasm stemming from the Fly Fishers Club of London and the English press.

Mather, an angler, an outdoor writer and a fish culturist, attended the International Fisheries Exposition at Berlin. Included in the trip was some trout fishing in the well-managed streams of the Black Forest. What he saw, what he hooked and what he heard tell by one, Herr F. Von Behr, president of the *Deutsche Fisherei Verein,* sold him on the advisability and potentiality of the redistribution of the species—back home.

It was in the charmed year of 1883 that the German liner *Werra* steamed into New York harbor. Stored in moss-lined trays were 80,000 brown trout eggs from Von Behr. The precious cargo was transferred to the State hatchery at Cold Spring Harbor, Long Island, where Fred Mather took charge.

In due course more eggs were secured from German and English hatcheries and introductory plantings were made. The makings of an introduced species is the breeding or spawning season of the first wild generation. The stream-bred offspring of the planted fish reproduced in marvelous fashion in watershed after watershed to re-populate abandon trout water with a more hardy substitute, a fish which grew larger than brook trout and a crafty customer that loved to surface feed on aquatic hatches.

The new trout, however, did not confine its range to the warmer trout water. Pre- and post-spawning migrations spread it over complete watersheds and it took its places beside the brook trout as well as downstream, as Mather had hoped, from the limited brook trout range.

Local wet-fly fishermen were skeptical. They were experiencing difficulty in taking the free-rising browns, and now and then a trout larger than any they had ever caught would roll up and snatch a fly for keeps. Exasperation and leader trouble led to condemnation. The idea became established that brook trout water should be reserved for brook trout. Fred Mather was faced with a problem: Was his success succeeding too well?

The preservation movement sought by Schurz, then made a reality by Teddy Roosevelt had no name. A Pennsylvania forester and skilled and dedicated angler, became a part of the Federal Administration. The influence on and assistance to President Roosevelt by Gifford Pinchot was great, and each in turn utilized his powers to the hilt. Pinchot had founded the Society of American Foresters; and the President thought so highly of the dynamic young forester that he broke all precedent for a Chief Executive by attending the weekly meetings in the Pinchot, Washington D. C., home.

At this time there was no word or term to describe the inter-relationship of waters, soils, forests, fish and game—all the natural resources. In his autobiography, *Breaking New Ground,* Pinchot wrote how he discussed the matter with an associate in the Forest Service, Overton Price, and one of them suggested the all-inclusive word "conservation." He did not recall which one conceived the term but there is no question about the identity of the individual who made it stick and added a dictionary definition. The President liked it to such a degree that "conservation" became the keynote of his administration. In 1908 he instigated The Governor's Conference, which featured conservation; thus it was introduced to the State level of government.

Tama Jim Wilson, in paraphrasing Thoreau, author of Walden, sounded the oft-quoted principle: "The question will always be decided from the stand point of the greatest good for the greatest number in the long run."

An accomplished disciple of Theodore Gordon was "the Moses who led American forestry out of the wilderness of confusion," Gifford Pinchot. It did not take him long after becoming the Governor of the Commonwealth of Pennsylvania to see to it that brown trout were propagated and distributed in his state under his capable administrator, Oliver M. Deibler, just as Fred Mather and Teddy Roosevelt had done across the boundary line to the north.

Angling technique of the fishermen of the East was under-going a change, which, to a large degree, was brought about by the writings of the leading lights of The Angler's Club of New York. As the population of brown trout increased, the practice of dry-fly fishing spread. Edward R. Hewitt, a New Yorker, emerged as the leading trout authority of the land.

Who, in this small world, should marry a relative of the great Hewitt but Gifford Pinchot? The two in-laws became close friends, fishing together, mainly in the streams of the Poconos. It was the concept of the latter to bring into being a state-owned showcase to demonstrate trout-stream improvement and promote the idea of greater sport by uninjured return. The revolutionary project called, "Fisherman's Paradise," was put into operation on Spring Creek in the geographic center of the state, the blue print having been sketched by Hewitt. (At this writing the death knell is sounding for that wonderful limestone stream, for the water is contaminated by a disposal plant.)

To this point the American conservation movement had been a defensive process designed to prevent squandering fish, game

This bodes no good. Quality trouting depends upon the release of fish and fly fishing.

and other irreplaceable natural resources. Following World War I a new concept was advanced by one who was primarily a forester, but this remarkable individual was also a naturalist, a philosopher, a writer and a lecturer. Aldo Leopold of Wisconsin theorized that there must be management which will positively produce rather than negatively protect. "Wildlife is a crop," he stated, "which Nature will grow and grow abundantly, provided we furnish the seed and a suitable environment . . . It is more important to build up carrying capacity than to build up populations alone without consideration of environment . . . Society should know about important fatalities in that new argosy of the intellect which seeks not the conquest, but the preservation of nature." The publication of Leopold's revolutionary work, *Game Management,* in 1933 marked the milestone in wildlife administration. The game technicians rapidly accepted this concept, but fisheries divisions, dominated by hatchery men reacted more slowly.

During the depression years trout food was cheap and the hatchery product was produced in great quantity at "fish farms" built in some instances with P.W.A. monies. There followed an era of drum beating and glowing predictions. It is not strange that the best waters received the most fish. Fish truck following became a common practice and a limit catch was regarded as a goal rather than a danger point beyond which we must not trespass. Angling sunk to a very low plane marked by a degeneration of tactics and ethics. By force of circumstance newly-planted trout are concentrated and they must experiment in their feeding activity. The fishermen learned to get them while the getting is good and that something big and bright and deep is the answer, even though it might not merit anything better than a passing glance from a wild fish. A generation of fishermen was educated to regard fisheries management to be a put-and-take trout program.

The fish culturist of the East became enamored with rainbow trout because greater tonnage could be shown for the food consumed. But the rainbows would not stay; they permitted the current to carry them downstream, tail first. Unless quickly caught, there was a confounding disappearance. Hewitt stated before The Fly Fisher's Club of Harrisburg, "rainbow trout have a strong desire for a diet composed of 20% zoo plankton. There is not sufficient nitrogen in fresh water to produce the necessary quantity of this microscopic food, so nature guides them to the sea where it is available." The hatchery man who

[103]

thinks in terms of catch rather than in terms of sport advocated immediate fishing for optimum recovery. The future, so important to the biologist, was not a consideration in this policy.

But if the migratory tendency of the rainbow was its downfall in the East, it was its greatest asset in the far West. It was discovered that 15% of the stocked 6 to 10 inchers later returned from the Pacific Ocean to the stream in which they had been planted as jet torpedoes which weighed pounds. Thus steelhead fishing was given a bright future.

The hatchery rainbow also proved to be a great asset in cool landlocked waters. Spawning runs developed in streams which feed stocked lakes, the best known being the run into Catherine Creek from Seneca Lake in New York. Strange thing though, the hatchery ancestors were fall spawners, but the offspring in the wild state turned out to be spring spawning trout.

The sea-run trout of Norway and Scotland is the brown trout, that of the Canadian streams flowing into the Atlantic is the brook trout, and those of the Pacific coastal streams the rainbow.

The manufacturers of fishing tackle took a leaf from the book of the arms and ammunition manufacturers by establishing a counterpart in the outdoor world of the Wildlife Management Institute. The Sports Fishing Institute is to the fishermen what the Wildlife Management Institute is to the hunter. Objectives of both are to bring about the best possible management at all levels based on scientific findings and educate the public along the line of sound practices. There have been glaring examples of today's facts becoming the myths of tomorrow, so there is considerable to be unlearned. Under the capable leadership of first, the late Dr. Robert W. Eschmeyer, and now Richard H. Stroud and William Paul, a powerful and wholesome influence has been exerted.

The fisheries manager possesses a unique tool which makes the game technician green with envy: he can permit the trout angler to drink his cup to the fullest in return for a limited take-home kill. Many an ardent angler has grasped the significance of this and as a result has imposed upon himself unofficial limitation. Thus he reaps the reward of personal satisfaction stemming from the return of caught fish. This has become the hallmark of distinction of the dedicated and the skilled. May it grow, and grow, and grow.

The disturbance of the '40s wrought change. The subsequent combination of inflation, meat scarcity, wage increments, and decreased fishing-license sale complicated hatchery output. Sud-

Following the turn of the century, August Beck was a most prominent outdoor man. He was Teddy Roosevelt's taxidermist and President of the Pennsylvania Game Commission. The walls of his fishing camp, beside his beloved Loyalsock Creek, were lavishly decorated. The above is a reproduction of a Beck water color the author has fortunately come by.

denly "development," "management," and "acquisition" became charmed words. The stature of the biologist enhanced tremendously. He was faced, however, with that generation of anglers which had been given to believe that a put-and-take trout program is fisheries management. The technician, however, rose to the occasion. A fairly accurate fish census can be taken by means of an electric shocking device which temporarily stuns fish. Stocked trout can be marked by fin clipping. Thus it became a reality to be able to conduct a fact-finding expedition by stocking then shocking. The facts remain: the hatchery product experiences a very rough time of it in the wild state and the loss of stocked trout is appalling. Michigan fishermen were the first to distinguish themselves by requesting that some of the State hatcheries be closed.

A new champion for more and better sport has come into

being, an organization patterned after the water-fowl organization, Ducks Unlimited. The objectives of Trout Unlimited are to bring about the most sound management practices possible and to elevate trout angling to a higher sporting plane. Under the guidance of George Griffith and a staff of nationally-recognized experts there will be influence exerted that should make some back out of blind alleys and turn down a beckoning boulevard to a brighter future.

What lies ahead for our children and the unborn generations? A speculative cast into tomorrow is in order. Fisheries management will be refined. New trout waters, cool and clear and plankton-laden, will be created below the deep taps in the dams of many new water-storage impoundments. As the water problem is intensified by an exploding population there will be more reclamation and less exploitation. Detergents will be outlawed unless some process is devised to remove them at disposal plants. Insecticides may be controlled. Watersheds will be protected, planted and subject to zoning in the age of Megalopolis and Striptown. The economic and recreational value of fishing will be more generally recognized and more vigorously championed. It can be said with accuracy that today the price of pure water, like the price of liberty, is eternal vigilance on the part of the conservationist. Tomorrow, the basic element for existence, clean water, will be the sacred cow of the land; and in it will be the normal aquatic life. By force of circumstance everyone will be a conservationist.

Trout anglers will come and go. There may be less killing but there should be more catching. When the discriminating angler counts his blessings, he will thank his lucky stars for the foreign import of 1883, *Salmo trutta*—the brown trout. Fishing will be generally regarded as very big business and protected as such.

CHAPTER 13

The Other Half of Angling

A FINE PIECE of trout water possesses more than fish. Prior to the telecasting of a so-called "football game of the week," a picture was shown of the site of the pending encounter. This part of the show was not live, for there was not a person in the great structure. The commentator divulged some interesting historical and statistical data then apparently broke away from the script and commented, "but a stadium without people lacks personality." Isn't it true that a trout stream without a head of trout and without fishermen also lacks personality? To add luster to the former, there must be a game and a crowd. To add luster to the latter, there must be rising trout and fishermen trying to deceive them. The fact that a rise form advertises that here is a trout and that trout is on the feed stimulates interest and activity and it captivates one's fancy. This is the sought-after challenge. There is no personal satisfaction in fishing in the trough of a hatchery and the tendency on the part of the fish of the stream to rise freely is worth all other assets put together.

Tagged Trout And Net Results

Some years ago I ran into something quite by accident which was not only thought provoking but it sparked a chain of activity. It started with the tagging of fish, but ultimately went far beyond that. Information about the procurability of fish tags was obtained from Gordon Trembley, who was conducting tagging experiments for Pennsylvania State College.

When the stiff tongue and groove tags, each bearing its own individual number, arrived from the National Band And Tag Co., Newport, Kentucky, they were altered to facilitate placement around the lower jawbone of the fish. After being straightened from their triangular form, the tongue was filed longer and thinner to better fit the groove, thus making attachment faster and easier. Then they were bent into semi-circular shape. The point of the tag was simply punched through the thin skin and brought through the mouth over the teeth to ring the jawbone before being inserted in the groove and bent down and thereby locked. After some excess metal was filed away from the tip of the sharp-nose pliers, the bending of the tongue was an easier operation.

[107]

A well played trout, exhausted to a degree, is less difficult to tag than a fresh lively one. It is more simple for a right hander to place the tag on the right jaw of the fish. When a trout is returned, it will be too tired to swim away, thus it is best to place it in quiet water along the bank where it can rest undisturbed then move at its leisure. If exposed to the current in a weakened condition it will be carried away, head downstream so the water forces its way through the gills and causes drowning.

The practice soon became more than a one-man campaign, for the fellows who frequented the stream were interested in what was going on and once this was understood they wanted to keep abreast of results. Frequently a call bore the suggestion, "Here's one; how about tagging it?" Some of these fishermen were employing dry flies, some wets, while others fished with minnows and garden hackle. Everyone had the same thoughts: if you return little ones, do you ever enjoy repeat performances from those particular fish; how fast do they grow; how far do they travel; can they be fooled more than once the same way?

In order to get more tags on more fish, some ordered their own. The two-legged predator was eating less fish and returning more—all cataloged. Recoveries were made and spaces in the record sheets began to fill. In due time the facts were forthcoming and interesting sidelights developed. This business of tagging fish had all the sure-fire elements of a good play—anticipation, disappointment, suspense, and, of course, eventual triumph. Ideas about trout seem to conflict as much as those about the unicorn and women, but now we were getting facts. Here are some pertinent ones:

The rate of growth of the 6-10 inch brown trout in this rich limestone stream was usually between 4 and 5 inches in one year, however one fish went from 7 to 15 inches in 13 months and another from 7 to 22 inches (4 lb. 3 oz.) in four years. The larger tagged browns did not grow this much in length but the increase in weight was greater than the smaller brethren. Brook trout developed about half as fast as the browns.

Rainbows which were not retaken in a matter of weeks were never heard from again. No brook trout was ever recovered below the spot of release. The browns maintained their positions to an amazing degree, a number being taken from the same homes on successive years.

Unquestionably they became increasingly shy of man and line and leader, but the fact remains that some were taken more than once in the same way from the same spot demonstrated that not everything registered and was retained.

One evening during a rise to the dependable sulphur hatch I took a small trout feeding in front of some brush on a #18 Tup's Indispensable dry. On a subsequent evening a trout was seen surface feeding at the same spot. The Pale Evening Dun was removed and in its place went the Tup's. It was my old friend again taken on the same fly. Before the season concluded I caught that trout two more times from the same spot on the same fly.

The greatest time lapse between tagging and recovery was 9 years. One wonders how this brown trout, a two-year-old when tagged, avoided the wares of fishermen or escaped from them for what amounts to a long lifetime for a trout.

The quickest recovery was in about an hour but this was a case of hunger superseding suspicion. It was a newly stocked rainbow caught early on the opening day. This fish, along with some others, was confined the greater part of the day in the interior section of a minnow bucket. It was not until about 5 p.m. that I got around to putting tags on these fish and before the last of them was tagged, the first was caught.

Of particular interest was the fact that the tendency of a trout to rise freely was not deterred by the taking of that fish when surface feeding on natural insects. They continued to use the old spots and feed in the same manner but usually there was a lapse of a day or two before the behavior pattern was resumed.

During the three-season period in which tags were placed on 300 fish, trout and numbers began to mesh, individual fish having known habits and eccentricities—personalities. As we pried into the private lives of our friends, the adversaries, it was noted that some were daytime feeders only, whereas others fed only at dusk. Some created less dainty rise forms than others. Some developed great reputations, others not so good. The all-time star and popular favorite was #51. If ever there was a wonderful fish, that was it, for with its incessant but discriminating surface feeding it furnished an abundance of angler activity and concentration.

Then we utilized the tagging to make a rough stream-section census. It was our considered judgment—best guess—that there were (alive) in the one mile stretch of stream about 125 tagged fish. We were catching six untagged fish to every one bearing a tag. We estimated, therefore, that on the 6 to 1 ratio there were 750 legal-size untagged fish in the area in question which is not wide water, making a total of 875 catchable trout.

One day I was pursuing the record sheets and suddenly something which had escaped notice before became as prominent as a toad in the punch bowl. Maybe this was the real moment of truth which made the tagging campaign so very much worthwhile. I blinked and looked some more. The dawn had come up like thunder and once clearly visible it glistened gloriously. Here might be a key to selective breeding and sound management. Obviously there were two kinds of trout. Some preferred to assume a position and have the water deliver their food to them—the free risers—whereas others moved about in quest of submerged food—the cruisers. Fish being taken on the dry fly were not being recovered on minnows, worms or deep going lures; and the converse was true. This was thought provoking. Tagging had already confirmed the suspicion that trout are individualistic, each having its own preferences and personality, but here was a general grouping into two distinct classifications.

Now, I cogitated, like breeds like. What would be the effect on the number of free risers of a stream if there was a mating of the great surface feeders?

Side Stream

Adjacent to the main stream was an old millrace. It was no great engineering effort to bulldoze it so that it was converted into a 1600-foot side stream. Set in concrete abutments at each end were gratings through which brood fish could not pass. The flow from a strong spring by a barnyard was diverted into it. Here would be the place to confine some superior surface feeders, furnish them with some good man-made spawning beds and hope that prolific fish would produce their kind which would filter out the gratings into the main stream.

Barnyards create nitrogen and in turn nitrogen brings about the development of zoo plankton, a microscopic organism. The great Hewitt, who had visited us on occasion, had advised that zoo plankton not only provided elwins and fingerlings with their most valuable food supply, but stream-bred trout over one pound in weight utilized it when available in quantity. He believed that the downfall of hatchery trout when liberated was their failure to eat minute food after having become accustomed to feed upon a diet of coarse morsels.

The brand-new side stream offered the perfect opportunity to learn more about that before utilizing it for the site of the selective-breeding experiment.

[110]

Right after water was diverted into it which flowed over the newly exposed ground, Vince Marinaro and I transferred thereto 16 wild brown trout ranging in size from 10 to 14 inches. I then purchased 16 9-inch hatchery browns and 16 19-inch hatchery browns. With cover lacking, these fish could not hide and at a quick glance the group to which an individual belonged was recognized. The coloration of the backs of the stream-bred fish was brown, whereas the hatchery fish were greyish-green.

The three-pound synthetics lolled around and wasted away. As the weeks passed, they became more lank and darker in color. None survived the first winter. On the other hand, the 16 wild browns cruised about and fed heavily on suspended invisible matter. Now and then one would majestically rise and deliberately sip something from the surface. Their condition was excellent and the rate of growth good. By November one of these fish was 17 inches in length—no doubt one of the original 14 inchers. The 16 9-inch hatchery fish had their troubles, but not to the extent of the 19-inchers. Some began to pluck the suspended microscopic food, just as the wild ones did; and a few of them survived the winter.

It would certainly be interesting to design and experiment with a trout hatchery where the main food is zoo plankton—no hand feeding whatsoever until fish are either one or two years old and ready for stocking.

The following year some of the normal food of a limestone stream was planted in quantity. This was easily accomplished by placing in the main stream great slabs of bark from a nearby dead elm tree. In a relatively short time the many rough crevices of the bark were alive with sow bugs, shrimp, crayfish and assorted nymphs. The slabs, along with the wealth of living organisms, were transferred to the sidestreams.

Prior to the spawning season, which is very late in this watershed (December and January), man-made redds were constructed. The stream was restricted in spots with V dams and below each one of these was distributed a good quantity of ¾-inch river gravel (not crushed gravel or crushed limestone, which are too sharp).

During the course of the season the stocking of carefully chosen brood fish was accomplished. Only good proven surface feeders qualified. Once a tagged fish had demonstrated that it was a free riser, upon capture it was moved to the millrace.

Of course these super trout got together and paired up at the proper time and place. One thing though they demonstrated beyond all shadow of doubt. They greatly preferred the spawning beds with overhead cover to the exposed ones. As an experiment half of them, eight, had been covered with burlap attached to wooden frames. The first eight beds which were used were the ones under the overhead cover, but as the season progressed other fish appeared on the exposed beds. A number of the eggs hatched; that we saw. Just how many little fish sooner or later passed through the gratings to ultimately become legal-size surface feeders in the main stream was impossible to determine, but the fact remains, surface activity in the main stream increased.

Strains

To further improve the home water, another campaign was launched. In the general vicinity are three remarkable limestone spring streams, each unique in its own right, each featuring something extra special. Unstocked little Cedar Run harbored a wonderful and unusual strain of brown trout. The stream of Big Spring, steming from Pennsylvania's largest spring and possessing a perfect balance between carrying capacity and rate of natural reproduction, was long renowned for its excellent brook trout fishing. Falling Springs was and is, to the best of our knowledge, the only stream in the East which has natural reproduction from non-landlocked and non-migratory rainbow trout. All three have their share of surface feeding.

You will note in this writing at this time the present tense is used in conjunction with Falling Springs only. In recent years Cedar Run has become pretty much finshed business due to contamination and straightening and shallowing; and ironically Big Spring has been sacrificed on the altar of lust so that the inferior substitute for stream-bred trout may be propagated for personal gain, a situation made possible by political protection. The situation with the former may be hopeless but the latter still possess the old potential and the day may come when it will once again be of infinite value to the angler and the public in general—again Pennsylvania's finest brook trout stream.

Here was not only the opportunity to introduce into the Le-Tort top strains of the three species of trout, but good surface feeders within these strains. Instead of relegating these fish to the frying pan, we brought them home—to the LeTort—alive. Certainly no harm could come of it and the collective effort could very well greatly enhance sport fishing potential.

Now the LeTort in its own right has a claim to fame. The late Sid Gordon had completed his work on his proposed book,

[112]

How To Fish From Top To Bottom, and it befell my part to read the manuscript. The author, talented and knowledgeable all-round angler, was a stream improvement expert who had been employed by both the Wisconsin and Michigan Conservation Departments. He devised a method and formula for measuring the carrying capacity of water by chemical analysis. Lime content was the key to the determination of how many and what size fish the water would support, and he divided water into the following five categories:

very soft—0-5 parts per million of bound carbon dioxide will support 0-250 pounds of fish and fish food per acre.
soft—5-10 ppm CO_2, 250-500 lb. per A.
medium—10-20 ppm CO_2, 500-1,000 lb. per A.
medium hard—20-30 ppm CO_2, 1,000-1,500 lb. per A.
hard—30-100 ppm CO_2, 1,500-5,000 lb. per A.

Sid had traveled 32,000 miles beyond the bounds of his "two states" to measure carrying capacity in order that the results could be recorded in the appendix of his great work. His comment was, "I have not been able to find highly productive water in the East," whereupon I advised that I would send him some samples for analysis.

The outcome was that a carton of pint jars of water, carefully labeled, from the stream sections I fish was expressed to him in Saginaw, Michigan. The revolution was that the LeTort was the richest of all Eastern waters tested, possessing an estimated carrying capacity of 4,750 lb. of fish and fish food per acre. Results were inserted into the book.

This was for the upper LeTort, upstream and south of Carlisle; the larger downstream section is contaminated. The big job now is to try to convince the proper authorities and pertinent interests that the greatest tourist attraction of the locality is trout. Carlisle stands head and shoulders above Gettysburg, Hershey, Harrisburg, et al. in this respect, an important one to many people. The lowest 4 miles, the big water of the LeTort, from the Army War College at Carlisle to its mouth at Middlesex, is contaminated water—unsuitable for trout. The mid-point on the Pennsylvania Turnpike, with an adjacent intake and outlet, bridges this polluted stream section. It has been estimated that if it were reclaimed by piping the effluent from the Carlisle disposal plant into the larger watershed into which it is now ultimately delivered via a running sore, the annual value to interests in and about town would be approximately $50,000.

The history of the introduction of the exotic species of trout

Lorna Doone's brook. The famous novelist, Blackmore, was an avid angler. His short story, Crocker's Hole, is one of the greatest fishing short stories ever written.

to the LeTort, Cedar Run and Falling Springs is a matter of recorded history and worthy of note.

The following was published in the October, 1942 issue of the *Pennsylvania Angler,* publication of the Pennsylvania Fish Commission:

"About 1920 Mount Rock Run, which flows near the (then) eastern terminus of the Super Highway (Pennsylvania Turnpike) dried up. When the flow of water ceased, some brown trout of varying sizes were trapped in the pools. Mac Pittinger of Carlisle and some angling friends managed to net 418 brown trout. They were redistributed in the LeTort at Carlisle, a brook trout stream.

"They adapted themselves very well to the new environment and after a period of five years were well established . . . The scion of the introductory stocking has furnished great fishing through the years in spite of the fact that it has only been in recent years that brown trout have again been stocked in this stream."

The introduction of brown trout into Cedar Run, just 5 miles west of Harrisburg, was a happy political circumstance. It was probably the only stocking the stream ever received.

One day a Harrisburg newsman and G.O.P. stalwart, Gus Steinmetz, heard the voice on the other end of the telephone line say, "This is Herbert Hoover." Believing someone was pulling his leg, Gus shot back, "Well how the Hell are you, Herbie; have been expecting your call." Well, it was indeed the President, who explained that he wanted to indulge in some Pennsylvania trout fishing and it had been suggested that he contact fisherman Steinmetz to lead him to it. The outcome of the conversation was an appointment.

The nearer the approach of the auspicious occasion, the more concerned became the guide. Suppose the President doesn't catch anything. "This," explained Gus to friends, "is worse than waiting for the outcome of an election." In a panic-stricken moment he called the property authority in Washington for an emergency shipment of legal-size trout, "so the boss will not be skunked."

The consignment of 800 9-inchers arrived via the "fish train" and Gus transferred them in milk cans to nearby Little Cedar.

Pressing affairs of state made the planned trip to Pennsylvania at the appointed time prohibitive, and it never did materialize; but the trout, listed as Loch Levens, were in Cedar Run. Thus brown trout had found their way into another watershed. They waxed strong and it took them less than two decades to supplant the native species.

It is interesting to note that Halford was disappointed by the fighting ability of the brown trout of the Continent and he regarded the trout of his native England to be the superior of those located on the other side of the Channel. For the most part, it was the brown trout of Germany which found its way to American hatcheries, but some eggs from hatcheries in Scotland crossed the Atlantic too. Since the Federal Government designated this consignment as Loch Levens, Cedar Run may nurture an undiluted strain of the British fish. All who have played them are amazed at the amount of jumping which takes place.

Little Cedar, the stream with the great sulphur hatch, is now pretty much finished business. It will always be near and dear to me, for it was there where I caught my first brook trout and my first brown. For me, a country boy, it was the only trout stream within practical bicycling distance of home—just two miles.

One night at the 19th hole it was decided by our unofficial LeTort fishing society to shift some of these to the Carlisle stream; and in due time some of the "orange belly jumping jacks," all taken on dry flies while feeding on the little Yellow Drake, were given a new home.

Then we trained our sights on the beautiful wild brook trout of unique Big Spring, unique because in good light you could pick your fish. Resting over the clean gravel in the crystal water, even though a good example of Nature's camouflage, they could be spotted. A tiny dry fly on a long fine leader would move some of them. Any fish which exhibited any sign of interest in the gently drifting fly, though refused, was worthy of serious attention, because the chances were even that he would take it on a succeeding cast. This was certainly selective fishing, for it was possible to pick out the good ones; and, of course, only surface feeders were caught. Some of these fish in the same places day after day never could be enticed to rise—maybe they never did. It is reasonable to believe that some of the larger fish were of the same age group as some smaller ones, simply they possessed a higher rate of metabolism. At any rate, what were brought down to the LeTort were the largest fish which would surface feed, and between the group and over a period of time the number was considerable. The result is that there is now some brook trout fishing in the

LeTort but it is all near the source and not in the area where these fish were planted in the first place.

There flows through Chambersburg a little gem, another limestone spring stream, this one named Falling Springs. The history of the introduction of an exotic species in this stream, judged by Eastern results, is spectacular. Here are rainbow trout, along with the brooks and browns, which are stream bred, and they are not landlocked. The fact that they are non-migratory was worth more than mere speculation. Investigation revealed something which may be of great significance. The Federal Government furnished the information that following World War I a consignment of fingerling "steelheads" was assigned to William Miller of Paxtang to be planted in Falling Springs and these were the Shasta River strain. Further investigation revealed that Shasta River is landlocked! No one now knows the lineage of the rainbows in the hatcheries and undoubtedly the blood lines of various rivers are represented.

Some of the offspring of the misnamed rainbows of old are now fanning their fins in the placid LeTort. If Falling Springs, which is mostly Fly Fishing Only, were a little closer to home, there would be more of them here now.

What a talented collecting crew there was: Tommy Thomas, Norm Lightener, Ross Trimmer, Malon Robb, Vince Marinaro, Doug O'Hanley, Lenny Welsh, Ed and Bobby Weidner and Jim Chesneys. We even brought visitors into the act including Joe Brooks and Ernie Schwiebert.

This brings up the questions: Are any of the hatcheries— private, state or federal—making any attempt to breed for the ultimate in sport, in fact are the managers breeding for anything? What is known about hatchery strains? Has there been degeneration? The principle in stream management of protecting the free risers in order to provide the ultimate in sport can be applied to all natural-reproducing trout waters whether they be managed for the public or under private supervision. It is a combination of understanding and objective.

Stream Improvement

The character of waters change when *homo sapiens* interjects himself on the scene, and it is along the streams where man likes best to live and work. Life itself is contingent upon an adequate supply of good water and the engineers maintain that a prime function of flowing water is to carry away man's waste. The fishermen cannot take exception to the latter, but sometimes it is necessary to exclaim, "Horrors! A running sore.

[117]

As a health measure and for the sake of those downstream treat it properly first." There is plenty which is horrible and disheartening about a fish killing but that is not the extent of complication for the distraught angler. Activities include agriculture, timber cutting, irrigation, drainage and grazing which exert adverse effects but in a less damaging and more subtle way than pollution. Siltation smothers gravel spawning beds and it decays the eggs of fish and aquatic insects. Deforestation creates erosion, which in turn causes warming of the water and siltation. The fisherman can be proud of the fact that he spearheaded the somewhat successful drive for clean streams, selective cutting and reforestation. He was ahead of his time in thinking, far ahead of the general public. It required a population explosion and a water problem to spark popular interest and activity. The best way we can now make the most of our complication is to improve and restore watersheds. Individuals and groups can do effective work and accomplish results.

The father of stream improvement was Edward R. Hewitt, who produced a booklet on the subject. Possibly the first public display of it was the Fisherman's Paradise created by the Pennsylvania Fish Commission in the late '20s. By the time the child of the depression, the Works Progress Administration, came into being it at least was known.

It was my good fortune to have as a fishing companion Edward R. "Eddie" Jones, Pennsylvania Director of W.P.A. Eddie resided in York County; my residence was Dauphin County, and our fishing area was Cumberland County. Here is a rich valley where the limestone joins the freestone and water belches forth in strong springs from the ground water channels at faults in the limestone at the juncture, thus creating two fine water systems. Eddie advised that a considerable amount of money was allocated per county and he thought stream-improvement work would be ideal where proper arrangements could be made with property owners. Involved was fishing rights and rocks—for free.

It wasn't because I could not have used a job just then, but there would have been a two-way embarrassment for a young Republican state official to find his way to the W.P.A. payroll, so I straddled the line to do and dare. It probably wasn't bad, though, to have someone talking to the Pennsylvania farmers who spoke their political lingo and also who knew his way around in sportsmen's club circles.

The wheels were placed in operation and we did right well—

trout stream improvement projects on Hoagstown Run, Silver Spring, Big Spring, Boiling Springs and Trindle Springs. By the time all this was on paper, there wasn't much left for the manicuring of roads and the scratching of leaves.

Appropriately enough, some of the foremen were fishermen and officials of sportsmen's clubs and some of the workmen were club members too. Chunks of limestone were collected from fence rows, sink holes in fields and from abandoned lime kilns; there was plenty. The pattern was to form in the streams a series of V dams and wing walls properly angled and nicely spaced. It was assumed, and no doubt assured, that after completion, there would be periodic state stockings. A quarter of a century later a lot of it is still serving its intended purpose. The idea was to create trout cover and create more fishable water.

Some years later I was able to purchase a modest little farm. It wasn't a coincidence that the property line was the middle of the channel of a one-mile stretch of the looping Yellow Breeches plus a few hundred yards of an old millrace into which water spilled and through which it flowed.

Two bleak stretches needed attention—simply low dams to create downstream pools and upstream flats. The idea developed that pieces of broken concrete from torn up sidewalks, due to the great surface area and irregular crevices on the one side, would harbor more nymphs than is the case with rocks. It so happened that there was plenty of this available at a nearby town where redevelopment was in progress; so it was channeled to the Breeches. Physically the concrete did the anticipated job, but the biological result seemed to be just so many more carnivorous stone fly nymphs, possibly at the expense of the more desirable ephemera. Decent dry fly fishing did not materialize, so the farm in effect was exchanged for a section of the productive LeTort.

It was imminent that the regulars of the LeTort would turn their attention to stream improvement work to supplement other activities. We were in complete accord that the chief object here is to increase the rate of natural reproduction, to attempt to get it into better balance with the great carrying capacity. Old timers talked about extensive stretches of clean gravel bottom and great schools of fingerling trout. Deterioration in the form of siltation had covered much of this and in its place are beds of the water weed, elodea. It appeared to be practical and not complicated to make some new beds and

[119]

restore some of the old ones in the upper reaches where most of the spawning takes place.

The first effort was to put 14 tons of ¾-inch river gravel under the three bridges near the head, then sit back and watch. The next December and January, on this late-spawning stream, there was considerable activity on the three improved or reclaimed beds.

The following fall a good working crew converted 25 wagon loads of big limestone rocks into a series of V dams and wing walls in the headwaters, then placed 31 tons of ¾-inch river gravel (not crushed gravel, which is too sharp for the fish to work) in the spots gouged out by the limestone chunks. This

The famous fishing hut of Izaak Walton and Charles Cotton, located in the bend of the River Dove.

required eight weekends of hard labor by a good crew of strong backs.

To put it mildly, the spawning activity in this area has been impressive and the egg hatch has been heavy. The Fish Commission made a census by electric shocking in a part of this graveled area. In spite of the fact that schools of trout swam ahead of the two submerged charged-wire loops and others bolted downstream between them, the numbers which were knocked out, then netted, marked, weighed and returned made the technicians grin and chuckle. We were accomplishing our purpose, but there was room for more improvement, more wild fish of selected strains. This brings up a good question. How many truck loads of legal-size fish is one truck load of gravel worth in this situation?

Attention was then turned to another area of the stream which needed work of an entirely different nature. In the greater volume of water below the juncture of the two branches and below the major spawning beds are more catchable fish and less fingerlings. Here where the drop is slight and there is more silt, more dense beds of elodea have developed. Old timers advise that there was a day when the stream bottom was sparkling gravel and the weed growth, which at that time was mostly water cress, was limited to the edges of the banks. Over the years, however, silt from cultivated fields, road drainage pipes, and the watering spots of cattle has practically coated the streambed, creating a highly favorable environment for elodea.

The lush submerged growth develops to such a degree over the summer that in spite of the fact that the stream volume has diminished some since spring time, the weed has a damming effect which makes the stream higher and pushes it over the banks in spots. Channels close and the areas heretofore exposed bottom, disappear.

The trout are forced into tight pockets and many must assume feeding positions in the shallow water over the weeds. Normally predation in a trout stream is not a vital factor, but this condition alters the situation. Water snakes locate trout then move unobserved under the weed to sneak within striking range, whereas in open areas the sucker is the chief target, thus trout became the easier target. King fishers too seem to be more successful with the little trout over shallow "moss" due to visibility.

For many years the English met the weed problem by mowing in patch pattern then disposing of the cut crop. This temporary approach for us was impractical and complicated. By experimentation it was learned that a long submerged log, extending across the stream with water flowing over it and under it accelerated the current sufficiently that both weed and silt were moved for some distance, thus forming an open pool. If the logs protrude above the surface, a death trap is created for the emerging duns, and terrestrial insects are sucked beneath the surface. The placement of one of these anchored water obstructions every 30 to 50 yards would solve the weed problem and make the water more interesting to fish. Weeds are not a total loss, for they harbor quantities of certain organisms, but too much is too much. The Pennsylvania Power and Light Co. is cooperating by furnishing old poles for the purpose. Each year we expect to add some more.

The bigger trout prefer overhead cover. They seem to be annoyed by the presence or company of smaller fish. When this is not available, the better fish take over the open pockets and deeper spots and drive away inferior members of their kind. This discourages surface feeding on the part of the up-and-coming crop of catchables. Where overhead cover does exist, the large fish stay under it by day, moving out in the evening to cruise or surface feed and the daytime feeders pick their spots and feed unmolested.

The stream area in question lacked overhead cover, but it was a simple matter to cut brush, mainly box elder saplings, secure them into brush piles with copper wire and anchor to posts or logs at the chosen spots. A year after establishment they were covered by attractive beds of water cress which appear to be verdant natural stream edges, but they are open underneath.

The brush piles did something else too. There is a little drake, *baetis*, which deposits its eggs on submerged sticks after climbing under the surface on them. The emerging duns furnish some interesting dry-fly fishing. It is an odd hatch in that there are three or four broods per year. After the creation of the brush piles, this hatch improved.

A new type of stream improvement is functioning amazingly well and its scope is being expanded. Wing walls and V dams are made by the strategic placement of a series of oil drums with the ends burned out, then completely covered with rocks. Some are submerged so agitated water breaks over the tops. The largest trout spend most of their time in these tunnels and thus do not interrupt and interfere with the feeding activity of the smaller fish in the nearby open channels. A favorite feeding position at dusk is at the upstream aperture. Furthermore, it is anticipated that the permanently clean channels created by these stream devices and the additional amount of stone in the stream will stabilize the hatches, which are cyclic in this section, possibly due to varying weed beds from year to year and the shifting of silt. In addition to the drums, the more durable corrugated, highway, drain pipes are being utilized in the same manner.

There was the instance where a heavy trout upon being hooked above the pipe, swapped ends and bolted through the tunnel to wage his fight on the downstream side, the line and leader, of course, following the hollow course. This four pounder was successfully played, drawn back through the fortress and landed on the upstream side.

The most beautiful and effective piece of stream improvement work which I have ever seen on a wooded stream of considerable drop was done by an individual. The work encompassed a combination of Hewitt undercut, slab dams; wing walls; V dams; anchored brush piles and logs, and foliage trimming. The new look was engineered for right-handed dry-fly fishing. Hazards are surmountable, providing you are not left-handed. The stream section flows by the home of its architect and owner. It is a model of making something wonderful out of something insignificant.

Competition And Predation

Instances of predation under special circumstances have been touched upon, but there are related factors worthy of note. Close observation will lead one to believe that the carnivorous habits of various creatures is not as vital in the lives of trout on the vast majority of our trout stream sections as competition from coarse fish. Well conducted studies have revealed that when weed fish are removed, trout take their places; and the opposite is true. A given area of stream will carry just so many fish. Man can exert considerable influence on the ratio of the species.

On the surface it does not appear that there is conflict between suckers and trout, or even fallfish, chubs and trout, but the student of ichthyology knows better. Even though suckers do not eat trout and trout will eat some suckers, there are other conflicts. The same thing on a slightly different scale and for slightly different reasons applies to other coarse fish. All that is needed by some trout streams and some stream-fed ponds to set them off is a large-scale disposal of "trash fish." Suckers are vulnerable to trapping and corraling in the springtime on their spawning runs.

An amazing piece of legislation was enacted into law in stocking-conscious Pennsylvania. Fishing on trout streams was, and is, prohibited during the month preceding the opening of the trout season on the theory that some newly stocked trout will be poached. This is the time when suckers bite best, are concentrated and are fit to eat. Taken from the sucker fisherman is his greatest opportunity of the year and handed to the trout stream are just that many more spawning suckers. Isn't this a case where both lost? Combine sucker protection when it counts the most and liberal size and creel limits on trout and you have the formula to convert what was basically a trout stream into sucker water.

We hear that trout are notorious small-fish eaters. The old argument that a lot of trout are caught on minnows, therefore they eat a lot of fish is circumstantial evidence, but should it be taken seriously? How about food value, the digestive process and availability? Trout are protein eaters; their systems require an abundance of fat. The protein content of insects is much higher than that of fish. Hatchery trout cannot exist on a diet of ground fish because of a deficiency of protein. Trout in the wild state greatly prefer to feed on the easily-caught fat-laden insect-crustacean world. Nature, though, has dictated that they be a part of the sanitation corps, the job of trout being to mop up on the sick and the injured—a part of Nature's plan for the survival of the fittest.

Naturally it is no simple matter for a large fish to move un-observed into close quarters with a small one. Fish cannot close their eyes; therefore they sleep with them open. They see in their sleep just as we hear in ours with our unclosed ears. It is no simple matter either for a large fish to be agile in shallow water. Once in a while we see a large trout chase a small one, but more frequently we observe one chase another nearer its own size. It does not appear that a cannibalistic trait is the driving force; rather it seems more logical to believe that con-flicts for homes and feeding stations must be resolved. The very fact that the huskiest trout take over the best places and when a good fish is taken from such a spot another has a way of

[124]

taking its place demonstrates the point.

Trout in hatcheries have to be segregated according to size to prevent cannibalism but have you ever watched the feeding in a hatchery? Some get considerably more than others, therefore some remain hungry. With no other available food, necessity would make some look at others with hungry eyes.

The digestive process of trout operates at a maximum in a water temperature in the low 60's and Nature provides the greatest amount of aquatic insect food at this stage in the spring and the greatest amount of land-born food at this stage in the late summer. The process slows down proportionately in cooler and warmer water. If a 20-inch trout in freezing weather were to eat an 8-inch fish, what length of time would be required in the digestion of it, or would it have eaten itself to death? Incidentally, the hatchery men feed their charges less in the winter than at other times and most hatcheries are near or at springs where water cold enough to manufacture surface ice and anchor ice is nonexistent.

It seems to be the thing to do to kill the water snakes—to most of us a repulsive looking critter. I'll admit, I don't like them, but if my trout water had too many coarse fish and a greater rate of natural reproduction than the carrying capacity could adequately handle, I would live with them. It is surprising how big a fish a snake can handle once that mouth is unhinged and the skin stretches. But the reptile family does not eat frequently.

On the other hand, king fishers eat three times their own weight daily, and they neither hibernate nor migrate. A great amount of food is necessary to maintain that fast heart beat and high body heat for their rigorous lives. Suppose the problem on rich water is to increase the rate of natural reproduction to better fit the carrying capacity, would you like to have king fishers around? They are beautiful and interesting but in their deadly dives they are coming up with some baby trout—but some little suckers too. Are you going to convert some of their quills into trout-fly parts or are you going to choose to leave this beautiful bird on the wing?

Balance of Nature is touchy. Hewitt told of skunk trouble at his private hatchery on the Neversink. They were fishing out some experimental, dwarf, freshwater salmon from Norway, so he directed that a campaign be leveled at them. The result was that the skunks were dispatched but this was followed by a veritable plague of snakes in and about the hatchery.

[125]

Coons have their big inning with trout in the mountain brooklets during low-water drought periods but did you ever see one of these unsilted little mountain streams where the rate of natural reproduction did not far exceed the food supply? Sometimes when hunting grouse along these beautiful, fast-falling, shaded mountain streams I have seen four-inch brook trout working the clean gravel in the spawning act. That means, to be sexually mature they were at least in their second year. By necessity "hemlock trout" are little trout—and hungry trout. The unsilted mountain streams can take a lot of fishing pressure and killing too. Wouldn't it be great if the surplus migrated to bigger and richer water which could use more wild trout?

"He's a belly fisherman. He follows fish trucks."

Nature is cyclic to a small degree but the force which really upsets the balance is man, a fierce predator. Possibly he possesses a greater ability to manage himself than to manage other predators. The first and greatest step to bring about more sport with trout where it counts the most is to exercise logical restraint. That, of course, is less killing, not less fishing.

Are there any fields, including politics, in which interest on the part of the devotees has greater intensity, where difference of opinion is more divergent, and the facts more difficult to determine than in the field of fisheries management for trout?

The Build-Up Principle

Every city in the world, and the vast majority of the towns too, are located by a stream. Picture if you will a wonderful trout stream flowing through a typical American town. Each generation of town folk has spawned its quota of keen anglers who depended upon the stream for their major recreational outlet. Some think of it as, "my stream, the home waters," although they may not own a foot of land along it. Over the years during the evenings of late spring and early summer grandfathers, fathers and sons have fished it in their own way. Some employ worms and minnows; in this age there are some with spinning outfits; and, of course, there have been and are fly fishermen. It is also a favorite place for "outsiders," particularly on weekends.

For several generations things went along fine. The stream produced and supported many beautiful brook trout; brown trout then marked their appearance and practically took over. Fishing continued as usual.

But finally things became complicated. The State began to plant trout in it, mostly rainbows, the stockings being legal-size fish and well advertised. Early season pressure increased but this was soon to be exceeded by the fishing traffic which moped up on the in-season stockings. The stocked trout which were taken by the limit-seekers went out fast and then the amount of fishing became normal again. There were troubles though. Property owners, whether they fished or not, were not happy with the periodic mob scenes and the accompanying parking complication; and the regulars of the stream hated to see some of the little legal-size natives go out with the new synthetics. In their own fishing they returned all of the up-and-coming crop they caught, so this kind of killing was a sacrilege.

A situation such as this happens to be the case on the stream which is the major object of this chapter but it could be anyone of a number of other natural-reproducing trout streams. The regulars of the LeTort who shower tender care on it were faced with a problem. In the consideration of all circumstances, factors and interests, how could things be handled? Possibilities were to close it, have fishing by invitation only, charge to fish, make club water out of it, assign fishing rights to the Fish Commission for Fly Fishing Only or do nothing. Some who fished with fly only were in a strong position to do very much as they pleased but they respected other stream regulars who did not fish as they did and then there were the kids who did not have or could not secure fly rods.

At first the above seemed to be all the possible alternatives, and none were good, but then another idea cropped up. Certainly a property owner can specify the terms of trespass on his own land. And the property owners involved could join together and all specify the same thing. That was it. Utilize the trespass law as a stream-management tool. You are permitted to trespass and fish here provided you abided by the prescribed regulations. Upon inquiry, the State Justice Department advised that such a procedure is legal and binding.

We were in business. That led to the question, what regulations will develop and maintain the best possible fishing for those who depend upon the stream? The fishing property owners went into a huddle and to the best of their ability answered that question. The matter was then taken up with the other property owners who would be involved, and they signified accord. The next step was to present the plan to the three local sportsmen's associations for sanction, and that followed. All that was left now was the printing and posting of the signs bearing the specifications of trespass. Basically it was less killing and barbless hooks for everything.

This preceded the 1960 season. Fishing quickly improved; so did ethics and enjoyment. The State discontinued stocking and fishing continued to improve; so did the head of trout. The limit-seekers canceled the stream from their list, following the fish trucks elsewhere.

The system spread to a second watershed but in this instance it stemmed from the fishermen and was taken before the local sportsman's club, which in turn formalized the regulations with the property owners and printed and posted the regulations.

Thus all fishing was for wild trout, in any legal manner, at any legal time, by anyone, but with barbless hooks only and a

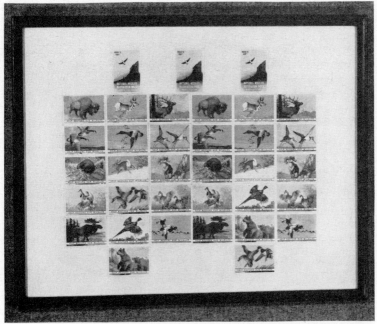

Annually, during National Wildlife Week, the National Wildlife Federation issues stamps. One dollar not only secures a beautiful sheet of them, but it is a way in which the individual can support the cause of conservation. This is the first sheet, all of which are copyrighted. Courtesy of the National Wildlife Federation, Washington, D. C.

minimum of killing. There have been no prosecutions, not even any wrangles, and to the best of our knowledge, no chiseling. Gracefully the whole thing has developed into an honor system and there is honor among anglers. Should the regulations be removed, a hue and cry would go up; they are that popular. We never had it so good and it should continue to improve for a few more years before it levels off—a new way of life with trout.

There was a concern though, would there be much loss on deeply hooked fish? Studies revealed that there is with barbed hooks but how about all barbless hooks. No one knew. No doubt there is some loss but it appears to be negligible. Dying trout struggle on the surface and bloated dead trout float. In two full seasons only one casualty has been observed and there isn't a day of the season that observant fishermen are not scattered along the meadows.

But mark you, the trout in this stream section are shy.

[129]

The following is the wording on the posted signs.

From the standpoint of constitutionality—legality—Fly Fishing Only is a dubious restriction in the State administration of public fishing. West Virginia, in 1961, was the first trout state to rescind it, the grounds being that this type of management discriminates against a segment of the licensed fishermen. As test cases and the rulings of Justice Departments crop up, others may go the way of West Virginia. When such is the case, there is no alternative for the effective management of waters open to public fishing other than to adopt appropriate restrictions comparable in philosophy to the LeTort regulations.

In the foregoing pages of this chapter is told the story, and the story behind the story, of the treatment given a cherished little river. It is an account of how some trout with tags on them made some anglers think and spurred them into activity. That is the way it is in trout country. It is the streams and the trout therein which develop techniques, anglers and interests, and therefore deserve credit for refinement. Henceforth that is the way it is going to be with management too in its various ramifications—just a question of time and many stream sections will be treated right.

Transplanting Mayflies

The only situation which is responsible for a heavy rise of the better trout of a stream is the presence in quantity of some large insect floating on the surface of the water. When this condition does not exist, the most cherished fish which are inclined to rise, feed below the water's surface and are not tempted by the dry fly.

Of all the aquatic hatches, the Green Drake—*guttulata*—enjoys the reputation of bringing about the ultimate in angling for trout.

Roger Wooley, in his excellent book, *Modern Trout Fly Dressing*, writes: "The sight of practically all the trout in a stream rising well at the same time has given the impression that the trout's 'silly season' is the duffer's opportunity to make large captures. This will not be found always or even often the case, and frequently just as much skill will be found to be necessary when fishing the mayfly as when fishing the imitations of the smaller *Ephemera*. So let not the mayfly carnival be looked upon as a time for great slaughter, but rather as a time for extra careful fishing for the big fish of the stream, the fish that may have an inclination to turn cannibals and that rarely give the opportunity of their capture with smaller flies. Happy is the angler who can be on a trout stream daily from the beginning to the end of a mayfly season, with a good rise of fly on, for most interesting and instructive will be his experiences, if only he is not too keen on catching fish and has the observant eye to notice the wonders that will unfold themselves."

Ironically this spectacular hatch, so highly regarded, frequently pursued and carefully observed by the angler, does not exist in every cold water stream or even every section. The fact that it marks its appearance in all of the limestone streams and some of the freestone waters of the central counties of Pennsylvania and some other isolated sections but does not appear in the great limestone section of southeastern part of the state prompted the thought that it might be successfully transplanted to this area where it is nonexistent. Members of the Fly Fisher's Club of Harrisburg were determined to make an honest effort to introduce the insect.

[131]

There are three possible methods of approach in the matter of redistribution. The first is to transfer the nymph. In view of the fact that the larva of the insect in question is so difficult to capture, this is not practical. In regard to the nymph Dr. Lyte, eminent angler of Allentown, wrote as follows in a personal letter: "Some years ago a friend and myself gathered a bucket of mud from the side banks of the Little Lehigh, containing some water and a good number of mayfly nymphs. It was late in the evening, so we put the bucket in the cellar over night. In the meantime the larva emerged and our cellar was full of mayflies. It was our intention to plant them in another stream." He adds that the nymphs were difficult to catch.

The second method is to transplant the fly. In the dun (subimago) stage, they are delicate. Spinners (imago) cannot be captured, transplanted and released, for sufficient time does not exist between the nuptial flight and the depositing of the eggs to permit transportation.

The third alternative is to transplant the egg. This method makes it possible to deal in volume and this was the system that the Club elected to adopt.

After missing the hatch on four or five streams in late May and early June of 1946, it appeared that it was over everywhere for the year; then the information was relayed by a long distance telephone call that a heavy hatch of duns was in progress on Honey Creek. A hatch of spinners should follow this emergence by 48 hours.

We chose a spot at an island along the hard road approximately three miles above the point where Honey Creek flows into the Kishacoquillis. There was a wooded area one-quarter of a mile downstream, which should harbor many flies during the molt.

Upon our arrival at six o'clock on the evening of June 9, 1946, it was bright and clear, a condition which brings about a late evening hatch but a concentrated one. Some duns were emerging. Many male spinners were flying about the tree tops but no females were in evidence upon our arrival.

About one hour before dark the female spinners left the foliage almost simultaneously, and the nuptial flight quickly developed. Forty-five minutes before dark the fertilized females descended and started their slow migration upstream, which immediately precedes the laying of the eggs.

This is a large drake, pale in color and identical in appearance to the Spring Creek specimen. Along with it was another fine, large drake, dark brown in color and later identified as *Ephemera simulans.*

A boiler one-third full of water was placed on the island. Two men with nets were stationed in each channel beside the island. The flies in their slow cumbersome upstream migration followed the water course and did not travel over the island. It was our first thought that netting could be accomplished from the island and from a wooden bridge 20 feet above the water, situated 100 yards above the island. It was soon discovered that it was necessary to operate from the water, for the concentrated flight was near the surface and confined its course within the shorelines.

The hatch was heavy. It was possible to swing the net back and forth until a mass of 25 or more flies was in the bag, before emptying into a wash boiler. At times at the peak of activity two or three females were captured with one swipe of the net.

After being dumped into the boilers they quivered on the surface of the water. This action apparently accompanied the expulsion of the egg masses. The eggs fill the thorax up to the head in two parallel sacks. It is our belief that a gas is generated which forces the eggs to drop in masses but not all at one time.

During the 45 minutes of concentrated flight we believe we averaged 15 flies per minute or 675 per net, making a total of 2,700 flies. Halford had written that according to microscopic count each female carries slightly over 7,000 eggs. On this basis the total number of eggs secured that evening was approximately 19,000,000, 90 per cent *guttulata* eggs and 10 per cent *simulans.*

The following evening was probably more effective, for there were five nets in operation and a refinement was the addition of a removable cloth bottom in each boiler to which great masses of eggs adhered.

Upon arriving at the LeTort, approximately two hours later, the following steps were taken. The dead and few dying females were placed in a wire box and submerged, on the theory that some eggs had adhered to the bodies and wings. The milky colored water of the boilers was poured into the stream. The cloth bottoms on which there was a layer of eggs one-eighth of an inch deep were ripped into strips and pegged to the stream bottom. These strips were literally heavy with egg masses. The boilers themselves, to which eggs had adhered, were submerged. Finally the cloth liners of the nets, to which eggs had adhered were planted.

[133]

Halford had written that the eggs of the mayfly hatched in nine days in an aquarium.

Dr. B. W. Kunkel, former head of the Biology Department of Lafayette College, is of the belief that a loss of eggs was suffered due to overcrowding. This could readily be overcome by the insertion of additional cloth bottoms during the netting operation.

The three leading authorities of the United States were requested to comment and pass judgment on this enterprise following the 1946 endeavor. In addition to the method of capture, transportation, and stocking the following facts were set forth. The streams stocked are less than 100 miles distant from the area of great hatches, and about 40 miles further south. The difference in elevation is less than 1,000 feet. A mountain range segregates the two. The stream characteristics appear to be similar in respect to bottom and vegetation.

Contents of a letter from Dr. Paul R. Needham, Director of Fisheries, Oregon in 1946, formerly of Cornell University and author of *Better Trout Streams:*

> "It seems to me that if conditions were suitable in the area described, *guttulata* should certainly be present, in spite of the fact that the two sections are separated by a mountainous area. Winged forms such as mayflies distribute themselves long distances and if conditions are suitable will usually be found in waters to which they are adapted.

> "A number of years ago, we introduced the burrowing mayfly nymph into Mr. E. R. Hewitt's waters on the Neversink River in the Catskills. I do not believe that they ever 'took' there because conditions were not suitable. You might write to Mr. E. R. Hewitt about this and ask him if he could give you the latest word on it. His address is 127 E. Twenty-first Street, New York.

> "The green drake in nymph form is a burrower in silt beds in both lakes and streams. If the stream that you described did not possess deep beds of silt it is likely that they failed to find conditions suitable, and as a result never developed.

> "It seems to me your method of introduction was satisfactory and if conditions had been suitable, they should have developed.

> "I, personally, am quite pessimistic about your chances of being able to establish them in an area in which they are

[134]

not already present. Often times small changes from their home habitat are enough to block success. Your approach was all right and you are correct in the assumption that usually the green drakes require three years in the nymph stage.

"I am sorry that I cannot give you more specific aid in this problem."

Contents of a letter from Charles Wetzel, author of *Practical Fly Fishing:*

"Your method of redistributing mayflies opened up an entirely new avenue of approach. I had never thought of that angle; however, I don't see why it should not work, providing the eggs were properly fertilized before being put out into the stream. As you know copulation occurs in the air only a short time before the female spinner starts depositing her eggs on the water. I have never been definitely able to determine how the latter operation is accomplished, although I have caught many female spinners that had two sacks of eggs protruding from her abdomen, which leads me to believe that they are deposited in a mass. What is your theory on this angle? As I mentioned, if the act of copulation occurred before the flies were put into the wash boilers, then your chances of success are very good, providing the same stream bed conditions as applied to the parent stream are encountered. I have found that this is a very important matter. Some streams will just not harbor certain species.

"The fly on Spring Creek is *E. guttulata.* There was some doubt in McDunnough's mind (he is the Canadian Mayfly specialist) because the Spring Creek fly is somewhat larger than that found on other streams; however, he took the matter up with Speith and Needham, and the consensus of opinion was that it was the same fly, only somewhat larger. It is hard to tell if the flies on Spruce Creek and Stone Creek are the same species. I am convinced that it is possible to transplant different species on the same water and get hatches at different times—but the stream bed conditions should be the same. I should think that by the third year you will begin to see results, although in my case the flies started emerging about a week after they appeared on the parent stream, that is three years plus one week to be exact,

"When I originally transplanted the Green Drakes in Middle Creek, I did it by the nymphs; that is, the nymphs were collected and transplanted, but the method was wrong. Many of them were injured in collecting, and it was too big a job to gather them in abundance. The successful program was accomplished by transferring the sub-imagoes in wire cages to the stream, and then liberating them. The fly now comes on yearly in abundance, although I don't believe there were more than 2,500 in the original stocking. The ratio of females to males was about three to one, and the following evening after liberating them the spinners were observed laying their eggs naturally on the water."

Contents of a letter from Edward R. Hewitt, dean of American trout anglers and author of *Telling On The Trout:*

"Your mayfly stocking will probably succeed to some extent, but you did not adopt the best method. This transfer of mayflies is very common in England, where the hatch is quite often all killed out from a stream or a section of stream by bad rainy weather when the flies are in the bushes changing their skins. If rain occurs then, they all perish. Mr. Lunn, the Keeper at the Houghton Club on the Test, worked out the best method of transferring mayflies, which is in regular use in England. He catches the flies about to lay eggs and puts them under a wire cover such as is used to keep off flies from pies in restaurants and puts the cover over a china plate which contains water. When the eggs are laid he stacks the plates one over the other, with a strip of board in between them to keep them apart, the stack is taken to the place to be stocked and the plate placed on the bottom of the brook in a suitable place. They should be well scattered so as to get good distribution. When the eggs are hatched the plates are recovered. This method is completely successful.

"While the mayfly makes a very short time of very good fishing, it does not furnish any food for the trout during the rest of the year, and when the mayfly hatch is over the trout are stuffed and won't take surface flies well for some time. It has the advantage of bringing up the big trout to a fly better than other flies. They have a whole series of flies in English chalk streams, which hatch all during the season and provide good dry fly fishing all the year. I have arranged with Lunn to ship over a large number of the eggs of these flies for the Castilia stream in Ohio. They will arrive next June. The Castilia stream is very similar to the Test in water and in vegetation, and I am sure these flies will do well there.

"The mayfly is variable in streams. It will exist for many years in a stream and then die out entirely, probably due to the weather killing the females. I have known many streams which had them at times and then they all disappeared. They can be reestablished by planting the eggs. The flies will hatch out at various times, from the same female; the

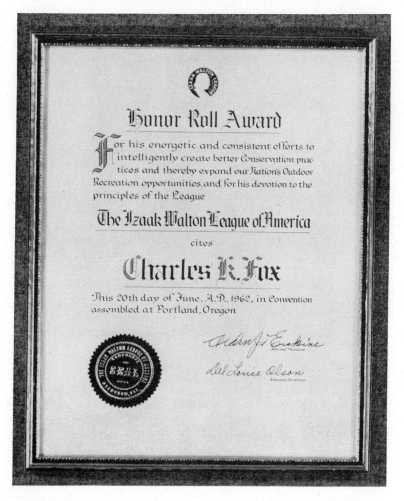

flies will hatch in one, two, or three years from the same hatch of eggs. Lunn proved this in his aquarium. There are many families of mayflies. In some the nymphs can live in sandy bottom, in others in gravel, and in others in stony bottom. If the mayfly selected for planting is not suitable to the bottom, the plant will be a failure. The bottoms of the streams must be similar when a transfer is to be made.

"In some streams the water conditions are such that every few years all the nymphs are killed out. This is true of any stream where the ice freezes on the bottom. I got mayflies started on the Neversink and they persisted for three years and then all were killed. This is why there are none on the Neversink. The conditions become impossible for them every few years. This may be true of the streams you are trying to stock. You may get them started and then they may all disappear in a few years. This is probably why they are not already in these streams. If your planting fails later on, don't be worried. You will then know that these streams have conditions at times unsuitable for mayflies. Only a few streams in this country will continually carry a mayfly population for many years at a time.

"The Willowemoc above Livingston Manor had the largest mayfly hatch I ever knew about fifty years ago. None have been seen there in twenty years now. They exist in the lower river but have never come back above. I don't know why.

"We don't know very much about the conditions which are suitable for the mayfly. These conditions must be suitable over the whole year and no one ever studies a stream for every day in the year and many years on end. It is quite likely that you will succeed in getting a mayfly hatch in streams where there are none now, but it is very doubtful if such a hatch will persist over many years in succession. If conditions were really suitable for mayflies they would already be there."

The practice was followed for at least two evenings of the hatch for each of the three following years, 1947 through 1949; and in each of these years distribution was made in four limestone streams of Cumberland County, Pennsylvania: Yellow Breeches Creek, Big Spring, the LeTort, and Cedar Run.

There are several refinements initiated after the two experiences of the first year. In order not to crowd the eggs more than necessary, several wash boilers were utilized instead of one. In addition to lining the boilers with cloth, small stones wrapped in cloth were placed on the bottom of each boiler, thus creating greater surface area and facilitating distribution. The boilers were three-quarters filled with water so the eggs could adhere to a greater area of cloth.

Observation revealed that both the scuds and sow bugs (shrimp and cress bugs), which abound in limestone streams, collected on the strips of cloth bearing the precious cargo; and the assumption was, that being carnivorous and scavengers, they were preying on the eggs. No doubt the crayfish in their nocturnal feeding activity did the same. To afford the utmost protection, the strips were placed in tubular containers made from hardware cloth, the ends being stapled after insertion of the egg-laden cloth. These cages were then submerged in appropriate channels.

It is common belief that the Green Drake is in the nymph stage for three years. To bring about quickest and surest possibility for a sustained hatch, it was decided that the experiment should be carried on for at least three consecutive years at the same spots. (Actually it was conducted for three years under the most exacting scale possible, with the first of the four years charged to experience with the hope that some results were achieved.)

Much to our amazement the first emergence occurred the first year following the planting, proving that at least a few complete the metamorphose in one year. Probably others hatch in two years, something which could not be proved, and the predominant hatch taking place the third year—Nature's method of perpetuation in the event of catastrophe.

Each season the spinners were netted between the 8th and 14th of June. Surprisingly, the duns and spinners observed on the stocked waters appeared between the 19th and 29th of May, indicating that the variation in temperature accelerated development.

As the years rolled along, no bona fide fishing hatch—either duns or spinners—of the Green Drake developed and during the seasons of '54 and '55 none at all were observed, although it is possible that some did emerge and return to deposit their eggs. The fact of the matter is that this hatch does not appear to have become acclimated in this environment, a really great disappointment. But the effort was not in vain. *Simulans,* the other big mayfly which was netted at the same time, however in

[139]

smaller quantity, is apparently here to stay and in quantity. *Simulans,* almost as large in size as *guttulata* and as interesting a hatch in every respect, has taken hold well on two of the four streams. It may have become established on the other two streams and may be emerging at the same time. Due to the fact that the interested individuals are capitalizing upon the result-ant fishing hatch on two of the streams, they cannot be sure just what is transpiring in other parts over the same period of time.

The accepted imitation of the imago of *simulans* (now locally called Brown Drake) is a number 10 Adams with a canary yel-low body. In one respect the fly has a tremendous advantage over the Green Drake: the fall of spinners sometimes settles on

Three reasons to go trout fishing, anyone of which is self-sufficient.

the water as early as 6:30 p.m. whereas *guttulata* usually holds back until dusk. One interesting aspect to date is the fact that as yet *simulans* has not spread over its normal span of time. Two evenings a year is the limit to date. The sub-imago must emerge at night, for very few duns have been observed on the water or leaving the water in spite of the fact that spinners occur in quantity.

Dr. Paul Needham is of the opinion that so long as there are a few remaining pairs of an aquatic insect in a watershed there is hope for the reestablishment of the hatch. Both *simulans* and *guttulata* may through the years become thoroughly entrenched in the limestone spring-streams of the Cumberland Valley. However, prospects for the former appear to be excellent, the chances of the latter, poor.

(This story of the attempted redistribution of *guttulata* and *simulans* was a paper prepared for and delivered to the Fly Fisher's Club of Harrisburg.)

Management

Compare present trout fishing with that of the past. There may be as many trout caught today but certainly they are taken by a lot more people and in fewer miles of water. It is a case of a diminished resource for the individual, a sharply reduced horizon, and increased competition. There are more and more frustrations and vexations for the distraught angler, stream pollution not causing the least.

A Frankenstein monster has been created which complicates matters. The practice of put-and-take—fish-truck following—has altered some thinking and some procedures. There have been a deterioration of sport fishing, a breakdown of stream ethics, and something else too. We have witnessed management and promotion geared to belly fishing for brand-new counterfeits which are well concentrated and along with this the utilization of our finest stream sections for sordid trout derbies of sorts. A generation of fishermen has been brainwashed to believe that fishing for newly-stocked trout is trout fishing—and sport.

Think what a school of hand-fed transplants from the quiet water of a lentic environment to the push of a lotic environment must undergo in their fight for survival. To further complicate matters, many are transferred from alkaline water to acid water. Where the pH is below neutral, a certain amount of consumed food must combat acid, whereas in hard water it all goes into physical development. Concentrations of newly stocked trout have their way of making the limit a goal rather than a danger point beyond which we must not trespass.

It must be recognized, though, that given the opportunity, some stocked trout become worthy fish and furnish fine sport. Some learn to feed normally and with selectivity and thereby furnish a challenge and bona fide angling.

There is good reason for the dedicated angler to be skeptical of the technician who speaks and writes of crop harvesting and optimum recovery, for he is thinking in terms of take-home catch and not in terms of sport.

Now the trout fishermen find themselves in the middle of a muddle. On one hand is a vocal group of truck-followers and limit-seekers of provincial interest who have a way of being able to foster the mating of fisheries management and politics. On the other is a group of inveterate anglers who are so interested in having consistent fishing and sport for tomorrow that they return most of the fish they manage to catch. The ideals and desires of these two groups are inimical.

Thus a conservation agency is on the proverbial spot. The easy way to meet the problem is to let sleeping dogs lie—stick with the old, avoid changes, and this in spite of the fact that it is becoming increasingly expensive to continue put-and-take and keep its advocates lucky.

There is where we are right now. Certainly there should not be civil war within the ranks of the fishermen, for strength in unity is needed to protect and improve the water situation and to exert an influence for sound legislation. Is there a logical answer? What is the best possible blueprint for official trout management?

It is my fervent belief that the following is the only workable solution: First there must be a classification of stream sections to provide a framework for management. There are three logical categories: One, natural reproducing stream sections with a high carrying capacity which with good management need no stocking. Two, stream sections with a limited hatching of eggs and a good holdover quality which with some supplementary stocking and special management could furnish consistent fishing. And three, the strictly put-and-take places where no trout eggs hatch, such as certain cold-water ponds and the silted lower reaches of some streams. With this framework, management can start. Less killing and less stocking go hand in glove; so do less killing and sport fishing.

This, zoned trouting, is the only way all-season quality fishing can be developed. Blanket regulations are obsolete. Trout stream sections should be managed primarily for trout, not for fishermen, and each should be treated as an individual problem. It is necessary to encourage and capitalize on the bounty of nature.

Ours is a great heritage which must be perpetuated. It should not only be our desire to preserve it but to improve it too. Our children and the unborn generations deserve the same opportunity which has been ours and our forebearers.

Most of us had our start on waters open to public fishing. Most of us fish there, at least on occasion. All waters, and the finest club waters are no exception, are subject to droll periods. Some sections cannot produce in hot-weather drought time. Others do not come into their own until late May. Still others have voids between hatches. But while some are undergoing seasonal droll periods, there are others which are in full bloom. Certainly one stream section offers infinite variety, nevertheless it is nice to be able to move around, to have safety valves in the form of greener pastures.

The Province of New Brunswick, in its excellent fisheries program, has made an honest effort to strike a happy balance between private fishing, which costs real money, and public fishing, which better fits many pocketbooks. The point is, there can be both, Hampshire, England to the contrary.

What is going to happen though if some open water is not managed for sport fishing. In self defense individuals and groups who will not put up with poor fishing will purchase or lease the finest stream sections and manage them privately. Officialdom will be relegated to the keeper of brooklets and warm water. On the other hand, top brass engineering a noteworthy program of acquisition, development and management will be championed by all trout fishermen and trout fishing in the old American tradition will have a future. Yes, the angler and his children deserve more for the money than just another load of trout dumped in the stream.

Today we stand squarely at the juncture of two roads, but oddly enough both—the high road and the low road—lead to the same destination, that destination being improved management and improved fishing. Only the stewardship is in question. I hope for the sake of my boy and yours it is the New Brunswick blend, not the English overtone.

The rallying point and the force for good is Trout Unlimited. Consider the philosophy of this national organization.

"Trout Unlimited believes that trout fishing isn't just fishing for trout. It's fishing for sport rather than for food, where trout are the means, not the end, where the true enjoyment of the sport lies in the challenge, the lore and the battle of wits, not the full creel. It's the feeling of inner contentment that comes from limiting your kill instead of killing your limit. It's communing with nature where the prime reward is a refreshed body and a satisfied soul, where a license is a permit to use, not abuse, to enjoy, not destroy our trout waters. It's subscribing to the proposition that what's good for trout is good for trout fishermen and that managing trout for the trout rather than for the trout fishermen is the fundamental solution to our trout problems. It's appreciating our trout, respecting fellow anglers and giving serious thought to tomorrow."

Reading between these wonderful lines is a screaming message: Trout must continue to rise; henceforth there must be less killing; the swing must be back to nature wherever feasible.

CHAPTER 14

The Odds Were Long

EVERYONE had taken his place and the two cameras were set to roll. When a big TV channel places things in operation to make a show, no detail is overlooked. The amount of elaborate equipment which had been moved into place from the special station wagon was impressive; so was the technical personnel assigned to the project. Nothing was taken for granted and there were directions for everyone and plans for everything. It was super-colossal Hollywood style. The idea was to make a picture sequence of the casting of a fly, the trout taking it on the surface, the hooking of the fish, the power run, then the playing, landing and releasing of the trout. Of course it had to be a big one.

Bruce Brubaker, the International Casting Champion, who had won his laurels by breaking a world record at the International Casting Tournament at Brussels, was set. Harry Allaman, the moderator of the program, The Call Of The Outdoors, had taken his place. The star performers, trout, were between the cameras and their would-be captors. They are the special fish of the Krystal Klear fishing preserve, the eggs having been flown in from Oregon, hatched in special glass batteries, then the fish raised in a series of troughs and ponds, each pond in turn simulating more closely natural environment.

"Fox," the director announced, "are you ready to make the first cast? The fly must land over that bare spot where the big lens is focused. You are in the field of the wide-angle lens of the other camera. Ready?"

Then he hesitated. "Wait!" and he intently peered through the ruffled surface of the clear water. "The biggest trout out there," he advised, "has a red-and-white thing on his back. That's our fish."

Everyone intently gazed in the direction he indicated. "Sure enough," remarked the proprietor, "there is a Dare-Devil spoon caught in the dorsal fin of a big brown trout."

From my angle the shine on the water made it impossible to see any fish but I could make out the spoon and it was moving in the general direction of the window of the telephoto lens.

Then came the voice of the director, "Shoot the big one." Apparently it never occurred to him that "the big one" might not want any part of the fly or that a smaller quicker one might get there first. "We might get a picture of him breaking the pole," he adds, hopefully I thought.

Now this fish was one of a large number of varying size located in the pool. Furthermore, my "pole" was a precious 2½ ounce stick of split and glued bamboo which had cost more than I could afford to replace.

As all eyes followed the spoon, I worked out line.

"Let'er down, now!" screams the director. So I dropped the fly on the surface in the prescribed area.

About half a dozen wakes converged upon it and the fly disappeared in a boil. An angler is supposed to answer such trout reaction by a lift of the rod tip to sink the point of the hook. When that rod tip came up, there was no give; so I knew I was into a big one, not one of the 12 inchers.

"Keep 'em rolling, fellows," roars the director. And the cameras ground away.

First there was slow, deliberate big-trout movement; then it built up into a powerful surge, which peeled line from a screaming reel. The fish was in command of the situation and ran and lunged exactly as it pleased. Everywhere that moving leader pierced the surface, there, nearby, was the little spoon. It seemed impossible to turn the head of the fish ever so little even with the rod low and to the side. Old hard-head would simply slow down, stop, then start out again. But there was no "pole" breaking.

"Great heavens," exploded Bruce. "Your fly is not in the mouth of that trout. You don't even have the fish hooked. Look! The fly is attached to the spoon." The two Harrys—Allaman, the announcer, and Smith, the proprietor, gaped in disbelief. So did I. But the technical boys took it in stride, just a normal circumstance in the course of good planning.

In due time, and a long time it was, the stubborn head-free trout found his comely proportions nestled in the mesh of the landing net. Before our eyes the barbless hook of the sodden dry fly rolled out of the tiny ring of the little swivel, a fixture to the spoon. The pesky spoon was removed from the fish and thereupon the big trout was returned to his pool. Without proof a truthful fisherman would hesitate to tell such a tale but here was motion picture recordings and witnesses.

Those who are interested in the computation of odds can work on this. There is a fish in a pool, a large slow fish, among

250 others. One cast is to be made. The fly is a floater. A spoon, a metal wobbler, is attached to the back of the big submerged trout. The eyelet of the spoon's swivel measures about 1/32 of an inch. What are the chances of catching this fish with a barbless hook engaged in the eye of the swivel attached to the back of this trout?

Of all the things which I have experienced this is the one that hits on super-colossal odds—bad odds, that is. Never again can Dame Fortune be expected to smile such a smile in the same direction.

> (Evidence can be provided by:
> Harry Allaman
> Channel 8 TV (WGAL)
> Lancaster, Pennsylvania
>
> Bruce Brubaker
> 2018 Harvard Avenue
> Camp Hill, Pennsylvania

And the tens of thousands who watched that Channel 8 outdoor show.)

LeTORT
Carlisle R. D. 6, Pa.

July 20, 1961

MY DEAR SUSIE,

This is the first occasion which has presented itself for me to write to you since your school days began almost two years ago. About the time this letter crosses the partly leveled Appalachian Mountains on its way westward, you will be seeing for the first the rugged peaks of the Rocky Mountains. You are doing things which I have never done, you are seeing things which I have never seen and you will be in places where I have never been. This includes crossing the Mississippi River, seeing the Air Force Academy and passing through certain states. Keep your eyes open and remember what you see. In the way of wildlife, which interests you so much, you may get a glimpse of a band of antelope, prairie chickens and prairie dogs and even a bear and a mule deer.

You like puzzles; so here is a word question, but first a clue: In your group is a school teacher, an English major student, a voluminous letter writer and a little boy just learning to talk.

When you show this page with the question on it to each, the only one who has a chance of giving the right answer is your little brother.

The question is, how do you pronounce the word

ghoti

Here is the second clue: The *gh* like the *gh* in the word enou*gh*, The *o* like the *o* in the word w*o*men, The *ti* like the *tion* in the word na*tion*.

That is tough, isn't it? How about the final clue? The picture on the letterhead depicts the word you are after. Now you've got it, Fish.

Affectionately,

DADDY

CHAPTER 15

A Nine Pounder On A Floater

"HOPE SPRINGS eternal in the human breast;" but when an angling heart is involved, a beam is cast rather than a ray. Ed Koch was big-fish minded. Three times that angling year the door of abundant satisfaction slammed in his face when the fish of his dreams, the perfect wall decoration for his tackle shop, parted company with him. Twice it was a severed leader; once, a broken hook. Then the fish left the old abode, its whereabouts unknown. It had proved difficult, if not impossible, to re-locate this one; and the sands of time were running low on another season. In spite of previous disappointments, the extra effort of an early break was still in order. He would put up with a jingling alarm clock which interrupts slumber in its soundest hour and the preparation of a pre-dawn breakfast. That is the kind of drive, or call it urge or optimism, which burns in the angling heart.

This early-morning angler witnessed the birth of a new day, just as he had done on other occasions when in quest of the big trout. The first rays of an August sun made the dew drops sparkle on the weeds and grass like a myriad of diamonds and every spider web was outlined in a pearly sheen. Here was an illuminated fairyland rivaled only by its anthesis, the flickering of fireflies under a velvet firmament attuned to the katy-did chorus—his two favorite times on a stream.

Visibility would be good as he cast toward the western bank on a piece of right-handed dry-fly water. A low clear stream exercises its exacting demands and finishing pressure of many weeks duration makes for sophisticated fish. These things he understood.

When the lid of the chest kit was flipped open, there in the separate compartments was an imposing array of counterfeits from which to choose. The lifted hand hovered over a hopper, the popular choice at this time of year; then the eye was drawn to the ebony form of Eddie Shank's deer-hair cricket. A fly has a way of beckoning, then calling out, "Look here! Change your mind. Call on me." Every fly fisherman knows how an afterthought overrules. As the thumb and forefinger withdrew the second consideration, the hinged compartment of the box snapped closed behind it with finality. The angler assured himself, as though to back up the decision, "After all, only two evenings ago my fly-tying partner was into a big one with his cricket."

Just before the fly was directed toward its intended target, and as the line and fly were being dried with false casts, a keen pair of eyes scanned the water ahead. The prime targets were the channels and pockets beside the over-hanging grass across the way. The idea was to make the imitation drift tight against the cover. Just about the time drag would set in, it was his custom to give the fraud a series of little twitches, a sort of last-ditch stand in the adventure of each cast.

Slowly and methodically, and uneventfully, he worked his way around the serpentine bend and into the straight stretch above. It was good to be healthy and out, where he belonged, on a day such as this. Ahead was a log jam, a veritable treasure house of snags for trout abode. Beyond that some overhanging boughs dropped down to interrupt the water course, each obstruction in turn creating a backwater. Here was a complicated but an interesting challenge.

Low and cautiously he moved in closer. As false casts lengthened the line, the eyes were drawn to a light form upstream. Something seemed to be out of place. It looked like a log, but what would a log be doing submerged in one foot of water and resting on a bed of dense elodia? The front end was blunt and the back end tapered; looked like the club of a giant. Ed blinked behind his shine-cutting sun glasses. That could hardly be a log, but it was so big it could hardly be a fish.

The back part undulated in the current. There was a beady looking mark up front. Sure enough, it was the giveaway to human vision trained to search out and spot creatures of nature, the eye. Finally the spots took form and this was the clincher. It was a monster trout still out and feeding, overtaken by daylight. Dame Fortune had again smiled, for here was another chance during the course of the season to cast over the fish of his dreams. He slumped to his knees, trying to melt away, as the back cast died to drop the fly downstream so motion would cease.

The fish was undisturbed in the feeding position, watching and waiting. The angler's eyes left the spot as he appraised the situation. This job had to be cased. There was the log jam ahead; and just below him, was a deep open pocket in the aquatic weed. Suppose the fish took the fly, what would it do? Looked like one of two things to Ed; either it would bore its way under the entanglement or it would make a panic-stricken rush upstream only later to drop back into the over-head cover. The more he mentally turned over possibilities, the surer he was that there was only one chance. Such a fish hooked in such a place had to be denied the initiative. If the trout could be hooked on a stout leader and immediately thrown off balance, there was the possibility that it could be induced to swim downstream, away from the obstructions, and into the open area. Thus strategy was mapped.

To be able to turn the head of the fish, a better angle was needed. On all fours he worked his way to a spot where the cast would be quartering up instead of straight upstream. One does not boss a fresh heavy fish with a 6X leader strand testing 1.8 lbs. Off came the fly, then the 6X, the 5X, and the 4X. Would this fish take a fly on a heavy leader? That was the crux of the matter. Trout such as this do not become big and old by wreckless living and bold adventure. No doubt during his days of bigness this one had seen hooks and leaders aplenty and had alluded some good men too. Probably as a small young fish it had found itself rudely drawn into a net or slithered onto dry grass, only to be carefully released. Such is the life and education of a LeTort native.

Carefully he re-attached the hair cricket with a Turle knot, then tested the connection. Nervously he glanced up. The fish was still there. What is more, he was in business. A minute form drifted into the window and the trout moved slightly to look it over. Apparently it was rejected with distain. Maybe a particle of weed or a thistle seed, Ed thought to himself.

Ever so carefully, with a minimum of motion, he set up the pitch by false casting. As the cricket lit on the water ahead of the trout and a bit to the caster's side, the angler was almost afraid to watch for fear the great fish would be made suspicious by the heavy leader point and disappear from sight. But the quarry neither moved to intercept the drifting fly nor to evade the telltale presence of trouble.

Casts number two and three were apparent duplicates of the first, both in the matters of placement and result. This wasn't good. The angler figured he had shown that fly to the fish in just the right manner and there had been no response. Was the problem one of pattern or presentation? Should a change of fly or leader be made? Or should a cast be made so the fly drifts directly over the nose of the fish? He chose the latter, for sometimes trout seem to be too shy to move more than several inches to either side in order to intercept food.

[151]

The fourth pitch carried the imitation two feet in front of the fish, and the opaque form started its drift in the surface film of the placid water. Downstream it came until it appeared to the angler that it was over the fish. Of one thing he was certain: the trout was watching the fly.

Then majestically, deliberately, confidently the fish rose and the water bulged. The spiked maw opened showing a putty-colored interior, and the fly disappeared in a dimple to the tune of a slurping sound.

The planned reaction of the angler was not in keeping with the usual. When one employs a light leader, he simply answers the rise of a trout by lifting the rod tip to establish a hook-embedding connection. But this time the fly was attached to more sturdy stuff. In one progressive motion the rod tip was lifted high then drawn low to the left. The massive head of

A nine-pound brown trout taken on a floating imitation of a cricket from the LeTort by Ed Koch of Carlisle, Pennsylvania.

the trout was swung around so the fish was facing the angler's bank. It had been thrown off balance before the powerful influence of the wrist of its tail could be exerted. From the angling standpoint, this was good fishing, and that little stick of parabolic bamboo had gotten things off to a fine start.

Equilibrium upset, the fish continued to turn in a half circle; then it rushed downstream to settle in the deep water of the open area. Everything was right now. Ed scrambled to his feet and moved below the trout, all the while keeping the line taut. If the fish made a run for the jam, it would have to be a long one to carry all the way; and there was that heavy leader tapered out to 3.5 lb. test which could exert substantial run-checking influence.

The initial worry, smashed tackle, was now but a slight possibility. What had been the secondary hazard, the hook loosing its hold, became the chief concern. The angler was boss and he was ready to press his advantage.

Satisfied that security rested in depth rather than distance, the trout did not elect to run. The battle of rod against fish was routine. All rod pressure was to the side—the same side of the fish. To maintain its elected position, the trout had to utilize the same set of muscles and the same action time and again. There was no letup of pressure, a relentless drag to the port, a devastating sameness.

No longer could there be a power run, and the tenacious barbless hook held firm. For twenty-five minutes the battle was all one way, thanks to that wonderful start. The big break had been the acceptance of a fly attached to 3X nylon; and maybe too, the fly was just the right size and pattern. Ed was approaching the achievement of a cherished goal.

The broad tail began to periodically break the surface as the head tipped downward. The time for the payoff was at hand.

The relentless strain increased. The fish was drawn from the pocket, over the elodia, and into a bay beside the low bank. It slithered over an outstretched frame. When the net was lifted, the mesh sagged, loaded for fare-thee-well with handsome fish flesh. The last act was the makings of the '62 trout season for one, Ed Koch.

Back at the parked cars, three campers stirred. The coffee on the two-burner was beginning to steam and it was time to lift the bacon from the pan and give the eggs a sizzling reception.

[153]

Bill Thompson was the first to notice what was approaching. "Gad!" he exclaimed, "Look, fellows; look out there."

He ran for Ed, or was it the fish? Bud Hoeffer disposed of the frying pan and grabbed his indispensable, a 35mm camera. Harold Powell was only a step behind.

Appreciation and satisfaction welled within the happy angler. The massive broad-shouldered fish was the trophy of his life. The final resting place would be on the wall above the show-case containing colorful attractors and deceivers. One thing sure, he would maintain a supply of black deer-hair crickets on the top rung right under that trout as a testimonial to their worth.

The fish was hung on a scale and the dial hovered between the 9 and 9½ lb. marks. When placed on top a tape, 27½ inches were blotted out. Picture taking followed, but there was a problem. Ed looked fine, big grin and everything; but he couldn't hold that fish still. Nervous hands still trembled. Some-one suggested that he was supposed to be posing with a trophy, not "playing a banjo." Well, that is how he was affected, and that is the way it should be.

Some more fishermen entered the scene, and the story of the fight had to be re-told, blow by blow. If pandemonium can be generated by a small group, that is what it was that broke out around the bench at the 19th hole in the turn-around meadow by my house.

To add icing to the cake, the information came from the Pennsylvania Fish Commission that according to official record, this is the largest brown trout ever taken on a floating fly from the waters of the Commonwealth. History had been made.

CHAPTER 16

The Big Fling

A VERY excited, arm-weary and trembling angler first blinked in disbelief, then beamed in exuberance as he gazed at the great silver form on the bank. The details of all the incidents leading up to the feat of landing his first Atlantic salmon were crystal clear in his mind, ever to remain that way. There was that deliberate and almost majestic head-and-tail rise to the fly. The solid feeling as the hook sank home. The rough, strong run of a panic-stricken fish. The wild, noisy jumps and the way the water flew. Now here it was, a salmon, his salmon, on the bank.

Turning to his companion he exclaimed: "Three years, three thousand miles and thirty-thousand casts later, I did it!"

To be sure, that was quite an occasion—the high light of an angling career—but there is a pathetic note. This is not the Hollywood-script version of a success story. During those three seasons and those thirty-thousand casts such an incident should have transpired not just once, but many times. Under the same circumstances a Joe Brooks or a Lee Wulff would have had many a salmon on the bank.

Practically every ardent trout fisherman somewhere along the line has been told that he owes it to himself to give salmon fishing a try.

"It has the daintiness and refinement of trout fishing," those confirmed salmon fishermen advise, "yet you are dealing with honest-to-goodness battle wagons."

It was such fight talks as this which induced several of us to engage an accommodation back in '35 at Bill Craig's on the North West Miramichi. Our chief adviser was William E. Kidder, a confirmed salmon fisherman from Kalamazoo, Michigan. He was the recipient of a life fishing license from the Province of New Brunswick after he popularized the practice of tailing and returning fish uninjured in the days when the gaff reigned supreme. His forty-eight-pounder from the Blue Hole at the mouth of the Cains River, where it joins the South West Miramichi, was regarded for many years as a Provincial rod record. The elderly Mr. Kidder was to accompany us, but at the eleventh hour he suffered the loss of a digit in an accident; so two green-horns set forth without the eminent adviser. However, there were some famous last words involved: "The traditional method is to cast a large fly on a heavy leader quartering downstream, take two steps and repeat," he told us. "Most of the time, that is the poorest thing you can do. Don't listen to anyone," he continued, "and don't ask questions; use your own judgment, and experiment."

Since that trip, several of us have operated for the last two weeks of each September from a wonderful little riverside camp on New Brunswick Crown Land—we glorify our shack on a branch of the Miramichi by calling it a camp. This is the time of year when the rock maple light up the North country. We never see such flaming foliage around our homes near the Mason-Dixon Line. This is also the time of year when the weather has put an end to the punkies and mosquitos. Now and then, to add spice to our chosen avocation, one of us wends his way in June or July to some other river which has a heavy, early run of fish.

Due to the wonderful start from the old man who wasn't there, we always step into a fresh morning with the prospect of a great day. Optimistically we search for possibilities and problems; experimentation is fun, and we won't permit ourselves to be trapped for long in the bog of a monotonous, futile routine.

There are some basic conditions which must be recognized by the confirmed trout fisherman who takes the big fling at salmon. Now he is after a gregarious fish which is in the river to breed, not to feed, a fish which seeks comfort and cover, not feeding stations and prime lines of drift. The lies are not in the shallows and the riffles; it is a pool proposition.

Here is one wild creature which does not associate danger with man. He does not flee from the sight of a man's legs, his line or his leader; but the sight of any one of these may be so distracting to the fish that man's offering is refused. Just why a salmon takes a fly is debatable and of greater interest to the ichthyologist than the angler, but take it he does.

The salmon have stopped in the pool because they are tired. They will probably push on with the next rise of water, which means the improvement of traveling conditions. The earliest arrivals from the sea have the longest journeys to the redds where they spawn; the late-run fish will spawn lower in the watershed—nature's way of meeting possible catastrophe by not putting all eggs in one basket. It is generally believed that

[156]

a salmon returns to the river of its birth and then seeks the section where his original emergence from the egg took place. The natural history of the fish is fascinating. As for the fishing, it is tricky, but fairly "trackable."

The technique of the expert is based on these truisms:

1. Salmon are more interested in wet flies than in dry flies when the water temperature is less than 60°F., but the converse is equally true.

2. Differentiation must be made between what salmon fishermen call "lies" and "taking places."

3. The water stage, the degree of clarity, and the nature of the surface dictate the size of the wet fly.

4. Salmon prefer a swimming or drifting wet fly which is near the surface most of the time rather than one which is down deep.

5. Wet-fly fishing is a game of making the fly swim or drift properly through the taking places or over fish which can be seen.

6. There is a marked preference for a fresh, high-riding, dry fly, tied with the best of hackle, as opposed to a sodden or soft one, bogged down in the surface.

7. A floating line is highly desirable; a long fine leader is a tremendous asset.

Those seven generalizations, as true as any generalities ever are, amount to "the facts of life" for the salmon fisherman.

A September night in a Maritime province can be brisk: brisk enough so Jack Frost paints the ground and the glass on the car a sparkling white, brisk enough to make the early donning of waders a cold and clammy operation. Bluebird weather may prevail most of the day and the fisherman may put aside his jacket to fish comfortably in shirt sleeves if it is not breezy; however it requires a lot of bright sunshine on low water to produce dry-fly fishing. The fact of the matter is that late-run rivers furnish basically wet-fly fishing, but there are exceptional hours.

During the course of the September following World War II the salmon fishermen in New Brunswick, and probably the other Maritime provinces, were plagued with a heat wave. Our group was fishing over fish because we saw some, but try as we might we could not make them take. The only productive places seemed to be at the mouths of cold feeder brooks and there were not enough such spots to go around. Day after day the water temperature was over sixty.

I thought I had scraped the bottom of the barrel for ways and means—when by chance I discovered an accident in a fly box. By mistake two big trout spiders, given to me by Edward R. Hewitt, were found misplaced with the salmon flies. Although they had no wings, body or tail—just hackle—they were big. But nestled in that hackle ring was a short-shank,

A part of the tradition of salmon fishing is the association with the guide, and the Canadian guide is quite a personality.

light wire, number-16 hook. In spite of the fact that such a hook is totally inadequate for salmon, I decided to try one. The only way to attach it to a leader was to add a length of fine gut which would pass through the tiny eye of the hook.

What happened after that to those two Neversink Skater Flies I hardly dare to write. Fish took them, made somersaults over them, rocked up to them and drowned them—gave them the works in that soupy warm water. I hung onto those flies for several days before the hook was straightened out on each. Usually there would be the spectacular surface rise, either deliberate or violent, and I would momentarily feel the fish as the little hook snicked the teeth, then came back.

Since those days I have always been ready with the real McCoy—skater flies made from the best hackle tied on well-tempered, short-shank, number-8 hooks. Any time the stream thermometer shows that the water temperature is up to sixty, out they come. The color of the hackle or the combination of two colors does not seem to make much difference. The main thing is to utilize a long leader, at lest twelve feet, tapered down to 8- or 6-pounds test at the tippet. They can be fished straight across stream, but the most fun of all is to cast them quartering down over a taking place on a high lazy cast, then, about the time drag sets in, skate them off to the side before the pickup. A greased line and leader make possible a clean pickup without dunking the fly and this in turn keeps the fly fresh and light.

Guides and outfitters often say that "The river is full of fish, but they are not taking." Of course, there are times when that's true. Some of the salmon are impossible to take. It is not likely, for instance, to move anything from water more than ten feet in depth. It is the more shallow lies which are the prime taking places. The beautiful picture pools, big, deep and quiet, are often the tough nuts to crack; but an insignificant-looking little depression in a medium fast flow, near some big rocks or an irregular ledge where the water is about five feet deep, should be as hot as a Fourth of July firecracker whenever there are fish in it.

Rain on the water will work wonders for any pool, and in certain spots it may be the difference between taking and not taking fish. I have in mind a placid place where salmon are prone to stack up in an area ten feet deep in a long flat. It can be a discouraging location on a calm bright day, but come the rain I would rather be there than anywhere I ever fished.

[159]

A friend annually fishes the Matane, a Quebec river which has the deepest holes imaginable for a stream of this volume. For a few years he haunted a few of the name pools—all big water—and he experienced tough going. Now he is paying considerable attention to the smaller, more shallow pools, and the fish are snapping at his number-8 and -10 Silver Wilkinsons, Black Doses and Cossebooms.

American fishermen have been deceived by the results the English anglers have obtained in the salmon rivers across the ocean with their prescribed method: a very large fly, attached to a heavy leader, delivered with a brute of a rod, cast quartering downstream. No doubt they are efficient in their environment and correct in their procedure; however, there is a basic difference. The runs in the salmon rivers across the Atlantic are very early, from February through May. This is the time of year when streams are swollen, cold and cloudy. About the time the Scotch and Irish fishing ends the Canadian rivers come into their own. By comparison we are low-water and warm-water salmon fishermen.

The lower and clearer the water, the smaller the wet fly should be. The low-water fishing is the more interesting and the small flies and lighter tackle are more fun to use.

At our camp, we prefer the sparse low-water flies tied on relatively light wire hooks in sizes 6, 8 and 10; but we recognize that in high cloudy water the larger fly on the heavy single or double hook comes into its own. In comparison with the standard, our flies are small and sparse for their respective hook sizes. And, with the exception of a river in flood stage, we fish our little wet flies near the surface.

In flat water, the cast is directed at a right angle—straight across the stream—with an extended rod and as straight and taut a line and leader as possible. The retrieve is by the fast hand-twist method as the rod tip follows the course of fly downstream. The little fly, barely submerged, is swimming sideways, showing all its beauty to the fish. When a salmon "takes," the rise can be seen. In this respect it is as spectacular as dry-fly fishing. To a large degree this is a game of searching the water for a taker. Many fish are raised. Some come back time and again, either ultimately taking or refusing the fly. This is our favorite type of salmon fishing, particularly on drizzly days, even though some anglers and guides avoid flat water like the plague.

In slightly faster water which is ruffled, we slow down the

pace of the swimming fly by directing the casts a bit further downstream and by diminishing the speed of the hand-twist retrieve. The decreased angle of the cast compensates for the increased rate of the current. By leading the line with the rod tip, the fly can be made to swim sideways over what appear to be the most likely spots. Even though we may still be searching the water for fish, greater emphasis is placed on targets than is the case with flat water.

Heavy water is deceiving. In spite of the fact that it may be wild, even white on the surface, there may be a fine resting place for a fish on the bottom. Protection may come in the form of big boulders and ledge crevices. To induce a fish in such a place to move from the protection of the lie through rough water to take a fly, it is necessary to offer ample opportunity. A fast-traveling fly is not effective. The hope is to work one's way above the spot, and cast well downstream. The angle permits the fly to loiter over the lie, thus offering the fish opportunity to see the fly and move for it. The fly on the double hook holds better in such water than those tied on singles.

The unorthodox English salmon fisherman, the late Arthur Wood, who developed "greased-line fishing," has provided us with a useful technique. His method encompasses a sparse fly, made to drift naturally and side-wise over the taking places. To prevent the current from dragging the line, thus pulling the fly, he mended the cast by rolling the line upstream. This is accomplished by pointing the rod tip at the fly and making an upstream semicircle with the rod, exerting enough force to move the line, but not pull the fly. This is our last resort for the fish which has been raised, but seems not to want to come back.

When a big fish rises to a fly near the surface, water is going to be displaced and disturbed, and more likely than not part of the fish will come into view of the angler. Frequently the disturbance or the actual fish is seen before the fly is touched. A quick strike by the angler can result in snatching the fly from the salmon. A big fish, large trout and grilse included, will hold a fly longer before ejection than is the case with the smaller trout; therefore, there is plenty of time for striking. Permit the fish to close over the fly and turn back to the lie, then do your striking.

It is practically unanimous opinion that the worst possible wet-fly action results from a cast where the fly lags behind the line and leader in such a way that it follows their course in a downstream loop. In part of its path the fly travels downriver head first, increasing speed all the while; then it is rudely whipped around in a semicircle. When an upstream wind creates such a situation, shorten the leader and/or the casts.

It is possible to overcome the objectionable downstream loop when a right-hander casts from the right side of the stream by pushing the rod to the left during the course of the shoot, thus placing the line further upstream.

The hair dry fly—hair tail, hair wing and clipped hair body— has gained great favor in recent years, as witness the popularity of the Rat Faced McDougal and the Irresistible. Lee Wulff's specialties, the White Wulff and the Grey Wulff, have come to enjoy great reputations. The latter of the two is the pet of the genial and great Joe Brooks. There is another style of tie, featuring a hair wing flat over the back, which has taken the Medway River by storm. A sort of stone-fly effect, it is a dry fly which can also be fished wet.

To some of us a sinking line is an abomination, so objectionable in fact that we take time out to dry and dress it, and every several days switch to a reel which carries a duplicate that has been given the opportunity to dehydrate. The floating line with its clean pickup makes all casting more efficient, and distance casting on smooth water a reality.

A floating leader in fishing the wet fly on smooth water is equally objectionable, although this is not the case when the Skater dry fly is utilized. A good cleansing with soap or toothpaste, leaving a film of it on the leader, will remove grease and let the terminal tackle submerge.

Unless it is necessary to buck a gale, all the true artists we have ever met prefer a long leader. This is the defense against "line-ing" a fish and thus distracting him by the too-close slap of the line. A suitable formula for a Platyl leader is as follows: two and a half feet of 19.8 pound test, two of 17, one and a half of 14.3, one of 11.8, two of 9.5 and three and a half of 8.5.

A salmon usually lies still if given slack right after being hooked. The fish appears to be so indifferent to the jab of the fly that I believe it might rise to a second fly from another rod, making the old expression, "sting of the hook," ridiculous.

We always beach our fish, not because it is the quickest and surest way to get one on the bank, but because it is in itself an interesting operation, which makes for greater personal satisfaction. If one escapes, either during this late stage or at any other time, more power to him. After all, the uncertainty of landing salmon is one of the great appeals of the sport. We must admit, though, that generally speaking the Atlantic salmon is more difficult to hook than to hold.

The specific gravity of a fish is about the same as that of water; therefore submerged they weigh nothing. We feel their strength and the pressure of the water until a jump takes place; it's only then that the weight factor enters the picture. During the jump a wildly contorting fish has the best chance to break the leader. The rod tip must be lowered to eliminate tautness. So when a salmon jumps, salute his greatness by the lowering of the rod.

Shoot 'Em As They Jump

The cherished trophies are not dead fish—but live action snapshots of the jumps of hooked salmon. With a preset camera on the chest, one can be ready to catch the spectacular leaps in suspended animation. The free hand is transferred, back and forth according to demand, from the handle of the reel to the short cable release of the camera. A nervous movement on the part of the fish usually precedes an aerial surge, thus making it possible to anticipate the action and be prepared to shoot with the camera, chest-pointed, where the jump should occur when he comes out of the water.

It is a game of maneuver to try to get the fish to jump at the right place, sort of like bird shooting in that you don't hit them all. When salmon fishing, I am always trying to add to the collection of prints. The camera has become a part of my salmon fishing equipment.

I operate with a 35 mm. camera with the lens protruding through a hole in the front pocket of a fishing kit, which has another sack on the back, the two being connected with wide shoulder straps. Accessories such as rainshirt and extra fly boxes are carried in the back pocket. With the weight distributed on the shoulders, the camera can be carried with a minimum of effort and in comfort all day long.

The lens utilized is 75 mm. (3 inch), the film fairly fast. On bright days with the sun on the image I shoot with the camera set at the f 5.6 stop and the shutter speed 1/500 of a second. When the light is not so favorable, the shutter speed is reduced and, at times, the next lower stop, f 4, is utilized.

The depth of field can be determined by the hyperfocal distance scale for the lens involved. For example, with a 3-inch lens set at f 5.6, and the distance at 20 meters, everything will be in focus from 37 feet to infinity; at 13 meters everything will be in focus from 29 to 119 feet. The f 4 stop is more critical;

[163]

[164]

at 13 meters, everything is in from 31 to 62 feet.

Such a hobby makes fishing just that much more interesting. The spectacular fighters are appreciated more and their performances better remembered. A trip does not end when one takes leave of the river, for anticipation continues until the negatives have been developed and prints have been made. Then there is that permanent, visual memory-refresher—great decoration for the walls of the den or under the glass top of the office desk.

Certainly I am delighted that I was talked into trying this game, which was started from scratch, for I was not a camera bug, but I am now.

CHAPTER 17

ℱ*ly* ℱ*isher's* 𝒱*iewpoint*

THE ART OF fly fishing for trout never was, nor will it
ever be, a simple affair. The true greatness of the happy sport
is due to two features: the fascination of the problems presented and the glory of the environment in which the adherent
operates. Accumulated knowledge, the powers of observation
and analysis, experience and skill combine to meet the challenges of imitation, deception and approach, all of which are
complicated. The most beautiful places on earth, be they rural
or rustic, are the edges where land and waters meet. Success
is measured in terms of personal satisfaction, which when
abundant is the greatest reward of all.

The pages of literature are replete with statements of the
fundamental philosophy of the angler. One which could be
adopted as the immortal proclamation was penned by Col.
Edward W. Harding for his book, *The Fly Fisher and the
Trout's Point of View*. (Death prevented the completion of the
revision, which was anticipated to be definitive and the last
word on the subject.)

"To some all this may seem like taking a recreation far too
seriously. If these objectors can take lightly the sense of baffled
disappointment following on failure by the waterside; if they
are content to enjoy success as though it were some caprice of
chance; if, in short, they are content to be the slaves and not the
masters of their fishing fate, then perhaps they are right: but
to me the sense of bafflement robs me of half my pleasure and
casual unexplained success is but Dead Sea fruit to the palate
of enjoyment."

Eugene E. Slocum, in his book *Ye Gods and Little Fishes*,
writes as follows relative to technique:

"An infinity of details, constantly varying with conditions
which may change with the speed of lightning, bestrew the
pathway between fly casting and a mastering of the whole
game. The fundamental principles may be learned in a few
hours; to transform them into a finished art requires many years
of devotion."

A quotation from *Angler's Choice*, edited by Howard T.

[166]

Walden II, expresses the philosophy of the editor: "There are the lure of bright waters and lithe rods, the challenge of each bend of the stream, the delight of fathoming the infinite moods of the creatures to be hooked at the end of the line. And best of all, there are the fancies, memories and hopes that lodge in the heart and mind of the fisherman."

Edward R. Hewitt cataloged fishermen into stages of interest: "At first we want to catch as many as possible; then interest turns to trophy fish; and finally, the one who continues to progress enjoys most the challenge of problem fishing."

In retrospect, the memories which are most vivid and exciting to me are the captured visions of surface-feeding activity. It may have been the nature of the rise form, or the location, or the tempo of the individual fish or the intensity of the collective rise. Some of these trout were never touched, some were hooked and lost, some were captured. There was "the big slasher" at the buttonwood, "the beetle eater" in the draping weeping willow, the incessant rising of "the trout without a mouth," "#51," the sulphur eater against the brushpile, "Old Faithful," "The flue liner fish," "the jassid king." Then there were the heavy multiple rises to the blizzard of green drake spinners, rises to the early season rafts of Hendrickson duns, June sulphurs and August winged ants. These constitute the ever-deepening and ever enriching layer of cream, which builds as the seasons roll along. It is with great anticipation that one looks forward to more of this sort of thing—the sight, the sound and at times the feel of rising trout.

Howard Black had a special way of expressing his feeling about fly fishing for trout:

It's the song of rippling water
And the beauty of the stream,
It's the flash of trout when feeding
In the sinking sunlight's gleam.
        That's anticipation.

It's the way you gauge your backcast
And the way you drop your fly.
And it's how your line is tightened
As the fly goes floating by.
        That's fishing.

It's a symphony of music,
In tune with nature's best.
A rhyme of song and motion
That puts your cares to rest.
        That's relaxation.

So take your flies and leaders,
Your reel and old fly rod
And wade your favorite trout stream,
Then you'll be close to God.
        That's the truth.

Anticipation explodes with the initial cast of the year. Although flesh may be chilled to the bone in raw, grey, sub-spring weather as foreboding water tugs at waders and wind numbs the hands, the spirit of the inveterate angler is at fever pitch as the curtain rings up the start of another season. It is not the prospect of opening day, not to the one who belongs there; it is the magic of another open season. A strange outside power has taken over and will cast its spell for months to come. Opening day, with its strange traffic, is a means to an end, a ritual to be performed, like going to sleep. Gaily and uninhibited we set forth on a new campaign with nature, which will soon assume its regular dignity.

Just how wild-blue-yonder can one get? Well, this is sure to be the best season ever. Accumulated knowledge and experience will make it so—new flies, dreamy fresh approaches to old problems, new spots, old fish and repetitive hatches to be exploited. Thus we blow sky high with confidence and drive.

About the time shirt-sleeve days are a reality and a rise to the evening hatch is expected rather than hoped for, along comes the bonus, daylight saving time. As though the angler is Dame Fortune's fair-haired child, his evenings grow and grow until it is possible to discern a rise on a silvery sheen at 10 p.m. Those who hunt as well as fish possess a profound appreciation for the extent of the angling day and the longevity of the angling season. It is a carefree routine—fish, fish and fish some more, but not at the now-or-never pace of hunting.

Ever-changing conditions contribute variety, the spice of fishing. Over the years in the meadow by the house it has been Nip and Tuck between the imitations of the sulphurs, the jassids, the ants, the Jap beetles and the hoppers to see which produces the most fish and the best fish. Then along comes

Chaunce Livly with his John Crowe beetle and Ernie Schwiebert with his partridge caddis to add two more fly types to enter into contention.

Golden days speed along on unnoticed wings. Angling is becoming more tricky with a more wily quarry in a more exacting environment—pretty fishing, this. The night air sparkles with fireflies attuned, it seems, to the katydid chorus. Suddenly there is a realization: the sun is setting on another trout season; the charmed routine will be broken. "Let's see," we pause, "just how many more days of it are there?"

The last roundup, like the kickoff, is a ritual, but the mood has changed; so have the fish and the nature of the competition. Robert Traver, in his delightful book, *Trout Madness,* likens the last day fishermen to pallbearers, "pallbearers at their own funerals." In order to soften the blow and produce a finale, a few push on to a Maritime Province for Atlantic salmon and others go to "Matchless Montana" or "Wonderful Wyoming."

Some years ago the LeTort regulars staged a picnic at the end of things, which is now the established custom. It's a good thing, because misery loves company. During the course of the afternoon or early evening anyone who catches a particularly good fish releases it, takes down his tackle and retires with the realization that the last cast of the season was a mighty fine one. Twice for me it has been the best cast of the year—a satisfying cud for long digestion.

Grouped on the circular benches before the crackling fire the anglers perform the post mortem following the dying gasp of another trout season. All good things must come to an end. Like the underdog rival who never wins, we say, "Wait 'till next year" and part company at a rough hour.

Fishing and hunting is a latent desire to follow in the footsteps of ancestry. Before the dawn of civilization man depended upon wildlife for food. Through the ages necessity forced him to fish and hunt. It meant life; it was fun. Today it is sport only but deeply ingrained, a powerful pull out of the past.

Thus, it is not surprising that the business of outdoor recreation occupies the top rung in the economy ladder. From the financial standpoint alone, this biggest business of all is worthy of protection, expansion and stimulation; but it goes beyond that. A vital part of the pursuit of happiness is an answer to the call of the outdoors. Affected, therefore, is the welfare of the most precious institution of all, the great American home. It is wholesome to believe that what is best for the family

[169]

circle is best for America. It is not possible to crush the desire to fish and hunt, so it is only plausible that we plan and provide in order that those who follow us will have their day of it too. Re-creation for recreation is the obligation which must be met.

There are good reasons why it is not advisable to tell a man how he should fish. This interjects thunder into the air, the unnatural kind. Then there is the realization that it would not be conducive to the best of sport if everyone desired to fish the same way for the same species at similar places and times. It is to the good that there is variation in thinking, variation in interest, variation in approach and variation in the ingredients which make for personal satisfaction in the mind of the individual fisherman.

Now and then the barbed question is put, "Is the fly fisherman on his way out?" We smile wry smiles as silent laughs go up our collective sleeves. "Show me a man," we think to ourselves, "who loves the fly rod and I'll show you a person who cherishes warm-weather low-water angling; one who is interested in aquatic and terrestrial insect life and their relationship to the feeding activity of game fish; one who appreciates skill, finesse and refinement; and one who relishes the challenge of problem fishing. There will always be those who are interested in the science of angling; therefore, there will always be fly fishing. There will always be those who enjoy wading; therefore, there will always be fly casting. Let them say what they like."

Today there are more men and women highly skilled along this line than there ever were before. Undoubtedly one reason is because there are more people. But there is another reason. Under pressure fish become increasingly shy; therefore, successful angling requires refinement. Refined angling encompasses fine leaders, good presentation and the best of deceiver and attractor flies, the tying of which to many is a part of the pastime. Fly casting is an interesting target game, a game of inches.

It must be recognized that there are two kinds of trout and two kinds of trout fishermen. There are the newly stocked fish which by necessity must experiment in their feeding activity and there are the stream-bred trout and holdover hatchery trout which have established selective feeding habits. Then there are the fishermen who like to work over concentrations of newly-planted fish, with their goal a limit catch; and there are those who revel in the challenge offered by acclimated trout, their goal being personal satisfaction. In the parlance of

[170]

the outdoor writer, one is a "belly fisherman," the other a "sport fisherman." Trout management has been geared very much for the former in spite of expenses and property-owner complications.

There will come an awakening of the Chambers of Commerce and commercial interests of the trout towns that the development and maintenance of quality trouting is attractive to visitors. It will be realized that anglers concerned with quality sport fishing expect to spend and do spend considerable time and money in pursuit of their hobby. When they hear of quality fishing they arrange to sample it. If they like what they find, they return for more, month after month, and year after year. The tourist interests will learn that quality fishing is angling in an attractive environment in which is located a worthy head of catchable-size trout and it is fishing where one finds well mannered kindred spirits. Consistent fishing can only occur where put-and-take is curtailed by killing restrictions. Zoned trout fishing accomplishes the job.

The Pennsylvania Fish Commission has determined by survey that 10% of the fishermen catch about 65% of the fish which are taken. If it were possible to pursue this further, most certainly the fly fisherman would appear by comparison a highly efficient operator. The making of a conservationist is the realization that one has the power to destroy the thing he loves most. Among the ranks of the fly fishermen are many eminent conservationists.

Our scion, cast from the molds of their fathers, even as we were, deserve the opportunity presented their ancestors. Each generation in turn has the obligation of stewardship as every age produces its quota of spoilers. Like the price of liberty for ourselves and our children, the price of fishing is eternal vigilance.

Exploitation is no longer the bold brazen thing of old, thanks to watershed protective legislation, which received its impetus from the angler. Now, when it occurs, it is a subtle deal. Fred Smith of the Conservation Council stated before a Pittsburgh gathering: "It is amazing how a talented wordsmith can confuse the most genuinely interested layman by somehow making an out-and-out theft of a resource ring out as a thoughtful, considered measure to advance the cause of conservation." The term multiple use can be employed as an excuse for abuse. Then, too, the angler must beware of the chief panjandrum and the technician who know nothing about sport fishing and who, in speaking of trout fishing, advocates optimum recovery and crop harvesting. Until such time as both fishermen and fisheries manager alike think in terms of sport instead of in terms of take-home catch, complication continues and politics has its way of interfering.

A most unusual case of exploitation was the transfiguration of Pennsylvania's finest brook trout stream from a thing of stupendous public value to a meager endeavor to milk an irreplaceable natural resource. In its days of glory this limestone stream, which stems from the largest spring in the Commonwealth, was a living example of the perfect balance between a high rate of natural reproduction and a tremendous carrying capacity. Ironically it was sacrificed on the altar of lust so that an inferior substitute for stream-bred trout could be propagated for personal gain. Men in high places condoned the conversion and made possible the operation at the expense of those they represented and they deceived non-fishermen.

An appeal which won the hearts of a Legislature was the signing and mailing of the following hand bill:

Pollution, of course, has been the chief devastator, however, conservation thefts come in other forms and oddly-wrapped packages.

A speculative cast into the future seems in order. Competition and normal progress will bring about the advancement of tackle and methods; so it can be expected that our children will be better fly fishermen than we. Fly fishermen, a proud race and a sophisticated lot, will manifest interest in tradition, history and established techniques. The amazing recorded history will be appreciated more and more as time goes by. The trend of the fly-rod man to seek kindred spirits will intensify. There will be more local groups such as the Angler's Club of New York and Philadelphia and the Fly Fisher's Club of Pittsburgh and Harrisburg. The national organization, Trout Unlimited, will be a sort of clearing house.

The anglers today, but to a lesser degree his children of tomorrow, will be faced with that sanguinary idol cast in the dollar mark termed, progress. Because there are those who believe that collective rights in conjunction with an irreplaceable natural resource are nonexistent, the anglers' equities are impaired. There will be more donny brooks; there will be more legal vendetta and there will be instances when many will stand up and be counted on the side of conservation. In the end the conservationist will triumph completely, because a

[172]

Going, Going, . . . ?

PROTECT OUR FISHING!   SAVE BIG SPRING!

Once more the sportsman and conservationist is fighting and pleading for a cause which has been fought for and lost a thousand times over. Win or lose, this is one of the last battles simply because Big Spring, Pennsylvania's famous native brook trout stream, now threatened with destruction, is the last of its kind. Time after time the fisherman and the conservationist went down to defeat before the ancient and moss-backed argument that private enterprise must prevail over a "few little fish." A "few little fish" have blossomed into a multi-billion dollar industry to make sport fishing the most precious resource in the United States today.

According to the joint report of the Securities and Exchange Commission and the Federal Trade Commission, the capital value of the sport fishing resource is more than $50,000,000,000 (fifty billion)! More than 21,000,000 Americans pour an annual revenue of $2,000,000,000 (two billion) into the coffers of the business man. The capital value of sport fishing is 10 times that of the lumber and wood products industry! It is over 1½ times as great as the entire iron and steel industry! It is more than 2 times as great as the entire automobile industry! Fantastic, isn't it? But it is the absolute truth!

Every retailer who has a sign "Fishing Tackle For Sale" is involved here. Every manufacturer of outdoor clothing, tackle makers, boot manufacturers, boat builders, motor manufacturers, gasoline stations, automobile manufacturers and a multitude of others have a stake in this. It even reaches down to the modest clerk behind the counter, who earns a livelihood for himself and his family.

Big Spring is symbolic. You cannot have all this enormous wealth without Big Spring and more of its kind. Big Spring belongs to the people for all time.

Mr. Legislator, help save Big Spring.

A sportsman and a conservationist,

(Sign your name and address and mail)

[173]

requisite to sustain life is pure water. Additional trout water—cold clear water—will be created below deep taps from new impoundments. As the water problem intensifies there will be more and more reclamation and creation and less and less exploitation. The economic and recreational value of fishing will be recognized and vigorously championed. Ultimately the basic element for life, clean water, will become an inviolable thing across the country.

The immediate hope of future trout fishing lies in acquisition, development and management. Today the contribution of the individual is to champion the cause of the application of scientific findings and the practice of management for sport fishing.

Conservation Pledge

I GIVE MY
PLEDGE AS AN AMERICAN
TO SAVE AND FAITHFULLY TO
DEFEND FROM WASTE THE
NATURAL RESOURCES OF
MY COUNTRY — ITS SOIL
AND MINERALS, ITS
FORESTS, WATERS,
AND WILDLIFE

PART II

Rising Trout—Legend

Legend is a subtle blend of the actual and the ultimate, the area which lies somewhere between the way things are and the way we would like them to be. Fiction with recounting and rereading has a way of developing the roots of reality to produce growth which seems more natural than artificial in the wonderful world of could be.

Characters are the composites of companions and acquaintances, blends of personalities to create new individuals which better fit the scheme of things. Mental creation sparks lives which have a way of taking their places with those of the living generation.

Molded together are the real and the imaginary—people, places, and fish—to create the spirit of adventure along the waters where the trout rise.

CHAPTER 1

Brain Washed

A SUBSTANTIAL young fellow, a typical American boy, was trapped. A powerful urge to fish and hunt could not be answered; it had to smoulder. There was no fishing and hunting Dad, no escape from the concrete jungle. Suddenly, though, the picture changed. After high school was history and a job yielded money, money which was his very own to do with as he pleased, he became the possessor of an old-model car. Once the conveyance was made back-road worthy, Sonny was the owner of the primary fishing and hunting instrument. The strongest call, and the first which could be answered, was that of the trout stream. Knowledge would be acquired and battle gear assembled. There was a phraseology which haunted him, the title of a favorite book, *Call of the Wild*. It would soon be time to answer the call.

A piece of news reporting revealed that those who should know made a prediction: "This should be the greatest season in the history of trout fishing in the State." It added, "the streams are stocked as never before with legal-size spreckled beauties from the State fish farms." That was convincing, but there was more. "The supply will be replenished by a series of mid-season stockings." Then to clinch it was a listing of local "approved waters" and the route numbers of the roads which crossed or paralleled them. "The daily creel limit is 8, keep nothing under 6 inches," was more of a boast than a warning. The tone of the glowing release was, "come and get it." He would be there.

To date his only experience with trout had been at the annual fishing derby for kids in the municipal park. The last year he was eligible to participate, he won the grand prize for catching the most.

As equipment was in the process of being amassed, he asked questions; he learned. Things should go well, too, because the clerk at the sporting goods store had sold him an outfit which is "a great trout killer." He decided he would open the season at the clerk's recommended place, "right where the fish truck

[179]

stops." Hadn't he been assured, "you'll get your limit there, if you get there early?"

He was there early, that opening day, but even at that, parking was a problem. It wasn't difficult, though, to get a place between two others in order to fish the big pool below the dam. For a while everybody caught some trout, then things "quieted down," in fact all action ceased.

The next day the papers were full of it, listing anglers who reported limit catches. One man, it noted, had his goal of 8 before 8 o'clock in the morning "for the fifth straight year in succession." Maybe it was because mother did not know how to prepare trout for the table, or maybe he just didn't like trout, but that mushy grey flesh had a funny taste. The cat, though, seemed to enjoy what they couldn't eat.

It began to look as though things had "quieted down" for keeps. In spite of the fact that he could not catch any more, he kept trying. In spite of the fact that there were fewer fishermen; there were less fish, but he philosophized, that's the way it happens.

Then one day he read in the paper that the mid-season stockings were starting. Again he was Johnny-on-the-spot back at the bridge pool, and so were a number of others. He recognized that it was basically the opening-day gang. For a while everyone caught some; then it "quieted down." He was beginning to become perturbed by this term or condition.

It quieted down too fast and it stayed quiet too long. The next day there was some publicity about limit catches and he recognized some names which appeared in the first day reporting. That fellow who gets his before 8 o'clock did it again.

A few days later he was fishing his way through a piece of flat water which did not appear to be particularly interesting. But he would fish it out before he quit and started back to the car. When almost at the end, he suddenly became conscious that he was being watched. Two old fellows with fly rods set up were sitting together on a log, not conversing, just watching. Apparently they were tired and had given up. Wanting to be sociable, he directed to them some cheery words.

The two old cronies were anticipating a fall of spinners at dusk and an accompanying rise of trout. In due time Ben would slip into the tail of the long flat and Ollie would locate himself at the half-way point. If everything went according to schedule, wild fish—beautiful, strong, shy and selective—would move out

[180]

from under the brush piles and rocks to take feeding positions where the gentle current would deliver to them a feast of spent spinners. Each line had been carefully dressed and to the end of each 10-foot leader, tipped out to 4X, dangled a number 10 Cochy Bondhu Quill, their favorite imitation of the prevailing hatch. As the two sat chatting on a log, their eager eyes scanned the skyline at tree-top level for the nuptial dance of Mayflies.

"I see some, Ben, up there at the pine." Ollie's voice had a ring of excited confidence. Although the two were in the dull light of the floor of the woods, the last rays of a setting sun lit up the tops of the forest monarchs and played upon the glassy wings of milling insects.

"Good," answered the other. "I see more over there," and he pointed. "In ten minutes they should be down low; then in another five enough should be on the water to set off the fish. We've got our setup, Ollie," he smiled.

"Ben." The voice registered concern. "Look up at the bend." Two pairs of eyes attuned to catch movement and things foreign to nature's normal pattern peered at the riffled curve at the head of the flat.

"Do you suppose he's going to come down through, right when the trout are moving out?"

"Maybe he'll stick with the riffle," was the hopeful reaction.

But come he did, fast and hard. With every step wakes rolled out over the placid water and whatever he was casting landed with a splash. Hurriedly he plowed his way through the quiet water, dropping that thing on the end of the line with a plop, now audible to the unseen spectators. His stumbling and skating on the slippery rocks was offset by a great sense of balance and agile recovery.

Suddenly the fisherman noticed his gallery and caught sort of short he said, "Hi, how have they been biting?" Nervously without waiting for an answer he continued, "You know, they stocked some more a few days ago, but it seems by now what are left are scattered. I figure the best bet is to feel them out by covering a lot of water. Got two in the riffle," and he patted his creel as he glanced upstream. "Have you two taken some?"

Ben's answer began with a sort of sigh, "Well, we haven't started yet. We are waiting for a rise. Where is your car?"

"Must be a mile upstream. Guess I better beat it back through the brush before it gets dark. I'll leave these fish to you two. Hope you locate some. Nice talking to you. Good luck." And he plowed his way toward the opposite bank.

"Well," drawled Ben. "That's that. What should we do now?"

"Let's hurry. Maybe there is still time to hit a rise at the bridge pool," Ollie's speculation was at least a ray of hope.

As the two drove away they talked about the bad break. Then Ollie came up with a conjecture. "Poor guy, he doesn't recognize a setup when it is served on a silver platter. Right now he is running away from it, but he wouldn't know what to do about it anyway. Probably doesn't know that there is such a thing as a shy trout in the stream and a hatch in the air. Looked like a fine clean-cut young man, too, the kind a father is proud of. If he understood, he would probably become a real angler."

Ben took it up from there. "He is one of a generation which has been educated to believe that fishing over a concentration of newly-planted synthetics is trout fishing." As he finished lighting a smoke he added the words, "and sport. I tell you," he continued, "a Frankenstein has been created. Your fishing is not even safe any more a mile from a stocking point. Just suppose, Ollie," he reflected, "suppose the trout managers got their hands on more money for more counterfeit fish for more trout derbies."

"Just suppose," interrupted the other, "the publicity department could issue more releases about additional stockings."

The long silence which followed was finally broken. "What are we going to do for angling in a day and age of management for belly fishing?"

"I'm not so much worried about that. We've had it rich in our time, Ollie. What I am worried about, though, is my kid and his kids. What are the new ones going to do for their angling?"

As they arrived at Kellogg's bridge in the half-light, three other cars were just pulling away. Through the windshield of their parked car they looked out on a silvery sheen, and the erratic flight of insects was still visible. The surface was not marked by a single ring.

"Not like the old days; this place should be boiling right now."

"They have been put down for the count. Come on, let's go home."

There was some misgiving in a young outdoor heart and as the car chugged along, reflections developed into deep thought. Sure it's great to get into the country and the trout streams are beautiful, but somehow sporting elements are lacking and some situations are not what had been anticipated. Apparently in trout fishing the golden rule does not apply. You move away from a spot to land a fish and when you turn around, the place is gone. Then there was the fellow who waded where you were fishing and the guy who persisted in casting across the lines of others. And, too, those cans and other streamside litter were so badly out of place.

He thought about the incident of the blocked farm lane by a car, then how its driver got smart about it. For a few seconds he had been all for getting into it and, if necessary scramble the eggs of that wise guy, but second thought had dictated that one seeking outdoor recreation should not get fouled up in that sort of thing.

Even when you know right where the trout are and you are sure you are going to catch some, it isn't exactly wonderful; something doesn't fit right. Furthermore, when "things quiet down" it seems rather futile. Maybe trout fishing is not all it is cracked up to be. An idea flashed through his mind: photographing wildlife might prove more entertaining and rewarding—a better outlet. The hard-top road intercepted the concrete ribbons leading into the big city. As the car rolled faster he wondered how he would like to live in the sticks. His Dad had been a country dweller before he went off to war and his last adventure. Often his mother spoke about him. He had loved to fish, and he must have been successful at it too. His face clouded. There was a question he had never thought of before: how did they get the fish truck to the streams in Dad's country, back of World's End? There was something else which confounded him, a sort of haunting concern. What did that old fellow mean when he said to his companion, "Well, that's that. What should we do now?" Almost out loud he whispered to himself, "I wonder, I wonder, about trout fishing. Could there be two kinds?"

Would it not have been the great turning point in the young heart of a neophyte angler had there been a true meeting of the minds back there under the foliage and the flies, beside the placid water? Would it not have been a case of great personal satisfaction and abundant reward to two dedicated veterans had they but talked, talked about the thing they love to talk about most, talked about what makes angling for trout so very great a sport—and what is wrong with belly fishing for counterfeits.

[183]

CHAPTER 2

Buzzards At Large

ONE THING SURE: propriety cringes in a climate incompatible with the personal interest of the hobbyist. My ox has been gored. The stream which flows by the house has been depleted of its big trout, a circumstance brought about by collusion and a secret operation. So from my vitriolic position up the creek I herewith exact revenge by tearing aside the veil of concealment from the buzzards. Just what transpired and how it was accomplished is revealed to *all* would-be captors of lunker trout with the release of the following correspondence. Why should I care? I just quit fishing.

Richard F. McDougal

June 13, 1961

Mr. Byron S. Gordon
Northern Tier, R. R. 1, Pa.
My Dear Quill Gordon,
The other evening following a good afternoon of fishing to surface feeders, a stranger ended up at dusk opposite the house where I put in the brush piles along the edge of the stream. He had a light seven-foot rod and a long fine leader for the daytime rising trout. I could see him in the half light tear off several strands of the lighter tippets and tie on a big buzzard of a dry fly.

Well, a hefty trout deliberately sucked in that monstrosity, then after about half a minute the fly lost its hold.

As I sat on the water-side bench, he fished his way downstream to the next brush pile. This time a big trout plowed the water to get at the fly and took it, too, in a spectacular and noisy manner. In about half a minute the hook pulled out and came back in his face, whereupon he joined me on the bench.

"They were big," I offered.

"Yeah," he snorted. "Not enough of rod to sink the heavy hook. But trout come bigger than those."

Even though the light was failing, I had been able to see that he was not casting upstream as one usually does when employing the dry fly, so I asked him how he prefers to present the fly.

The answer was surprising and revealing. "They like drag on a night fly, so drag they get. Mostly I cast slightly downstream and just let the fly swing slowly across below me. Some of them jump it; some inhale it."

"You do a lot of this kind of fishing?" I ventured.

"Yeah. I like to catch big trout and that's the way to get 'em—right after dusk and just before dawn." He spat a tobacco stream which plopped in the water, then in a sort of reflective mood added, "that is, trout over 4 lbs. Tonight I was lazy. Should have gone back to the car for the night rod."

Now, Quill, you and I belittle large trout because they won't take our dry flies. We expound on the virtues of 14-inchers as grand fly fish. If by chance we would get a 2-footer, we would think seriously about having it put on a board. We think in terms of a ruler. This fellow is getting them on top and his measure is a yardstick. His idea of a real one is twice the size of ours.

He told me that he does better on smooth water with the floating fly than with the standard large wet fly they use upstate. I offer the observation that in order to help the fly along in smooth water there should be a hand-twist retrieve. It appears that he has something hot which we should apply.

Couldn't help but think of the water and brush piles in the stream above your dam and that dust-covered cigar box loaded with salmon dry flies with the clipped deer-hair bodies and hair wings, which you showed me.

Unquestionably we should eliminate the big cannibal trout from our waters. Now we know how to accomplish this in a sporting manner. Keep it a secret.

Kindest regards to you and your fair lady.

Cordially,

R. F.

Mr. R. F. McDougal   6/15/61
Cumberland Valley R. D. 3, Pa.

Dear Rat Face,

The message came through. In answer to your SOS a box of buzzards will be on its way. Why don't you learn to tie them yourself. Having watched you at the fly tying vise, I believe you could produce two in the course of a long evening, providing there are no rejects. Let's see, that would set the unit cost at $3.50, minimum wage rate, of course.

Since you are so sure of yourself, I hope the flies arrive before that fellow returns and catches your big trout.

You champion conformity. Do you regard the sort of thing you describe as orthodox?

Our best to all of you,

Regards,
Quill

Mr. Byron S. Gordon
Northern Tier, R. R. 1, Pa.

June 20, 1961

Hello Quill,

Am I happy and laughing? I took one of Old Tobacco Juice's big trout. Wonder what he will think when he returns and finds the cupboard bare? And return he will. It measured 19½ inches and took right in front of the brush pile—same as before. This is the one that sucks it in. Am going after the slasher tonight.

You better get busy draggin' the buzzards up your way!

The fly of yours to score was the one with the light tan body and the light brown wings.

Yours for bigger and better trout,
R. F.

Mr. Byron S. Gordon
Northern Tier, R. R. 1, Pa.

June 27, 1961

Dear Quill Gordon,

I must report that Old Tobacco Juice returned last evening. Right after dark he made a bee line for the brush pile trout and this time he had his night rod.

A strange thing happened. When he fished the upper brush pile, that's the one where the sucker was, he hooked a gawd-awful trout which measured 27″.

He said something significant. "That wasn't the fish I expected to take. Thought I would have to remove one about 19″ first then come back later for the good one. The smaller ones are faster than the big boys."

Incidentally, he got the slasher, too,—21½″.

Get going with this on your flat water!

Tight lines with the dry fly,
Mac

Mr. Byron S. Gordon
Northern Tier, R. R. 1, Pa.

July 12, 1961

Dear Quill,

Are you there? Why don't you write? This night dry fly
fishing is an effective and worthy game. The flies, the technique
involved and the rise forms constitute an exciting phase of
fishing the floating fly. Really, it is obtuse to refer to it as
"buzzard fishing."

I feel that I am serving the cause of conservation. To date I
have removed two. That means there are two less cannibals to
molest the young and up-and-coming crop.

Took the last one on the pattern with the dark body and
dark wings.

Crawl out of bed and get busy,
R. F.

Mr. R. F. McDougal
Cumberland Valley R. D. 3, Pa.

7/21/61

My Dear McD.,

Do you not regard the large trout as the finest possible brood
fish in the stream; is it not true that they work up the best
redds and deposit the most eggs, that these are the fish which
remove the trash which competes for the food supply and eats
trout eggs? In short, are they not the valued policemen which
patrol the beat?

One time you said that you and your 3 oz. rod, along with a
leader pointed out to 6x, are inseparable on a trout stream.
Have times changed, or is it you?

Sincerely,
Quill Gordon

Mr. Byron S. Gordon
Northern Tier, R. D. 1, Pa.

July 27, 1961

Dear Boy,

How silly can you get? If you practiced this night-fishing top-
water art, you would regard it as the acme of fly fishing—sport
supreme with superior trout, a game of tempting the great unknown. And, too, you would learn what a big trout is. Don't
be dogmatic, or is it a case of jealousy? That was a sour-grapes
letter if ever one was conceived.

[188]

Suppose I had the flies on hand and in ignorance knew no better than to store them away in a cigar box; then you demonstrated their value and application in a most convincing manner; would I be derogatory? Of course not; gratitude would prevail.

For your information, my score with the brutes is now up to 5. The grey fly has accounted for the biggest trout—23″. Some fish!

You don't know what you're missing.

As ever,
R. F. McD.

Mr. Byron S. Gordon
Northern Tier, R. R. 1, Pa.

Aug. 29, 1961

Dear Q. G.,

Although I haven't heard a word from you since your silly letter dated 7/21 was received, and I have written twice since then, it is possible that you have undergone a wholesome change of attitude. The curtain is about to ring down on another season. It has been far and away the greatest I've ever experienced. My best trout is in the hands of a taxidermist, and the fact that it was taken on a floating counterpart of nature makes the feat of its capture all the more cherished a memory. As you well know, it is no small order to equal 23 inches with the dry fly.

There is a moral obligation on my part to render an accounting of the flies you presented to me and which I have applied with success in a revolutionary effort. However, as time progressed, the big fish became increasingly difficult to locate. I'll tell you, they are shy creatures. Nevertheless, your flies accounted for 6 superior specimen. Think that one over! Of the 6, 1 was taken on the all-grey, 2 on the light deer hair and 3 on the dark—an imposing success story!

Next year you will have to climb down from that ivory tower and capitalize on the superlative opportunity. Only don't let the cat out of the bag—play this one close to the vest. The salmon rod would be admirable for this specialized art. Stubbornness never did anyone any good.

R. F.

Mr. R. F. McDougal
Cumberland Valley, R. D. 3, Pa.

10/2/61

Howdy Stranger,
   It's cold out there.
   The amount of dust on that cigar box full of flies was not as
deep as you would suppose. Why would a fellow tie up and
keep on hand 300 buzzards when he fishes only 14 days a year
for salmon and on some trips it's all wet fly fishing? Now,
Sonny Boy, who calls the buzzards, "salmon flies?"
   One of these seasons you're going to find out what a big trout
is. Just keep pitching those things on the black flats and use a
heavy leader. How come you didn't catch more and bigger ones?
   There is one surprising thing about this whole affair and that
is that Tobacco Juice spilled his insides. I told him where he
could find some real fish which the property owner would like
to have removed. Altogether he was down about 3 dozen times,
caught a hellava lot—his best trip produced 7 lunkers. From the
conservation aspect all this, no doubt, is good news to you.
Tobacco Juice favors the fly with the yellow body and black
wings. So do I. Between post-dusk and pre-dawn fishing, we'll
take the latter every time. How about you, Lazy Bones?
   For more and bigger trout,
                                    Toodaloo,
                                    Quill Gordon

cc: Dr. Alfred "Tobacco Juice" Bartlet, Northern Tier, Pa., who
   should pay more attention to patients and less to victims.

Telegrams dated Oct. 3, 1961
To Mr. Byron S. Gordon—Northern Tier, R. R. 1, Pa.
To Dr. Alfred Bartlet—Northern Tier, Pa.
   Did you ever observe a pair of buzzards soaring above a
prostrate body stop
                                    Richard F. McDougal
                                    Cumberland Valley, Pa.

CHAPTER 3

The Object of His Affection

THE INCREDIBLE defied the laws of angling. One day each trout season the genial restaurant proprietor was a marked man, the winner.

Through the years the sporting-goods store had staged a big-trout competition on July's last Saturday. It was no artificial derby-type affair with newly-stocked fish in a confined area; it was wide open, catch-as-catch-can, anywhere.

The nature of the trophy and local tradition made length the criterion; weight and girth didn't matter. Whoever brought the longest trout to the store before 10:30 p.m. on the big day got his name, with the length of the trout and the type of lure, engraved on the novel trophy.

In the early 1900's Boas Rupp, a jeweler who took his trout-fishing as seriously as his business, built an elaborate measuring device. A candidate trout was laid on a lateral rule, its nose touching a metal block. Then a sliding arm was nestled up to the tail-tips.

A husky optimism set two feet as the total reach, for back then there were only brook trout to enter, and an 18-incher was a veritable giant. But the long reach was just as well, for after "the war to make the world safe for democracy" brown trout of Germany ancestry were the perennial winners and their propor-tions considerable exceeded those of the vanishing native.

The measuring stick was mounted on a silver slab that bore the data on each annual champion. In time it became the duty of the store to supervise the contest, polish the block, and finance the engraving. No honor in local anglerdom was so cherished as having your name on the trophy with those of famous fishermen of the past, many of whom were making their casts from the other side of the River Styx.

About a hundred contestants entered every year, each free to choose the spot that his experience and judgment named as most promising and to use whatever tackle seemed best under the circumstances. With a little give-and-take for varied knowledge and ability, odds were about 100-to-1 for each participant.

The strange thing though was that recent years were an un-precedented era in which the same person won. The name of

Adam Beck had a nine years' straight run on the trophy. His fish was always about 22 inches long, and after the numerals designating length came the words, magic to him, "Dry fly."

Old Adam had a passionate fondness for the natural-floating artificial, always maintaining that if he couldn't take trout fairly and cleanly he didn't want them. Nothing irked him so much as to hear someone belittle the use and effectiveness of his beloved dry fly. Whenever he heard that it's bait or hardware that gets the big ones he was positive in declaring that you don't need to bottom-grub for a noble fish, for the dry will do a creditable job. Adam never gloated over his triumphs; the method of angling got the credit.

Habitual skeptics pointed to questionable factors. During the rest of the season the crowned champ rarely took particularly large trout; no other contestants met him streamside on the competitive day or even saw his car; and his winners always were dark big-headed fish unlike the well-proportioned light ones so common to their rich limestone waters. "How does he do it?" and "Where does he go?" were the ever-nagging questions about the mystery.

Adam only said, "There's often some special piece of knowledge that'll bring you fish if you use it carefully. The right dry fly in the right place at the right time is the most effective and the most enjoyable practice in the grandest sport of all." Beyond that he was eloquently silent.

Full well Adam realized that his legs were weakening and his casting was not as strong and deadly as it had been for many years. He was getting too old for long days and hard work. Nevertheless, the dry fly must prevail.

Although the day had come when he no longer could carry the cudgel, he had chosen a standard-bearer carefully, leaving nothing to hope and chance. From now on he'd bask in tranquility, celebrating the victory of his beloved floating imitation of the natural.

Often he fished with Frank Hunter, whom he called "Boy." The keen, firmly-knit young man had a deep love of angling and his thought and conduct now bore the Beck imprint. A half-century's age difference meant nothing; each was perfect company for the other. To the youthful eyes of Boy, Adam epitomized the master angler, as "compleat" as Walton's own ideal. His knowledge and streamcraft, his handling of both tackle and situations were indisputably grand. And as protege, Frank came up to Adam's highest hopes. Some day he'd be the unchallenged expert in this cradle of the great water system. The boy had coached well, much better than obstinate Little Caesar, and it was a pleasure to be with him.

One night when they were returning from the stream, Frank innocently put the leading question: "Well, Mr. Beck, are you ready to defend your title next week when the big day rolls around?"

"I was never so ready for anything in my life," came the stout answer. "These last few years you and I have fished together a lot. We think alike, Boy; we cherish the same things; we fish the same way. You've come a long way with your angling and ultimately you'll have no peer." He hesitated. "Anywhere," he went on. "Your casting is better than mine; the flies you tie are superb. From now on it's you who'll champion the cause. The winning fish this year will be yours and your victory will again prove the superiority of the dry fly."

Frank was flabbergasted. "But suppose I don't produce. Suppose bait or hardware wins."

"I like the way you put those questions but you're ready. Everything'll go all right. The great Henry David Thoreau in *Walden* wrote, 'Nothing is so much to be feared as fear.' In the early days of TV another fellow used to say that, and folks thought it was original, like some new ideas in guns and tackle. But I'm not making a political speech; this is serious business."

"I've never had a doubt," Frank assured his elderly friend, "as I've had with L. C. and a few others, that you took your great fish on a dry fly, but I haven't been able to figure where you go to do it. Do we travel far?"

"Just a matter of a gallon of gas. Be here at the restaurant Saturday before daybreak and we'll take off in my car after breakfast."

Frank was fascinated with the prospect and gracious about his new role but concerned about results. Then, to his horror, a torrential thunderstorm came the evening before the big day. The streams would be wild and muddy. How could the dry fly have a chance now?"

When he reached the restaurant before the east brightened he looked dejectedly into the old man's face. It shone as serene as ever.

"The dry fly did it before when it was like this. It can do it again." Adam went on from reassurance to challenge. "Boy, you'll have to do it alone. I can't make the grade this year."

"What do you mean, Mr. Beck? Are you ill?"

"No," he shook his head. "But the storm knocked out the old road. We can drive only within five miles of the place instead of the usual one. It's a steep climb and partly through brush. Some laziness, you know, is a medical duty when there's nothing but snow in your hair. Let's see, this means you can't leave after eight this evening and make it to the store in time to record your catch."

Confidence bred confidence. Frank was ready but he was sorry it wouldn't be partnership angling.

As the car headed into the northwest Adam drew his verbal blueprint. "From where we park you follow the mountain road about four miles to where a trail leads off north. Then you're one mile from the spot."

"Spot? You mean one place?" interjected Frank. "Not a stretch of stream?"

"Take it easy." Adam's eyes twinkled. "It's quite a spot. You'll like it! Follow that trail half a mile till you come to a big oak den tree on the right. The hole's up about twenty feet. Cut directly to your right through the laurel and rhododendron and head for a giant hemlock. It'll be tough going.

"A strong spring comes out from the base of this tree and opens into a pond about ninety feet long and forty at the widest. Then it flows under a big rock and into the ground. This rock is your casting position. It's brushy on all sides except straight back, and there's room for a healthy back-cast. Your forward cast will have to go eighty feet, and the fly must ride between the V of two logs that point toward you. They're about five feet from the out-cropping spring."

The tang of adventure quickened Frank's blood. But he had a trust and he must produce.

The side road got steadily rougher and at the loom of a stiff hill ahead the car stopped. "This is the end of the road today, Boy. I'll be waiting for you here. Take this little box and good luck to you!"

As Frank began his easy, bent-kneed, uphill gait he checked his watch. It would take a good hour to reach the trail, then ten minutes to the den tree, and fifteen more through the brush to the hemlock-canopied spring. The high crisp air poured delight into his easily-pumping lungs. You lived all right in town but you really lived here.

Arriving on schedule, he peered through the laurel. There it was, deep in the big mountain's heart, festively colored and full of magical reflections, beauty enhanced by its setting like

[194]

a pretty woman in a home she's made. Above the rippling of the water and the spring songs of birds he felt the imminent wilderness silence.

A slight boil broke the surface under the patriarchal hemlock, creating a slow flow through the V of the logs that would carry a dry fly. Downstream, the big rock lay embedded to its mossy equator in woodland mulch and water, anchored where it had rolled centuries ago, and under it tumbled the total outpouring of the spring.

Frank scanned the dark brown water. No living thing was in sight—minnow, newt, small trout, or even a fly on the surface. How could trout live here, let alone grow big? Had it not been for his unbounded confidence in Adam he wouldn't have looked twice at such a setting as the possible abode of a big trout. "This can't be, but it is," he thought aloud. "Actually it's too pretty a place to believe sterile."

On the key spot atop the rock he set up his rod, deliberately, as Adam might have done. A close scrutiny of the place was revealing. The backcast must pass through a relatively small opening but things were lined up just right. As his eyes searched the foliage they caught scars on the limbs. Dead branches littered the forest floor below them.

He smiled. "The old fellow found the trout before he fished for them," he murmured. "Then rather than dangle a bait he went to a tremendous amount of work to make casting possible. It's no place for casual fishing!"

Apparently whatever lived in this strange home hid under those angled logs. Stiff dead branches jutting up from them suggested that the water's shiny surface hid an abatis of snags. The only other possible hazard seemed to be the stream's slick escape under the boulder he stood on. A hooked fish might be sucked into its vortex.

He opened the little box. In it lay three large black-and-white flies, all alike. At once he saw what Adam's tying had imitated, although he never had heard of anything like them: big artificial hornets on #12 long-shanked hooks. He attached one to the leader.

As he made false casts he turned his head to watch the opening in the foliage behind him so that he could direct the back-cast perfectly. It was a nice trick to negotiate it just right.

The hornet dropped into the middle of the tiny pond. There it floated saucily. He gave it a twitch; nothing happened. He picked it off the water and shot it farther toward the logs.

[195]

Nothing again. A long third cast carried it into the narrow V.

There was a surge followed by that suction sound which delights an angler. When the dainty tip was lifted, the rod arched, then throbbed. The fish was not excited. It simply settled under one of the logs—no bolting, no jump, no perceptible force. Surely, Frank thought, the leader would snag on an underwater branch, but somehow all went well.

The fish started to move around slowly as large trout often do, without hurry or undignified alarm, just a strong deliberate cruise. In due time it violently shook its head in an attempt to unload the pesty thing that tenaciously clung to its jaw. Then, with its dorsal fin and tail in the air, it was clearly the last minute.

For an instant it wallowed ten feet from the subterranean channel before it was drawn slowly irresistibly toward the poised net. Frank got the big head over the net and it was all over.

Creditably and elegantly too, he had cast to, hooked and played the big trout. It was his largest, an estimated 23 inches. The secret spot in combination with the proper technique seemed as foolproof as ever a thing can be in angling. But it hadn't really been so simple. Frank found himself feeling more relief than elation.

He slipped the great fish into a live bag and sat down to rest the pool. As he watched the upstream V a hornet settled on one of those logs, walked stiffly to the waterline, drank its fill, and flew away. A few minutes later another did the same thing. Then another.

Every so often he pitched the artificial hornet into the V but nothing showed.

But after lunch it happened again. No two circumstances could have been more similar except that the second trout was an inch shorter than the first. Upon its release it made for the logs, all the fight out of it.

Frank was satisfied. He dispatched the first big fish, disassembled his tackle, and set off in that long lasting glow to meet his friend who had generaled their victory—if it was to be a victory.

As he neared the car a half-statement, half-querry greeted him. "You have one, haven't you?" His answer was to remove the big dark trout from his fishing vest.

Adam beamed. "That should do it. Hop in. Apparently everything went all right."

[196]

"There was only one thing to worry about, snagging the leader on the branches under the logs."

"You needn't have worried. There are no longer any snags under those logs."

"So you took care of that, too?"

For a while they rode in the silence of old friends who think alike. Then Adam volunteered the rest of the story.

"I ran into that place one late-winter day some years ago while hunting foxes. There was a bona fide stream right on down to the big creek and a lot of small trout had moved into the big spring-hole. When I came back a week later the snow had finished melting and there was no longer a stream from the spring to the creek. The entire flow went under that rock, just as you saw it, but the trout were still there. It was then I saw several large trout and about two hundred small ones, all locked up together. You know what happened.

"When I came back in July to fish it, all the smaller fish had been gobbled up. So had the tree-toads and polliwogs. The only thing left for the big trout was a little odd stuff and the hornets."

"And that was the first year you won the contest?"

"Yes, and down through the seasons I've returned only once each year. It's not our kind of fishing, Boy; we love the evening rises to the hatches and the incessant daytime surface feeding on terrestrials." After a pause he added, "It serves our purpose, though. You can count on it year after year. I figure there are always three to six big trout in there. Once in a while one of those fingerlings escapes being trout fodder to grow into another big one for the spring pond and for the contest. From now on it's all yours. In the future, if I can make it, I'll accompany you."

"By all means," responded Frank, "We'll fish it as a team."

"Speaking of teams, it's best that the others don't know of our teamwork. You put in your appearance at the store about ten. I'll show up shortly before ten-thirty."

When night had closed down dark and Frank had made his entry, the big trout roused quite a stir.

"Frank Hunter has the king fish," proclaimed the judge. Then, after judicious reflection, he nailed on a "So far."

The same question lay on every mind, that is, on all but one. "Can the old champ beat this?"

There were some good fish. "Spider" Webb, the fly-tyer, had a husky 19-incher. The lawyer and the professor had 17-inch browns. Because of tough conditions—high, muddy water—Little Caesar had hoped that his 14-inch prize might slide home the winner this time.

Just before closing time Adam entered. Everyone halted whatever he was doing or saying and looked at him quietly standing there in the doorway.

"Adam, can you beat 22¾ inches?" asked the store manager.

Adam shook his head in a silent negative.

The only disparaging remark came from Little Caesar. "Well, what do you know? What went wrong, Adam?"

"That means then, we have a new champion," stated the judge.

"Whoever he is," cried Adam heartily, "let him step up and receive my sincere congratulations."

He gave the muscular hand of young Frank a little extra squeeze and the crow's-feet around his sparkling grey eyes furrowed even deeper.

"Tell us, Boy, how did you catch your great trout?"

"On a dry fly, sir. It's the only way I fish."

"A purist!" Adam's broad smile was good to look at.

"The dry fly did it again," he added, satisfied at the victory of his chosen method of angling. A tranquil man, Adam had learned to live old Walton's maxim, "Sudy to be quiet."

Dawn Of A New Day

THE GREEN drake had danced its day but the memory lingered like that of a haunting melody. Only stragglers of the great mayfly hatch answered the curtain call that balmy early-June evening.

"It's over for another year," the anglers agreed sadly, though each had had his chances. The past week had endowed them with mixed memories, from those of tackle-smashing consternation to the supreme satisfaction that comes with the capture of a fine trout on the dry fly.

Strange, though: one fishless angler's smug, secretive smile reminded those who noticed it of a cat with a pet canary in his no longer streamlined stomach. Slick black hair and spreading mustache strengthened the resemblance.

On four successive nights Lucius Cribbs, well nicknamed "Little Caesar," had left, with empty creel, a bend in that stream of rare charms, the home of a mighty trout. No fish ever had exerted greater influence on local hopes and dreams. A phenomenon, he had made liars out of honest men. This great brown trout, well over the two-foot mark and a foot and a half in shoulder girth, never forsook the stage of life that dictated his feeding on the insect world by suction from the surface rather than by exertion down under. No doubt the rich protein diet made him larger and more potent than cannibalistic relatives. His accepted name was Jasper. On each of those four evenings Jasper had taken Little Caesar's imitation of the natural. Each time, on being hooked, he had bolted from the emerald slick to his downstream fortress under the deep ledge of the great pool. That was all there'd been to it. Taut terminal tackle can't withstand the shock of such strength and speed against edged limestone.

Engulfed in thought, L. C. hunched over his dinner platter at the far end of the long restaurant counter. Mechanically he forked in the steaming food, at times flushing down a mouthful with an unrelished gulp of coffee. Now and then the trance lifted when he advised pretty blonde Mabel, without even looking at her, to bring another "scup of scoff." If he could land the most famous local trout that ever had fanned a fin he'd have his most cherished desire. If he actually called the shot in advance, he'd stack up as that much bigger champion.

L. C. was a great angler—no doubt about that—but a jealous one, and therefore never quite happy. Although with typical lustiness he relished his gilded reputation, he knew its tottery base. Oh, he could catch trout in quantity and he'd even latched on to numerous "good ones," but never had he landed a fish that folks couldn't forget. Jasper was just what he needed and tomorrow would be the day.

Battle plans passed in vivid review. Impossible though it was to float a fly over Jasper's feeding place from the customary downstream position, a long high cast from above and the resultant slack leader would cheat the fish of the protection of the low over-hanging foliage. But when the great fish was hooked, the trunks of streamside trees made it impossible for the angler to race along to lessen the shock when the leader hit the ledge some hundred feet downstream. That was the Jasper fortress; that was his life insurance.

Three evenings, when the hatch was at its peak, Jasper's feast had been interrupted by the prick of L. C.'s well-tied counterpart. Each time the power run under the ledge had broken the leader.

It shook down to unquestionable if hardly beautiful simplicity. You had to hook that fish from above the ledge but you had to play him from below. That logic was as cold and clear as the element out of which Jasper could not live. In spite of all you might say against L. C.—and that could be quite a lungful—he was a smart schemer. He had utilized his plan that night, the last night of the hatch.

This time the fly line was not attached to the backing; it was loose and free. This time there was no jolting break.

L. C. relived each step of the campaign. In the half-light Jasper left his bomb-proof shelter for his fool-proof feeding station. Some of the big drakes were traveling his line of drift. L. C., crouched in the deep shadows, watched him inhale some three dozen of them.

Now that Jasper had a bellyful and night was coming down fast, it was time to swing into action. Retarded action was part of the plan: darkness let L. C. use a heavy leader and left Jasper comparatively inert with a full stomach.

The cast, of course, was perfectly executed. Majestically the fish rose. To the sound of a watery glump the fly disappeared and the barb sank home.

[200]

For an instant it felt to L. C. like the hooking of a log but that log-like form promptly reversed ends and surged down-current. To the reel's screaming accompaniment the line melted from the spool. Its loose end streaked through the guides like the tail of a fleeing snake and disappeared in the tossing mane of white water. There was no sickening snap—not this time—as the great trout went free from the would-be captor.

L. C. now had Jasper attached to a stout leader and a hundred feet of line. He pictured the turn under the ledge but this time there was no broken leader. It would hold, and the line, slowly sinking, would straighten out downstream to settle gently on the rocks at the bottom of the big pool. All that L. C. need do was recover the line, string it back through the guides and on to the reel, connect it to the backing, and play the fish on better than even terms from the tail of the pool. In the falling darkness and in deep water this would be quite a trick but tomorrow was a new day, a new dawn for Lucius Cribbs.

He pictured Jasper at that very moment balancing upon his fins, his gills undulating ever more smoothly as strength and composure returned. With the urge to feed satisfied he might even be asleep, though those eyes as large as nickels never closed. Certainly the limp line was resting on the rocks just waiting to be reattached.

Boy, the odds were wonderful! Jasper was a sitting duck—probably. L. C. decided to take the calculated risk and talk.

He picked up the check that Mabel, still unnoticed, had let fall face-down before him and advanced like a procession to the business end of the counter and the genial proprietor, who had been waiting him out before closing up. Lifting his hat to make room for a well-staged uncertain-looking scratch, he bade goodbye to his rusty conscience and broadcast the future.

"Tomorrow I intend to catch a tremendous trout. Before the day's over I'll have him here. There'll be a Number 8 dry fly sticking in his jaw, and, so help me, it'll be there when he's attached to a board to hang in my trophy room."

Highly regarded Adam Beck, a solid citizen, understood not only fishermen but also fish, trout in particular. His conduct with rod in hand was second to none, both from the ethical standpoint and that of the practitioner. Fishing companions claimed that he thought like a fish. All the visiting anglers sought him out with their where-to-go and how-to-do-it questions; it was Adam they wanted to converse with as they enjoyed a good dinner at the end of a fishing day. His personality and knowledge, along with the good food, had made his restaurant an anglers' emporium.

He looked at his lone and late customer and considered the proclamation. "That," he retorted, "is a very big order but a worthy goal. A doubly tough assignment now that the green drake hatch is over."

"Mebby so, but you can tell all the fellows that tomorrow I catch the biggest trout ever taken in these parts."

"That's all but firm? You make it sound so sure. Will it be easy?"

"He's as good as half caught right now. I have a plan. Tomorrow I get him."

"I, Caesar, have spoken," thought Adam, and aloud, "Will it be morning or evening?"

L. C. hesitated. Adam saw that this question hadn't been in the rehearsal.

"If you tell us the time and place," he prodded, "I'll bring the gang around to witness the show."

L. C.'s eyes grew hooded and flicked aside for an instant. "Won't go that far. Haven't I told you enough? Anyway, spectators might mess things up and I like to fish alone."

"Have it your way. I'll spread the word around that tomorrow L. C. hangs a five-pounder."

"I didn't say five pounds. You can double that," and L. C., who like other skilled anglers had a sense of timing, turned and surged out into the night.

The elderly proprietor was interested, deeply interested, probably more so than any other local fishermen would have been.

"You can go home, Mabel. I want to stick around a little longer."

How could anyone be so sure, mused the perplexed Adam, of a thing that by its nature is so uncertain. He didn't even hear the door sigh shut behind the pretty little waitress.

If the fish were already caught, L. C. couldn't resist displaying it to anyone—but *anyone*—who'd take a look. And by tomorrow it would be faded and dry, plainly not fresh-caught.

"No," he thought, "it's not that. The time and the place are secrets and that's strange for someone putting on a show. Then too, he's got a plan. Why, that fellow never even noticed Mabel this evening, and I've always figured she's the main reason why he, like a lot of others, regularly eats dinner here. That fish is 'half caught'; that's what he said. Tomorrow he finishes the job. There's only one way you can have a trout half caught: he's hooked but he isn't landed. Great Heavens," he exploded, "there's only one fish like the one he's talking about! Jasper's in trouble."

Chin in hands, Adam didn't notice that someone had come in.

"Sorry to interrupt such concentration." Young Frank Hunter's blue eyes seconded the smile of his wide, generous mouth.

"Boy!" exclaimed Adam. "It must be providence that brings you here just now. I was debating whether or not to go to your house this late. Boy, do you believe in hunches?"

"Only yours, because they're more than hunches. There's always a solid foundation."

"How'd you like to land Jasper?"

Frank's soft easy laugh was answer enough but he followed the old gentleman's lead, for Adam never sounded off. "No one can, I presume. He feeds under those limbs, always, and when you hook him he goes down the chute and under the ledge. He'll smash any leader fine enough to fool him in the first place. It's a hopeless situation."

Adam leveled a piercing stare. "Tell me, if you got him would you insist on killing him?"

"No!" emphatically responded Frank. "He's more than a fish; he's a legend. I'd hate to see him laid out dead and stiff."

"Good!" beamed the old fellow. "I expected to hear you say that. But I didn't mean put him back in his old pool."

"You mean," interrupted Frank, "start another legend in another place?"

"In a sense, yes. Curtis and I are experimenting with proven surface feeders as brood fish. All we want in his experimental station are the best of that sort. We've got a theory that they'll produce their own desirable kind, and his side stream is set up so that the offspring of his selected breeders can escape into the main stream."

"And," Frank continued the story, "a big brood fish like Jasper is the ultimate."

"Correct."

"Okay, but what am I supposed to do?"

"Slip out early tomorrow morning," half pleaded, half demanded Adam, "and look for a loose line in the bottom of the big hole. It's my hunch that one's there, with Jasper on the business end."

Boy's whistle was long and low. "You mean he took someone to the cleaner's, line and all?"

"Could be. Honestly, I'm not sure."

"What have you seen or who've you been talking to?"

"Little Caesar, but never mind that. I'm not sure of anything. But I don't want to see Jasper die and I'm afraid that's what's scheduled for tomorrow. It's all but made. If you find what I think is there, string that line down through your rod on to an empty reel. Reel up the slack; then play the fish to the best of your ability. Take along my big net and a wash-tub."

That night L. C. thrashed in his bed. Was it too many scups of scoff or was it something else? At any rate, visions rose of tomorrow as the biggest day in his angling career. Calling the shot on taking so mighty a trout would be sensational. He'd be Mr. Fisherman in this country.

The old town clock's bell went on short shifts before his restless mind dismissed his tired body to sleep.

He awoke with a guilty start. Birds sang and the sun shone high. He yanked on his fishing clothes, frantically grabbing from the cluttered pile beside his bed. After bolting a short breakfast he tumbled into his car and was off in a snorting start.

It was late but the day was bright and calm. The sunken line would be easy to see. It ought to be easy to raise, ever so gently, with a boat pole.

Relief flooded him when he saw the pool deserted. Old man Kreider's rowboat floated in an eddy, its anchor rope looped around a tree. Things were in order. No one must see him recover the line and string it to the rod. But later, if someone saw him play the betrayed Jasper, so much the better!

He poled the boat to the tail of the pool on the chance that the entire length of line had drifted below Jasper. It wasn't there.

As he eased the boat up the pool his sharp, beady black eyes methodically searched the clean bottom for that strip of yellow. Finally he reached the point in the clean-swept bowls where the undercut ledge was clearly visible. There was no line anywhere around it.

Grimness seized him. What could have gone wrong? Even if Jasper had rid himself of the fly or if the leader had parted, finding the line should be simple. He searched upstream and down but there was no evidence of any kind. Perplexed and chargined he returned to his room to brood and speculate.

Later, the afternoon sun looked down on this frustrated little schemer not only rechecking the pool but also extending his search farther up and down the stream. As in the morning, there was no one else around and no clue as to what had happened.

[204]

Night brought him an urge hard to explain. Misery does love company and, though he had no heart to face Adam and admit defeat, he somehow wanted to check in at the fishermen's rendezvous.

His spirit hanging down like a dejected tail, he set off to face the music. It was late and he was thankful to see that everyone had left but Adam, who was about to snap off the lights and lock up. Timing had been just right!

"Well, L. C., have you anything to report?" asked Adam, as they met on opposite sides of the long counter. "It was Teddy Roosevelt who said, 'Only shots that hit are shots that count.' Was there a hit today?"

"Nope."

"Did you come close, or didn't you put your plan into effect?"

"Nope." Mental effort seemed to be lacking.

"Here's something. What do you know about it?" And with that, Adam handed him a coil of yellow line with its attached leader decorated with a Number 8 dry fly.

"Jasper!" gasped L. C. "Is he gone?"

"Jasper is not a he and she is still around."

"Whadya mean?"

"The latest report has it that her adjustment is excellent. She was none the worse for her adventure and her new abode is a big flue liner in the lawyer's side stream. And such a trout— big, burly, small-headed and gorgeous. Why, that fish is as beautifully proportioned as the day she measured eight inches, the most highly-prized brood fish there ever was!"

Little Caesar was now as indignant as he had been dejected. "That's not right; I had that fish half caught!"

"Yes, I credit you with that. The end of the line is cut, not broken. The plan was smart. But remember, L. C., any trout in the open stream is fair game; 'public domain,' the lawyers call it."

"How did you know about this?" (L. C. no longer bristled.)

"Simple deduction. You talked so much last night you gave out the secret. The best I can wish you is that you hook some of her scions. They'll be superior fish."

"Did you get 'im?"

"No, Boy did. There are four of us who know about this. You will not tell this story on yourself and we won't talk. The rest of the fellows can still speculate about that great trout, where 'he' is and what might catch 'him.' They can anticipate and imagine and even lie a little if they please. The legend lives on."

Ensuing years brought Lucius Cribbs no closer to the taking of a really big trout, though every so often some angler claimed to have been broken up by the redoubtable Jasper in that stream of rare charms.

CHAPTER 5

Angling Tycoons

"YOU LIKE to talk fishing," the dentist observed as he adjusted the waterproof bib around his patient's neck, "but this time, Curtis, all you're going to do is listen to fishing talk. Now open up so I can put the juice-catcher in there. You're going to hear the wildest story you ever heard about a fisherman, and in open-mouth wonder at that. It's true, too, and that makes it great. I know because I was there—my only fishing trip. Memory's fallible but not about everything. There isn't much of that trip back in the summer of '29 that's got away from me."

The skeptical lawyer squirmed in silence as he thought, "This'll probably be worse than the tooth ordeal." He knew the dentist held a low regard for angling and delighted in ribbing fishermen.

"It started this way," the doctor told his captive audience. "I had to go with Uncle Wilt—rich Uncle Wilt who had no direct heirs or pet charities. Understand? All he cared about was fishing and playing the market. Those were his sports, in fact, his life. He was striking it rich, at least on paper and in fishing stories, in his halcyon cycle of buy, sell and go fishing."

He puttered around the instrument table, then turned, drill in hand, to the scene of trouble. Above the grinding and vibration his patient heard his droning voice.

"I was home from dental school—just finished—and he says to me, 'Get away from the market and things pop. Every time I go to the North Country big things happen. It must be a special way the angler is rewarded.' This was during the rising-market decade that went flat on October 29, 1929. You know," he sighed, "back when there was a surge of prosperity and it was solemnly promised that the income tax would never be more than one per cent. Back when you and I were kids.

"'No use starting your practice now,' he tells me. 'Start when business is good again. Better psychology. It's during vacations that people lose their teeth out deep-sea fishing and salt water taffy pulls out fillings and inlays. It's right before school that they get the kids fixed up, too. Tell you what: I'll take you on a real fishing trip before you open an office and buckle down.

[207]

I'll pay all your expenses. We'll go up in August for a couple of weeks. Then when you grind teeth and measure mouths you can tell them about the greatest angling of all!'

"That settled it; so I says, 'Sure, Uncle Wilt; that'll be fine.'

" 'There may be a third party,' he advised. 'I'm deeply obligated to a smart young fellow at the broker's office. Funny thing, he tips me off on what to buy and when to sell and his advice is wonderful but he doesn't play the market himself. If he'll go I'll pay for his trip, too. He never went up for salmon but he's red-hot on trout. Raised at Coburn on Penn's Creek. You better get to know him because you two might want to fish together around here and you gotta know a good securities man, anyway'." The dentist switched drills.

"Uncle Wilt had tackle enough to start a store. He fixed up five outfits: one for himself, one for me, one for the other fellow, and 'two just in case,' as he put it. The smart friend of his turned out to be a pleasant little fellow but all he wanted to talk about on the train up was fishing. He and Uncle Wilt kept batting it back and forth. Now and then, as a matter of principle, I'd ask a question—figured that was the thing to do.

"We got off the train 'way back of nowhere. All there was was a station manned by one and a fellow with a team of horses hitched to a big wagon. Uncle Wilt said, 'A lot of big-shots pass through this place each summer.' He decided to send a telegram to the broker's office to buy some more of something or other. The station master was telegraph operator too. Then we stepped outside.

"I was expecting to see a car drive up to take us to camp when Uncle Wilt announced, 'Load up.' Carefully as could be he put the rods and the case with the bottles in that flat springless wagon and the driver tossed the duffle-bags over the sideboard. 'Get in, boys,' he says.

"Uncle Wilt made a sort of nest in a corner out of his-and-my dufflebag and then put the case with the bottles on his lap. The other fellow pushed his dufflebag into another corner and sat on it. The driver was watching and as soon as he saw me settle down in the middle of things he says, 'Giddy-ap!' "

The dentist blew some hot air on the cavity and the recoil of his patient distracted him not one bit. "Uncle Wilt," he continued, "asked a lot of questions of the driver, Hubert, all of which got one or the other of two answers: 'The very best' or 'Few fish in the river.'

"We'd gone about half a mile when we came to a river, a

big one. 'There she is,' says our host and he had a strange look on his face. What do you think happened next?" asked the dentist as he looked the lawyer in the mouth. "The horses took to the river. Talk about a thumping and splashing! It was enough to knock out every filling. The wagon bumped and the horses floundered. Every now and then a wheel or two'd go over one of the bigger rocks and you'd hit bottom, your bottom, with a thud. I tried kneeling and that was worse yet, then Yogi Barra style, and that was no good either. Finally I crawled up on the seat and eased Hubert over to one side. This was an improvement but a lot of damage had been done.

"Above the noise I learned from my seatmate that, 'It isn't far to camp, only about six more miles.' If anything, the rocks were getting bigger and the jolts harder. Every time I looked back I could see the little fellow looking intently at something but the only thing to see was trees and water. Every half mile or so Uncle would shout out a strange name like Push-And-Be-Damned or Kate's Hole. A salmon flopped out of water and the others got very excited. I figured they'd be commonplace because we'd traveled so far for them.

"We came to a fine-looking house that seemed to be empty and not far from it two modest buildings which, judging from heads at the windows and clothes on the lines, must have been loaded. Hubert got the team out of the river and hollered, 'Hoe!' Uncle Wilt said something about a great environment for productivity: 'The winters are long and cold, you know.' This rocked Hubert with paroxysms of laughter. A bolder kid came to the wagon and was handed some mail from a bag. I realized we were being delivered to camp by the rural mail carrier.

"At last, at long last, the team pulled out of the river and we were met in front of camp by three natives who looked like lumberjacks. Uncle Wilt took over. 'Boys, it's great to be with you again!' He wasn't much at introductions but their names sounded something like Utex, Wetex and Playtex. Maybe they were brothers. 'One,' he explains, 'regularly guides Rex Tickard and the other the industrialist Eugene Ferris.' The third, of course, was Uncle Wilt's regular man. 'Three of the greatest' was his boast.

"It seemed that Hubert was also the cook. 'In celebration of the beginning of our trip,' announces Uncle Wilt, 'we'll break out a bottle of Gold Label as cookie works with his pans. Nothing like it in the States.' Then he reflects, 'Any more. One of Canada's greatest assets.'

[209]

" 'Look at the fog spot in the mountain gap,' says Utex. 'That means rain.'

" 'Good!' says Uncle Wilt. 'Let 'er rain. That means fresh fish.'

"About the time we started to eat fried ham, fried potatoes and fried onions it began to rain. 'Great!' hollers Uncle Wilt. 'That's what we want,' meaning the rain.

"The beds weren't soft and that ride had been rough. As I tried to sleep on my stomach the rain beat down on the tin roof. All three guides and Uncle Wilt had different kinds of snores. I thought daylight would never come."

He became so involved in pressing some filling into the hole he had drilled that he stopped talking. But that only gave him his second wind.

"Where were we? Oh yes. The rains came. After breakfast we put on our raincoats and took a look out at the river. They decided there couldn't be any fishing until after the run-off. 'We'll play poker,' says Uncle Wilt. 'Maybe that'll overcome the urge to get into the river.'

"Strangest poker game you ever saw. Nobody had any money except Uncle Wilt. 'I'll be the banker,' he volunteers and brings out a roll of dollar bills that'd choke a horse. 'Everybody gets a bonus of ten. Winners can pay me back later.'

"By lunchtime the three guides were out of money and out of the game. The little fellow had all the winnings but I still had some change left. You know, Curtis, I'm not too bad at poker but you should have seen that young broker. He was like a Univac. Knew all the odds, knew when to raise, knew how to bluff. The day wore on and every hour or so Uncle Wilt had to dig down for more. That little fellow was making change— ten ones for another ten. Uncle Wilt held just enough, drew just enough and knew just enough to get himself into trouble. Pretty soon he respected the little fellow's ability in this field as much as his judgment in matters having to do with the market.

" 'I thought,' he remarked, as he watched another pot get away, 'you never gambled.'

" 'That's basically correct,' the little fellow replies. 'My wife's opposed to gambling—matter of principle—and she considers playing the market a form of gambling. That's why we usually don't invest in stocks and bonds, just life insurance.'

" 'Silly girl, but what do you mean "usually"?' Uncle wanted to know.

" 'I have a secret little fund,' he explains, 'that I use for this unofficial purpose. Just before I left I put it into a sure thing, unbeknownst to her, of course.'

"'Of course,' echoes Uncle Wilt, and he reiterates, 'Silly girl.'

"'Bought 2,000 shares of Battery Craft. It's what I advised you to buy. Foreign submarine contracts and new inventions should make it double in the next few weeks. I asked the girl at the office to keep me advised by telegram.'

"'Fine,' responds Uncle Wilt, 'you're a pot-hunter in the stock market as you fish. I didn't follow your advice. Sunk all the extra in automotives. You know,' he reflected, 'too many females getting into male interests. Trouble is that Nineteenth Amendment that gives women complete equality. Bad as the Eighteenth. They're both against the concept of the founding fathers. Otherwise they'd have been in the Constitution at the beginning of things.' Uncle Wilt was against new laws.

"Two days ended the poker game. The little fellow came out of it with a vacation salary. Uncle threw in the towel. When the time came to refinance me, it was all over.

"To make a long story short, I'll give you a fragmentary description. It rained and it rained. Logs and brush were floating down the river and the dark water was coated with brown pine needles. After the second day the guides went home. About the fourth day Uncle Wilt said, 'We may have to make a little fishing go a long way,' to which the little fellow politely added, 'We're more richly blessed with water than with angling.' There were some sick jokes about the name of the stream, which I've forgotten but anyway it had the word 'Rest' in it.

"By the end of the week the Gold Label supply was exhausted. Our stomachs, particularly Uncle Wilt's, were indulging in barrel rolls. If cookie'd lost his frying pan he'd have been licked. There was a sort of thunder in the air—the unnatural kind. We were getting tired of looking across the table and seeing the same faces and hearing the same voices. Finally the rain quit and the weather was as fair as you ever saw it but we were still trapped.

"About the tenth day Hubert says, 'I believe I can make it to the station to pick up the mail bag.' At first Uncle Wilt was caught between unfulfilled desire and common sense. Then the Civil War in him ended and he announced, 'We'll go along. Come on, fellows; let's pack.'"

Fresh wadding went into the lawyer's mouth as the voice continued. "The trip downriver was worse than coming up because some water got into the wagon and the river bed was

[211]

no less rough. At the station we unloaded our dufflebags, sopping wet. The train was due in about an hour.

"The station master had no mail for Uncle Wilt or me but he had a stack of telegrams for the other fellow. 'As they came in,' he explained, 'I put each new one on the bottom of the pile.'

"The little fellow opened the top one, read it at a quick glance, and went for number two.

" 'Read 'em out loud,' says Uncle Wilt.

" 'Battery Craft 4, should I sell?'

"Then the next: 'Battery Craft 8, should I sell?'

"The little fellow says, 'Gad! I hope she has sense enough to sell!' The stack started to rattle in his trembling hands.

"Uncle Wilt says, 'Here, give 'em to me. Yor're getting too nervous.'

"He opens and reads number four: 'Battery Craft 12, should I sell?'

" 'Sell,' mutters the little fellow. 'Sell, you fool.'

" 'This is getting monotonous,' observes Uncle Wilt, and he pulls one from three quarters of the way down the stack. 'Battery Craft 75, should I sell?'

" 'Here!' he cries, 'the last one's dated yesterday: 'Battery Craft 165, should I sell?'

"With this edification the little fellow sort of blinked in a daze and staggered over to the station master but he couldn't say a word to him.

" 'Do you wish to send a wire, sir?'

" 'He sure does,' Uncle Wilt says. 'I better give it to you. It's to this name and address. The message is "Sell now." That was his counsel of worldly wisdom.

"But that's only the second act of the show. Here's the last." At this the dentist winced and slumped, much as his patient had done during the drilling. "Going back on the train the little fellow swore us to secrecy because he 'had a delicate situation on his hands,' which he didn't know how to resolve with his wife.

"It wasn't till mid-October, well after he'd settled down in his cage, that he came over to see Uncle Wilt and I happened to be there. 'I finally told her about it,' he admitted frankly, 'and Mary says, "We'll have to let bygones be bygones. You can't undo what's been done. But sell all the securities you have and put the money in the National Bank." '

" 'Silly, silly girl,' protests Uncle Wilt.

"The little fellow frowned. 'I don't know about that. Credits are over-extended, supplies over-produced, stockpiles too large.

It doesn't look good to me. It's a setup for a crash. If it were up to me I'd get out anyway and I recommend the same to you.'

"Uncle Wilt laughed. 'Ten years should prove that can't happen. Guess I'll have to look for a new financial advisor.'

" 'Yes, sir.' "

The dentist mopped his brow. "Uncle Wilt liked me even though I hadn't responded to his fishing. When he passed on he left everything he had to me—such as it was," he qualified morosely. "October 29 fixed him and his fishing trips, too.

"That was my first, last and only fishing trip." He stared at the blank unsympathetic wall. "I tell you, Curtis, those of us who're around fifty got off to a horrible start in this crazy world. The economic explosion that heralded the depression began a fatal decade for opportunity and now that there's money to be made, we're trapped by confining taxes. You can't salt away a nest egg. Complication reared its ugly head about the time we got out of school and it hasn't been beaten down yet. Why, even in this country we have to listen to a lot of guff as loose as a Communist's promise.

"The little fellow made it just in time." The dentist removed the fish-hook tube and the wadding from his patient's face, then untied the bib. "If I were to tell you his name, it'd register, for he's well known today."

The lawyer sat erect and tried to speak, but couldn't. He rinsed his dry interior, rubbed his aching jaw, then opened and closed his mouth a few times in the deliberate fashion of a baseball pitcher's windup.

"That story," he asserted, "bears eloquent testimony that it pays to go fishing. Furthermore, it illustrates the advantages rather than the disadvantages of domesticity. I too was in school the final year of that prosperous decade. Factories and people were doomed by the depression. I remember days when we had salt but no meat.

"That trip you told about isn't reason enough to take a dim view of angling. You're thinking in terms of 'firsts' and 'onlys' and you make the awkward and the ridiculous fair game for caricature. Fishermen and other sinners are composed of the same chemicals. If it's tranquility or activity, you're after, Nature provides the perfect outlet. Did you ever notice that the most beautiful spots in the world are the edges where land and water meet? Fishing is the outlet that many people desperately need. You can do it just as you please. It can be a passive recreation or an intensive sport. There are a hundred ways to fish and a

[213]

hundred motives for it. We can't define the undefinable but at least everyone should be openminded about fishing."

"I have an open mind," broke in the dentist. "That's just it, the reason—and a good one—for telling you that story. You've hit on what I was getting around to: a reversion to Nature as an escape from pressure on the one hand and boredom on the other. Would you loan me an outfit for a trial of fishing and let me come out to your meadow to see what I can do?"

"Certainly I'll do that but remember what President Cleveland said, 'A true fisherman's happiness is not dependent upon luck.'" The lawyer frowned and he inadvertently queried loudly enough for the other to hear, "Or is it?"

The dentist laughed. "Don't worry, Curtis. Fisherman's luck is one thing, financial luck another."

CHAPTER 6

Excelsior

THE QUESTION was whether trout angling was Adam Beck's vocation or avocation. Free as March winds, he went where he pleased. His only wedding was to the fly rod; his only responsibility was to make his small-town restaurant yield a decent living for him alone with some left over for charity.

Perhaps most men who pursue a hobby avidly have not incurred the responsibilities of fatherhood. Yet even this sort is prone to adopt an unofficial scion and shower on him companionship, wisdom and, to some extent, worldly goods. In young Frank Hunter old Adam saw the makings of a real great among fly fishermen and adroitly he passed on to him the intangibles that bring a true angler's rewards. Unspoken mutual understanding proved that each came from the same mold, a couple of generations apart—a chronological difference that leveled off to a half teaspoonful more than nothing.

The boy rated the best of tangibles and intangibles. The oldtimer was a rock-bottom friend and an accomplished artist and teacher, streamside. That's how they felt about each other.

They sat at a corner table in the restaurant. "Boy," began Adam hesitantly, "how'd you like to take a quick look tomorrow at waters that are steeped in tradition, the temple of the dry fly in America, the country of Theodore Gordon and Hiram Leonard?"

Adam's mind looked far back as he continued. "The old covered bridge at Roscoe, the pool where the Little Beaverkill and the Willowemoc join, the covered bridges at Beaverkill Post Office and Livingston Manor—those are the places—where I learned to fly fish. What say we run up to Liberty then meet one of the last of that generation of angling giants?"

Searchingly he looked at his fishing partner. "Or would you drive up tomorrow and would you do so alone?"

Frank felt something very special behind the revised question. Still, if Adam didn't care to explain, that was all right too.

"Sure, Mr. Beck, I'd be glad to go; It'd be wonderful to see the famous rivers and meet your friends.

"Fine!" Adam sounded relieved. "His name is Boyd Harrison.[1]

[215]

Give him my kindest regards. Better leave early so you can see him about noontime. He isn't well; so you can't stay long. On your way home will you stop in Allentown to say hello for me to Jimmie Leisenring?[2]"

"You mean the wet-fly authority?"

"Yes. The Poconos and the nearby Lehigh Valley were my second trout country. The big Dutchman and I used to go to the streams together. He always fished downstream and I went up. You know that isn't a bad arrangement at all for a wet-fly fisherman and a dry-fly man to team together: no complications, no interference and an interesting comparison."

"You said, 'second trout country'."

"Sure. One day I went from Roscoe to Easton to see Samuel Phillipe.[3] You know he built the first complete six-trip split-bamboo rod. On that same trip I met Jimmie Leisenring. He fished some over in Jersey, the Musconetcong and the Pequest and some Pocono streams, as well as waters around Allentown. He was always talking about the greatness of limestone water and we fished the Little Lehigh and its tributary, the Jordan, together.

"Fishing pressure was getting rough around Roscoe; so I moved to Stroudsburg. The Broadhead, named for Daniel Broadhead, is a great stream; so's the Paradise branch. Jimmie and I would meet at the Light House at Henryville. That was a great Mecca for anglers.[4] For a moment Adam was silent, trapped in the grandeur of those years.

"Why did you leave there?"

"No limestone, Boy. Jimmie got me interested in limestone water and its great potential. He'd say, 'Hadam, lissen to Chimmy. If you got ter haff der werry best, den try Pennsylwania chalk vater.' He knew where it was, all right. So did Theodore Gordon,[5] who fished both Spring Creek and Big Spring.

"So I moved in here to enjoy the best. We really have it, Boy. There isn't the tradition, there isn't the fame but we have the fish. Big, well-conditioned and wild; lots of surface feeding. It takes pretty angling to fool good trout in smooth limestone water. And fishing holds up—yes, improves—in hot weather, and we all get some of that anywhere, even in Canada. You fish in classic style, mainly to the rises on smooth water. As for flies, it is generally better to fish too small than too large. And you never know what to expect. As Shakespeare said of Cleopatra, 'Time cannot wither, nor custom stale, her infinite variety.'

So this is my last place to follow man's primal sport."

"You think it's like the chalk streams of southern Britain we read about in such-and-such books; River Keeper, Itchen Days and The Way Of A Trout With A Fly?"

"Exactly. Well, not quite," Adam hesitated. "The fish grow the same, but the hatches are different. All we need to set this up right is the famous blue winged olive hatch of the Test and the Itchen. You know, Hewitt had Lunn,[6] the old river-keeper on the Test, collect her eggs for our waters, but they never got beyond Washington airport. Some bureaucrat thought they might produce something that'd bite people and eat foliage; so he destroyed them."

"Why, that's ridiculous! Mayflies can't bite or even eat and they live out of water in the fly state for only a few days."

Adam nodded. "Beware of a naive 'expert' no matter whether he's involved in fisheries management or something else. The pity is, that hatch doesn't ride our water."

Like all the rest, it had been a pleasant and meaty talk but Frank was concerned. Could his aging friend have some pre-monition? "Has he appointed me an odd sort of messenger?" he wondered. At any rate, tomorrow he'd meet Boyd Harrison and Jimmie Leisenring.

No finer rods ever had been built than those by Harrison. An expert angler, he knew well the requirements of an in-strument to cast and false-cast and to protect fine leaders and handle hooked fish. To keep back casts high there must be backbone, plenty of it; yet to prevent leader breakage there must be a sensitive shock-absorbing tip. The trick is the con-bination of high quality cane, perfect design and fine workman-ship. The finished beauty must feel light but powerful, neither clubby nor like a buggy whip.

One day there showed up in a lot of Chinese cane from the province of Tonkin[7] a piece like none Harrison had seen before. Through a quirk of Nature a seed—and bamboo is a grass—had rooted in an extraordinary environment which produces a blade with extremely dense cells from the glistening outer edge to the inner surface of the hollow core, a pole straight and true and free of mold. This was the piece he'd been looking and waiting for so patiently,—as elusive as James Hilton's Shangri-La retreat. It would be fashioned into a two-piece eight-foot rod, the finest possible product of his craft, not for himself but for his son when he was able to handle it and ripe enough to appreciate it. Boyd Harrison's stream experience, workshop know-how and independent mind already had made him the initial champion of the two-piece eight-footer.

He smiled down at the little towhead, his only child, and assured him: "Sonny, someday you'll own and fish with the greatest rod ever made. You'll enjoy it and care for it long after I'm gone. It's my memento—for you."

The boy, Frank, didn't understand all the words, and the tone of his father's voice was one he'd never heard before but he smiled back approvingly.

Harrison used the greatest care in setting the mold, checking and rechecking the special measurements of the convex and converse tapers. A meticulous job of splitting and planing the strips followed, the nodes being arranged spirally. Glueing was done with a new hot vegetable compound and the individual strips were bound quickly together with his refined glueing machine. The resultant seams fitted so tightly that no gaps whatsoever were visible to the naked eye. Tolerances, when the sides were calipered at any point up or down the rod, approached the zero mark.

To insure a perfect ferrule-cane fit the stick was sent to Denver to dry in that clear damp-free air. Harrison traveled well across the continent just to fit those ferrules. Carefully he worked down the cane to the same diameter as the ferrule into which it must fit. Heat treatment expanded the ferrule and the cane was driven home. Back East again, the cane absorbed moisture and swelled so that the connection never could loosen. The exposed parts of the ferrule and the reel seat were lavishly gold plated and the satin-cork grip worked into perfect form.

When the completed wand was flexed, the action was superb. Never before had Harrison set into motion a rod that felt so light yet settled so quickly. Never before had he felt one with such delicate yet sure power.

The silk wrappings were scarlet, edged with black. Varnish went on in a dust proof room. On one of the six strips, right above the smooth grip, he inscribed one word, "EXCELSIOR." The opposite flat bore the legend, "TO FRANK."

At last Harrison confided to his wife, "Sonny's Excelsior is the greatest of them all. I truly think it's the finest in the history of anglerdom. Now we'll put it away till he's ready to take over its stewardship and enjoy its rewards."

But the little chap, the delight of their eyes, never lived to step into a stream to drift a dry fly over a rising trout. A reel never nestled in that golden seat and a line never was strung

[218]

through those oversize guides. Periodically the rod was inspected, then tenderly stored away again. To its creator it was the most precious thing in the world. Money couldn't buy it and, tragically, it seemed to have no future.

A nightmare brought the matter abruptly to a head. Boyd Harrison dreamed that he had died and in the disposition of his effects Excelsior went to one who never cast a fly. It journeyed to Canada for the lowly purpose of catching bait. Sometimes its owner, but more frequently his boatman, would dangle from it, over the gunwale, a baited hook and sinker attached to an old five-foot piece of braided line tied to the tip guide. Shiners and perch were catapulted to hang wriggling over the boat, whereupon the rod was tossed aside to let both hands reduce the elusive little creature to possession. Going to and from the fishing grounds the rod wasn't even taken down, let alone placed in its bag and tube.

When its owner was turning it over to a boy, directed to "go catch me some frogs on red flannel," Harrison awoke in near-nausea.

Right then in the darkness he realized that the most purposeful thing left in the sunset of his life was to dispose properly of his masterpiece. Long and hard he mulled over the possibilities. He knew many anglers personally and a host of others by reputation or through business but he couldn't pick the logical recipient with a sure "He's the one!"

The long rectangle of the window near the foot of his bed was just not quite black when the plan came. He would explain the situation and ask advice in a form letter to all the anglers on his mailing list. It took, at last, this expression—which after all was Boyd Harrison at his most natural.

Dear Sir:

Over two score years ago I built a rod for my son. It was made from the finest piece of cane that ever came my way and the design and workmanship were the best I have been capable of producing.

It was God's will that Frank should never use the rod. As a memorial to him I wish to place it in the most deserving and appropriate hands. I would appreciate any suggestion you might have to offer.

Good fishing,
Boyd Harrison

[219]

Responses came from many quarters. Each earned his study. They varied widely in nature and tone. Many writers felt the pathos of the request; a few missed it completely.

Some thought the rod should be a museum piece and others believed it should be offered as a prize of a specified sort. A number suggested that the rod should be sold and fabulous offers came as a matter of course.

One day a letter arrived from an old fishing crony. Its detailed information was startling. Harrison re-read it many times, musing on past days shared by the bright waters. Apparently he had found his man before it was too late. He must meet him.

When Frank Hunter turned out of Pennsylvania's Cumberland Valley the eastern sky was less dark than total night. As his car hummed along that Sunday, the day became as blue as a sapphire. At Roscoe the sun played on the weather-beaten boards of the covered bridge, some loose planks casting deep shadows. In the sparkling water stood some anglers.

"Too many fishermen to keep wild fish in business," he thought. "Too many slingers of hardware."

For fleeting moments he had visions of a time before his birth. The current tugged at the waders of a delicate little man who faced upstream and cast in the air a good deal—Theodore Gordon. Then there was a tall, lean, bearded figure—Hiram Leonard.[8] Wobbly Edward Hewitt,[9] dapper George La Branche,[10] stocky Roy Steenrod,[11] keen Emlyn Gill,[12] and a host of others passed in review. This was the Temple, these imagined figures the patron saints. A great artist should do justice to this spot.[13]

At Liberty, Frank found the Harrison home. As he crossed the cobblestones to the porch he saw sitting there a gaunt old man. From under a silvery thatch, eyes as piercing as an eagle's appraised him.

"I'm Frank Hunter. I've come to pay the respects of Adam Beck to Mr. Harrison."

The long frame stirred with difficulty and the man was on his feet. As the deeply lined face lighted up, Frank grasped the hard, bony hand.

"I was never so glad to see anyone in my life! So you're Adam's young friend, Boy. And how is Adam these days?"

"Mr. Beck is in fine health, sir, fishing every day of the season. He's a remarkable man and a wonderful angler."

"Yes, a remarkable man and a dedicated angler. Sit down; make yourself comfortable. I suppose you know I sent for you?"

"I'm afraid I don't understand, sir. I came at Mr. Beck's suggestion to convey to you his best wishes."

"Well . . . I see. Then Adam explained nothing to you. You must have unbounded confidence in him to make such a trip with so little cause."

"The reasons *are* great, Mr. Harrison. I'm honored to meet his friends, you and Mr. Leisenring, and I wanted to see the Neversink and Beaverkill."

Frank felt as if those sharp eyes were looking right inside him.

The lined old face brightened in wonder. "I can hardly believe what I see. The same sharp violet eyes, the curly blondish hair, the husky frame with the chest that was so deep even when he was just a little fellow! An open face, sincerity, unqualified confidence in friends. Yes, even the same initials and the same birth-date . . . You're exactly as I'd picture my boy—if he were here today. Providence has taken a hand."

Frank Hunter's embarrassment ended as the past world turned to the present. "But I'm forgetting my courtesy," Harrison was apologizing, "and you're an honored guest indeed." He motioned Frank through the hall and into a lived-in room with mantel bearing a pair of mounted trophies—noble trout they were—and walls hung with yellowed photographs of days along clean waters, faded prints, but in them the currents still wound their wreaths and the faces still smiled.

"Son, there's something you must have." Harrison swung open an oak cabinet's finely fitted door and with sure reach brought out a long round tube.

"I call it Excelsior. It's the rod of my Frank, the best I could ever build—and never used. Take it, my boy; enjoy it; use it often, as you both deserve."

"I—I don't know how to thank you," Frank stammered. "I'll certainly cherish this rod." Then, as the stunned feeling passed, he added, gently, "In due time my own Sonny will do the same."

"Perhaps you can't realize it," explained Harrison, "but a heavy cloak of anxiety has been lifted from me by placing this rod in your hands. Good luck to you always and God bless you."

Jimmie Leisenring was at his home that soft May evening with his friend Dick Clark[14] from Philadelphia, for in those days there was no legal Sunday fishing in Pennsylvania. They wanted to hear all about Adam and the incessant surface feeders on his limestone flat waters.

"Oi," said Jimmie, "vot fun! Der Adam catch 'em now?"

"Yes," Frank assured him, "he does right well with his flush-floating dry flies and fine gut."

Then Jimmie reached over and took the rod case from Frank's hand. "Vould it be a goot vun? Ve'll see." He uncased the rod and set it up. He flexed it, inspected it carefully.

"Gott in Himmel, Dick! Look! Boyd's jewel. Ach, dis is der greatest! Has it come to you, Boy?"

Although it was late when Frank returned to his limestone valley, he had to show Excelsior to Adam. And the old angler was awaiting his arrival. At Frank's approach his face shone even brighter than its happy normal.

All he said was, "Wonderful, wonderful! Boyd's jewel. Wonderful!"

Better than ever Frank realized that he was living in the golden age of trout angling, one of established tradition in which anglers know and respect each other, an age in which they are well informed, too.

Suddenly he had become Excelsior's curator, the recipient so critically chosen. He was a marked man. "He's the one," they'd say "who was given Harrison's jewel." All right, he'd live up to the challenge, keeping the sport of sport.

Rising trout and that unequaled rod, what a combination! Golden days lay ahead, and such days for his son Frank too. And best of all was the clan to which they belonged. It had tradition; it observed tradition.

Notes:

1. The name is adapted from the last names of two great rod builders, Boyd and Garrison.

2. Jimmie Leisenring of Allentown, Pennsylvania, was a keen student of wet-fly fishing who authored the first great American work on the subject.

3. The latest possible date of the first complete split-and-glued bamboo rod was established by Vincent C. Marinaro. It was the work of Samuel Phillippe of Easton, Pennsylvania, who was making such six-strip three-piece rods prior to 1870.

4. The Light House at Henryville on the Paradise branch of the Brodheads was destroyed by the August hurricane of 1955 and has not been rebuilt.

5. The father of the dry fly in America, Theodore Gordon, thought highly of the Pennsylvania limestone streams. He was probably the first to cast a dry fly on Big Spring, which stems from the largest spring in the Commonwealth and on Spring Creek, on which the Pennsylvania Fish Commission operates Fisherman's Paradise.

[222]

6. William J. Lunn, 1860-1947, was the renowned manager of the famous Houton Club on the Test and the subject of J. W. Hill's great English work, *The River Keeper*. As reported, he collected eggs of the b.w.o., the Welshman's button and other aquatic hatches for Hewitt to introduce into Eastern limestone waters, and they were confiscated at Washington, D. C.

7. All fine cane for split bamboo rods came from the Chinese province of Tonkin, now under Communist domination. Anticipating a cessation of trade, the current builders of bamboo rods accumulated great reserve stockpiles.

8. Hiram Leonard, early rod-building great of Central Valley, New York, shifted from bamboo rods with tips and midsections of split bamboo and butts of solid wood to 100% split bamboo rods in 1876. Like Phillippe, he was also a gunsmith.

9. Edward R. Hewitt, eminent trout-fishing authority, authored *Telling On The Trout*, published 1935.

10. George M. La Branche, Hewitt's fishing partner, wrote *The Dry Fly And Fast Water*, published 1914, and popularized dry-fly fishing for Atlantic salmon.

11. Roy Steenrod, beloved New York State warden, created, among other fly patterns, the Light and Dark Hendrickson.

12. Emlyn M. Gill authored *Practical Dry-Fly Fishing*, published 1912.

13. Painted in 1925 by renowned artist Ogden M. Pleissner for the Anglers' Club of New York. Color plates were made from this watercolor and 221 prints were run, whereupon the plates were destroyed to enhance the value of the prints.

14. Dick Clark, fishing companion of Jimmie Leisenring, is an active angler who still resides in Philadelphia.

CHAPTER 7

Gadgeteer

EACH DEDICATED fly-rod man had made his last cast as another trout season curtained down in the evening shadows. Nostalgia for past years, including this one—most of it that mattered, that is—was relieved but little by faint too-early dreams of the next.

It was the night of Labor's big day. September haze hung over the distant mountains but the wide fertile limestone valley spread under a turquoise arch. For a painter who could have depicted it justly it would have made an arch of triumph.

An incident of that evening was just too rich and rare to let float away in the stream of silence preserved and so on down the river of time.

Therefore, Curtis Q. Prentice, man of laws and trout student and angler of note, uncradled his phone to invite two fishing cronies to his country home. As he suspected, one call caught them both, veteran dry-fly enthusiast Adam Beck and the highly skilled young friend, Frank Hunter, who were at Adam's restaurant, conducting a postmortem on the season just ended. The stars were bright when they settled down on the porch overlooking Prentice's water meadow with its serpentine bends.

"This day," Curtis told them, "I witnessed the most amazing sight I ever expect to see out fishing, the sort of thing that sticks with you till the last chapter. Here's the story for our books, ours only.

"My fishing season officially ended about seven o'clock when I landed a fine trout with which I've had more than a nodding acquaintance—and my son has, too. I was so satisfied that taking another would have been an anti-climax that I let that well-to-be-remembered cast be the last of the season. I started home thinking the things we all think the last evening."

They were silent for a moment. The soft scratch of Adam's kitchen match sounded loud. Curtis went on.

"As I rounded the bend by the half-downed old willow I saw some distance ahead an undulating movement in the jewel weed and elderberry. I sat down on a handy log and watched the scene of agitation. Soon a hat appeared, then a squat human form. Alternately it disappeared and reappeared. I was about fifty yards away but finally I recognized him, then realized what was going on. It was only Lucius Cribbs—'Little Caesar'—catching grasshoppers and my thoughts turned to other matters. Tufts of brilliant green grass on the banks blended with the overhanging verdure and the reflection of each in the water made a changing study in greens; so there was no monotony to the eye. We had a beautiful evening to end it on, didn't we?

"Although not actually watching him, I saw L. C. come out from the high vegetation and sneak up to the head of the pool where the stream takes that grand wide curve. I was interested when he tossed a hopper into the confused current. It rode the surface, twisting and turning. L. C. knelt in the high grass and watched its progress intently. Once down in the pool proper, it began to kick.

"Its struggles must have been the attention-getter, for a heavy rise followed and the luckless hopper disappeared. L. C. threw in another and the same thing happened. Altogether he fed that fish about half a dozen.

"Satisfied that he had a big trout on the feed, he made, very cautiously, a wide detour to the tail of the pool. Ever so carefully he waded into casting position, so slowly that no tell-tale wakes would carry upstream. I thought to myself, 'This is a good lesson. You must move more cautiously on a still day than when the whole orchestra is playing'."

"Well put," said Adam, nodding his gray head.

"Thanks," smiled Curtis. "Well, you both know what I mean and those things mean the same to us fellows. Lucius froze into a rigid mold to give that wise old fish time to forget, just in case he might be suspicious. As you can well imagine, all the time my interest was boiling up pretty smartly. Finally he decided the time was right for the critical step, the presentation.

"We three know that casting is a manipulative art gained by developing a set of conditioned reflexes. Even from where I sat I could see that his fly was big and buzzing, no doubt as fine an imitation of a "hopper" as ever was fabricated. The phenomena of nature are the scientist's materials. This scientific angler was both keen and accomplished.

"As he false cast, carefully measuring that length of line in the air so his fly would land at precisely the right place in the proper line of drift, I studied L. C. even more carefully. Here was an angler with all the trimmings—like a Christmas tree. The key to *his* fishing personality was his gadgets. The scientist in him showed everywhere. He was a sort of one-man band.

"On his head was an all-weather hat with clips to hold small flies and a strip of sheep wool for the larger sizes. The high vest with many pockets was made from camouflage jungle cloth. Down the middle of his back hung a stained net, built with the same care that goes into a fine tennis racket. Around his waist, over the waders, was a canvas belt with compartments for plastic boxes. And trailing in the water on a leather thong was a wooden wading staff with a lumberjack tip.

"L. C., the gadgeteer, is indifferent to human frailties; his gadgets will pull him through! Just looking at him reminded me of Pope's assertion over two centuries ago: 'The proper study of mankind is Man.' How well L. C.'d fit into a Madison Avenue store window! How well would he fit on a trout stream, this exacting angler?

"But his cast, of course, was perfect and the fly must have been right, too, for the trout engulfed it just as he had the live 'hoppers. There was nothing wrong with L. C.'s response, either. As he lifted the rod tip, the steel sank home and he cried in a gust of passion, 'Gotcha! I'll play you till you're dead'."

Frank frowned and Adam did, too, though less severely. They held no grudge against any game of woods or waters, nor did Curtis.

The latter went on. "First the fish held position as a big one often does. Then there was a deliberate big-fish movement, a gentle tug building up to a powerful pull. That flawless angler stood still, rod arched just right to protect the leader. I could hear the reel clicking and I knew the line was throbbing. I moved in close to get a ringside seat for the battle.

"Suddenly pandemonium cut loose. The water heaved; there was a mighty surge and this time the reel screamed. The big fellow threw his comely proportions into the air. Then as he crashed back, L. C. dramatically pushed his rod forward in a sort of salute to soften the shock on the leader. 'Oh, no, you don't,' says he, and quickly regained his statuesque pose with rod tip pointing toward the firmament—in perfect command of the situation."

Here there was a faint snicker from Frank, who was more natural than dramatic in his ways; but so were the other two— even Curtis, except in office or court of law—and no reproving eyebrow rose.

"The trout took off again," Curtis resumed, "but quickly reversed field and cut back. Frantically L. C. stripped in line by hand, reeling being too slow for that fast run, with loose line trailing in the water. To help re-establish firm connection, he took some backward steps. Naturally such fish technique had taken its toll of human technique. But now the big trout was like a punched-out boxer. L. C. says, 'I gotcha you tamed down now,' and he proceeded to get excess line back on the reel.

"What came next would have disconcerted the Almighty Hades. The picture changed from the sublime to the plumb ridiculous. The little man started edging toward the center of the pool with the front of that vest sticking out in a point toward the fish. The low rod bent in a wide arc, its tip near the surface. On the far side of the pool the tired fish was exerting a steady strain on the line, rod and man. As it moved closer to the far bank, the fisherman moved with it.

"Obviously the trout couldn't pull away another inch of line; neither could the angler get back any, had he so desired. It was a sort of frozen stalemate. All the while L. C.'s right hand fumbled alternately with the thong of his wading staff and the soap button on his front.

" ' What seems to be the difficulty?' I called.

" 'Oh!' he answers in surprise. He shook his head, but it was like the shake of a setter's tail when he's not certain whether or not there's game out front. 'I guess I need help.'

" 'Help with what?' I inquired.

" 'Can't you see I'm in trouble?'

" 'Yes, I see, but I don't understand the nature of the trouble.'

"Just then the trout decided to move a bit. The rod bent lower and the vest protruded further. But our angler was up to the occasion. To relieve pressure he waded toward the trout and the water began to pour down inside his waders.

" 'Hurry up! Help me!' he implored.

" 'What should I do? I don't understand the problem.'

" 'Can't you see, you fool? The line's hitched around my wading staff.'

" 'Fool?' I asked. 'Who's a fool? It seems to me your vest is the trouble spot.'

"The trout exerted more pressure. L. C. again moved toward him but this time he went in up to his chin and the rod and line disappeared. By the way his head bobbed I judged he was on tip-toe.

" 'It's my soap button, too.' His words sort of gurgled.

" 'You mean double trouble?'

"He ignored this remark; so I went on: 'All I have is boots

and it's too deep out there. What do you expect me to do, snorkel for the fish?'

"He tried a new approach—on me, that is. 'The trout is awful big but he's licked.'

" 'Are you sure?' He seems to maintain the chain of command."

" 'Hell, yes!' he exploded. 'He can hardly swim.'

" 'Is he so big,' I asked, 'that one who doesn't have him hooked should get wet, too?' And I even ventured, 'Is the water cold?'

"This silly question didn't merit an answer, even a silly one. Now one thing was obvious. With L. C. out there in the middle of things, the trout couldn't smash the leader unless he left his home, the pool, for the length of line was the radius of his swimming area.

"About that time L. C. must have slipped or stumbled on a rock, for his head went under and that pretty hat came off. I expected it to keel over and sink with all those attachments but it floated away.

" 'I'll get your hat for you,' I told him when his head reappeared.

" 'The hell with the hat! Get over there and net the fish.' Then he added, 'Hurry!'

"His attitude was odd, for he was telling me and asking me in one breath.

" 'I'll try to oblige,' I answered, 'but I don't intend to get wet.'

"I went down stream and crossed at the shallow riffle, then with net in hand approached the trout. I got near enough for a good look and he was a dandy. When he saw me, he circled in a perfect arc to the other side. L. C. pivoted with him; so now the fisherman was facing east instead of west. Other than that, the situation was unchanged and it sure needed changing.

" 'Go back, go back,' he sputters; so I retraced my steps.

" 'Now sneak up on him and net him,' came the directive. 'Go in slow and low.'

"This time I managed to move into very close quarters. With the net in the water I tried one more step and made what might best be described as a desperation shovel-scoop. I missed the fish with the interior of the net but not with the rim. I could feel it prod him.

"This resolved several questionable factors, to wit: sure enough the trout had got his second wind, he could be activated and he had plenty of poop left. The poke of the net rim was also a mental stimulant. From the start it had seemed that he'd regarded the home pool as security, but if so, his conviction had

[229]

changed. Security and distance became synonymous.

"The desire to survive is a powerful urge. Like a bolt, tail upstream and churning, he bored head-first and pell-mell into the riffle. Line, rod and arms jumped straight out, there was a watery twang, and the line flew back into L. C.'s face. A big wake melted into the broken water below—*tout de suits*—as we gawked at this cataclysm. Even as American history was written in gun-smoke, angling lore and legend are written in smashed tackle.

"Poor L. C. was in a comatose state, the picture of complete finishment—and if there's no such word, there should be. I actually felt sorry for him, figuring his spirit was as dead as a last year's birds' nest after his blood sweat and tears. He gave me an icy stare.

"Then what do you suppose happened? He pantomimed significantly—shook his fist at me. Then he screamed, 'You blundering idiot, you lost my fish!' and his face turned one degree darker than thunder-heads—the purple passion of some people.

"In injured innocence, as unconscious of guilt as poison ivy, I looked at him as he went on—and there was a lot more before he quit to cough up some last holdout water from the bottom of his lungs. But I'd become a little sore.

"'Lucius Cribbs,' I addressed him, 'no wonder they call you Little Caesar. You're a dog in the manger and as unstable as milk weed seeds.'

"But I'm sorry for my outburst now. What I should have done was laugh because it was really funny, hilarious in the ridiculous sense."

CHAPTER 8

Reconstruction

WHEN THE sap rose in willows—and in angling spirits, too—
the lawyer always threw a little pre-season party for his fishing
cronies. Once a year the men took over the Prentice home to
talk trout before, during and after the serving of nutriment, the
women folk and Junior having gone elsewhere.

Cagy old Adam Beck and talented young Frank Hunter stood
apart from the rest as experts in solving dry-fly fishing's ever-
varied problems. Old Professor Grant from the English department at State and "Doc" Keller the dentist were but a short
down-wind cast from angling bunglers. One spent most of his
time in admiring the lush, serpentine meadow stream and the
verdant country it drained, murmuring now and then a line or
two from his rich store of well-relished Elizabethan poetry. He
would as soon thrill to a rising trout from his seat on one of the
rustic benches along the stream as to lay a fly along side that
dimple. The other, who at middle age had seized upon angling
as though life depended on it, covered the maximum amount
of water, promising or not, with as many casts as he could
negotiate.

The host, Curtis Prentice, and Dr. Hoffman, the eminent
surgeon, were in-betweens in fishing skill. The doctor was a
duellist, his specialty a knowledge of the whereabouts and habits
of individual fish. Prentice, the theorist, promoter and so kindly
an extrovert that you couldn't help liking him, was a clumsy
though persistent performer.

This unofficial little angling fraternity often got together in
the long meadow behind the lawyer's house. Today it lay cold
and gray, waiting for the soon-due transfiguration of spring.

Each year Prentice planned something of special interest and
now it would be particularly appropriate. He'd tell his story
after they'd eaten the last course and gone to the livingroom
for a cordial in front of the crackling oak fire.

It was then he brought out two matched rods and reels,
antique and priceless. "These are Phillippe rods and Hardy
reels," he announced, "and they date back a hundred years. Each
went to war, the prized possessions of two dedicated fishermen.

[231]

Their tradition's a part of American history."

He fondled the four sections of one rod as the other, set up, made the rounds. Each man in turn examined the glue seams of the split bamboo, the German-silver ferrules, the antiquated ring guides, the elaborate wicker-wrapped grip, the ash butt piece and each appreciatively flexed the long rod.

"We're celebrating a centennial," Prentice went on. "The gathering war clouds were rent asunder one hundred years ago today, April 12, 1861, with the bombardment of Fort Sumter. The Confederacy comprised only eleven Southern States and down there the thing for an able-bodied man to do was enlist.

"When young Foster went to war he took his beloved fly rod with him. The two were practically inseparable. If his outfit camped near likely-looking water he made the most of it. Fighting was in Virginia's river country and so far activity—or inactivity—always had been along or near one of those great systems that feed Chesapeake Bay. His favorite, mainly because it was home water, was the wadeable Rappahannock.

"The campaigns had been intense, for always, it seemed, General Lee could maneuver his outnumbered Army of Northern Virginia so the invading Army of the Potomac was decisively defeated—and driven back across the nearest river. Brilliant victories at Fredericksburg and Chancellorsville built the legend that one Rebel was worth two Yanks. So the plan came to invade the rich North and cartographer Jed Hotchkiss provided the blue-prints, the maps.

"Foster was with Heath when they marched into Chambersburg in late June of '63. Confederate high brass had trained their sights on the deeply populated areas beyond the Susquehanna. Right then, too, Federals were threatening Richmond. Lee's forces were deployed like a serpent with the deadly head in Pennsylvania. I guess every statesman and every general here and in Europe would have been holding his breath had he grasped the portent."

He laughed self-consciously, embarrassed at his own vision of those earth-shaking times. No one moved. A long ash fell, unregarded, from the dentist's cigar.

"Well, war is small things, too. As Confederate officers were drum-heading a citizens' committee in Chambersburg, demanding supplies, the young captain saw a little teenager with a couple of fish hooks in the band of his straw hat and he sidled over to him.

" 'Sunny,' he asked, 'where do you fish?'

[232]

"The scared kid looked up at his face. It wasn't the cruel type he'd been led to expect of a Rebel. It was nice and friendly.

" 'Are you going to burn us out?' the boy countered, Yankee fashion, question for question.

" 'Of course not! We do have to get some food, though. There's no other choice but to live off the land. Don't worry. Now, how about your fishin'?'

" 'I fish for trout in the stream that flows through town. Like it best a couple of miles up.'

" 'How about you and me going out together? You show me where and I'll pay you for your trouble. It'll be in Confederate money but you'll soon be able to use it. By the way, what's your name?'

" 'John Richie. My Uncle Edward's on the citizens' committee.' He hesitated, then added, 'I'll go with you.' "

Prentice paused for refreshment and admired one of the rod tips.

"The two started working their way upstream," he continued, "the fisherman casting to the places his little guide recommended. Even though he was the best caster the boy had ever seen, the trout weren't interested in his flies.

"The Rebel's pleasant easy-going ways built confidence in the boy. 'Do you catch trout back home on those big flies?' he asked.

" 'Don't have trout back home; only bass, the new fish. They take these flies well. Don't they look any better to you than they do to your trout?' he laughed.

" 'Uncle Edward uses little flies, mostly brown or gray ones.'

"After some two hours of fun and good casting, but no catching, the two were well above town. The captain knew, though, that he was fishing over trout. Now and then he'd see one bolt like an arrow for cover and the boy assured him that those little surface rings were made by feeding trout, not 'minnies.'

"The two rounded a bend and up ahead a rod flashed in the sunlight above the bushes. The Captain, followed by the boy, walked directly to the spot. The angler was a tall young man with his arm in a sling. Methodically and accurately he searched the water with his cast of three flies, delivered quartering downstream. Suddenly there was a mark on the surface and the long rod sprang into a throbbing arc. In the trout's struggle for freedom, the officer noted, it splattered and twisted a great deal, sort of stood on its ear, but it didn't jump. At last the fisherman skidded it into the grass where the bank sloped to the water.

" 'Nice going!' cried the Captain. 'You've proved to me that these trout can actually be taken on a fly.'

"The other looked up startled. 'I'm surprised to see anyone on the stream this afternoon, particularly'—he hesitated—'a Confederate officer.' Then, with apprehension, 'What does this mean?'

"'Invasion of the North is in full swing. Didn't you know? My friend and I came up from Chambersburg.'

"The fisherman look into the familiar face of the boy, who by an affirmative nod confirmed the report as fact.

"Captain Foster continued. 'By this time Early is probably at York, maybe even headed for Lancaster and Ewell should have Carlisle and possibly Harrisburg. We are unstoppable because your armies are down on the Potomac around Washington and near Vicksburg. Lee will walk right into Philadelphia and probably New York. That'll end the war; the civilians of the North will demand it. France and England will intervene soon, too, because they need our cotton.'

"'You make victory sound easy but you're misjudging the attitude of the northern citizenry and the desire of the Army of the Potomac to do battle with your Army of Northern Virginia. Look out, too, for the new Federal rifles. We have a revolutionary weapon, the Spencer repeater. Muzzleloaders and single-shot breechloaders can't compete against this eight-shooter.'

"'Where are you from?' queried the Captain.

"'My home's over the mountain, near Gettysburg.'

"'Could it be that you're a wounded soldier on furlough?'

"The other nooded.

"'When were you wounded?'

"'I got it at Chancellorsville, May second. A Minie ball in the shoulder. It happened the same evening that your Stonewall Jackson was fatally shot. I was hiding in the bushes right near by, waiting my chance to go back. I could hear your fellows telling about how they shot him in the dark by mistake.'

"The Captain changed the subject. 'Have you caught any other trout?'

"In answer the angler rested his rod against his shoulder and with his one free hand lifted the top of the creel. In it lay a half-dozen speckled forms, the most highly-colored fish the Southerner had ever seen.

"'They're positively gorgeous! But they sure enough don't like my flies.'

"Each intently eyed the other's equipment. 'I see you have a Phillippe rod,' observed the man in civilian garb, 'Do you know

[234]

much about these new rods built in Pennsylvania?'

" 'No. Nothing except the name of the maker. It was given to me.'

" 'Samuel Phillippe is more than the maker,' the Northerner explained. 'He's the creator. He lives in this state—at Easton. A remarkable man. Besides being a rod builder he's a gunsmith and a violin maker. He's the only person who's produced six-strip bamboo rods—makes his ferrules and guides, too. You notice the upper three sections of your rod are six-sided, six strips of planed bamboo glued together. The butt joint is ash. It wouldn't surprise me if he started making complete rods of split bamboo.'

" 'That is indeed interesting information. I suspected that I had something very special. Now I know it.'

"Just then a horse whinnied back in the trees and its strange love-call was answered from downstream.

" 'Soldier!' crackled the voice of the boy. 'The Rebels are coming. Hurry!'

"As fast as he could with his slung hand, the Yankee opened a red leather fly-book. From one page he extracted a brown fly, from the supply on another page a gray one and from a third section a white-winged fly with an iridescent green body. 'Take these, Captain; they'll do you some good. A Ginger Quill, a Starling and a Coachman. I tied them.' And from an envelope attached to the book's inner binding he drew a coil of gut. 'You'll need a fine leader, too.'

"As he slipped through the bushes toward his horse, his parting words came back to them: 'Good luck, Captain; and keep your head down.'

"The officer smiled at the boy as they heard the hoof beats of a lone horse fade toward the South Mountain.

"The small reconnoitering party drew their horses to a halt beside the stream and the leader, a gray-haired sergeant, saluted smartly. 'We're contacting farmers for food, sir. They sure enough have rich farms here 'bouts. How you all doin' with the fesh?'

" 'No good,' replied the Captain, 'but we expect to get some before long' and he winked at his young accomplice.

"When the wounded Federal turned from the headwaters of his favorite trout stream toward the Cashtown Pass in the South Mountain, he made hot haste to Gettysburg. Valuables needed to be hidden and maybe women and children evacuated to some point east. Even now, the upper Cumberland Valley was overrun with Rebels. It was only a matter of time before they'd cross

[235]

the mountain and swarm through Gettysburg's orchard country. Pennsylvania was in trouble.

"Much to his surprise on arriving in town, he found advanced units of Federal cavalry, sabers a-swing and stubby Spencer carbines cradled across saddles, their high hammers at half-cock over charged chambers. General Buford was there and he sought him out to report what he'd learned from the Confederate Captain. Buford told him how Meade had succeeded Hooker in command of the Army of the Potomac, whose entire force was pressing North to intercept Lee. Cabbot then realized that neither army knew where the other really was and that a major collision was imminent.

"Back home, it was decided that his father would drive the rest of the family to his mother's old home in Frederick, Maryland, and he'd stay at the house to care for the stock and bury the silverware and other precious articles. 'If the rest of them are anything like that little band of Jenkins' cavalry that passed through Gettysburg last Friday,' reflected the head of the house grimly, 'it'd be best not to be around.'

"Next morning Cabbot walked over to nearby Seminary Ridge. Heavy firing broke out northwest of town, presumably along the junction of the Hagerstown and Chambersburg roads. To the east he saw Federal forces assembling on gently sloping Cemetery Ridge about three-quarters of a mile across the flat. As he bestrode a boulder deposited by the last ice age he watched his team-mates to the north retreating into town. Firing began out in the direction of the Harrisburg Pike. Then, several hundred yards down the line, he made out gray uniforms coming his way under the oaks of Seminary Ridge.

"He ran back home. He wasn't going to be a candidate for Libby prison if he could help it and he wouldn't leave the homestead unless forced out by fire. He'd watched the Union forces massing on Cemetery Ridge and he felt sure the Confederates were pouring in from Chambersburg, Hagerstown, and apparently Dillsburg, too. The fortunes of war could make this engagement bigger and more decisive than Fredericksburg and Chancellorsville and it might seethe back and forth for days.

"Fortunately he had decided to hide the family valuables, including his fly rod and reel, the night before in the fireproof place he and his father had chosen. Hurriedly he threw extra hay to the steers, which had been rounded up right after the family had driven away. Wellington, the big English setter, was in the almost-empty corn crib with a bucket of water. The best place for Cabbot to hide was under the steps of the little back porch.

"First he pried loose a foot-wide side board, his escape route. Then he entered the house, returning quickly with a blanket under his good arm and a loaf of home-made bread and several tomatoes jammed into the sling. He shoved them in by the loose board. Next was water. He filled an iron kettle at the pump and lugged it over.

"Underneath the porch at last, he pulled the board back into place. With a flat rock he forced a vertical board between the steps so that a half-inch crack opened as a peep-hole. Off east in his clear but limited field of view stood Cemetery Ridge. He settled down for his accidental date with destiny.

"Before an hour passed, Confederate soldiers entered the house by the back steps. Their worn boots thundered across the boards above him. Finally some officers arrived and set up a headquarters upstairs. Long after dark and throughout the long night there were muffled voices and much to and fro trampling. He heard one man tell another, as they passed overhead, 'Ol' Pete Longstreet's on his way here now.'

"Through the slot the stowaway saw in the morning light, men in grey by the thousands pass south between his home and Seminary Ridge. Except for the movement of troops, horses, caissons and cannon, things were relatively quiet, considering there were so many opposing armed men within a short mile of each other. From his hide-out he conjectured the Confederates would go to the great rock mass, Devil's Den, then occupy or circle Big Round Top. Among them were Hood's Texans and the Louisiana Tigers. Almost to a man the whole of Lee's army that he saw—though tatterdemalions some of them were—looked bigger and taller and harder than the legionaries pictured in his old copy of Caesar's *Commentaries,* and a thousand times more grimly dedicated to their cause.

"He was fearful that nothing could stop such men from working or fighting their way behind Cemetery Ridge and cutting the Federal line of communication.

"A check of his watch revealed that it was four in the afternoon when firing started. He could see puffs of light-gray smoke from cannon on the brow of the ridge; then beyond was violent rifle fire. The din and tumult were terrific. It sounded as though it was around the Sherfy, Trostle and Wentz homes, maybe in the peach orchard and wheat field on the Seminary Ridge side of the Emmitsburg Road. Then it broke out near Big Round

Top. Certainly the two main forces had collided—another slugfest between the Army of Northern Virginia and the Army of the Potomac. This time it was the redoubtable Lee and the recently promoted Meade. Cabbot was sure the Confederates were attacking the Federal left flank.

"Only darkness stopped the fierce engagement. Continuously during the night heavy overhead steps interrupted his dozing. He wished that he could understand what the voices in the livingroom were saying.

"Wet with perspiration, Cabbot was awakened by cannon fire. He realized that he had slept the enire morning, for it was one o'clock. Through the crack in the steps he could see Federal shells exploding over Seminary Ridge and puffs of smoke from the Confederate guns on the crest of the hill. The artillery duel grew in intensity. There'd been no exchange like this at Fredericksburg or Chancellorsville. An hour later all was painfully silent for a few minutes; then the rifle fire and distant boom of field-pieces grew terrific. Obviously the Confederates were attacking the Union line lodged on the opposing Cemetery Ridge. The sharp smell of black powder filtered under the steps and the sky was darkened with a death shroud of smoke.

"Finally he heard a far-off cheer beyond Seminary Ridge. Confederate soldiers were streaming back, first by the dozens, then by the hundreds, finally by the thousands. They were walking, not running. Stretcher bearers were part of the procession. Soldiers assisted wounded comrades and a few used rifles as crutches.

"Then he saw the fishing Captain walking toward the house. His head was not bowed like those of the rest. Intently his eyes searched the home. He paused for a moment to look at the barn, the sprawling fields and the orchard. Then he passed out of view and his steps sounded on the boards overhead.

" 'This,' realized Cabbot, 'is the first clean-cut victory of our Army.' He expected to hear more shooting and see men in blue appear on Seminary Ridge but darkness fell and the counterattack didn't materialize.

"Saturday, July 4, 1863, was another hot one. Between him and the brow of Seminary Ridge were many grey uniforms. Most of the men sat in groups or slumped on the baked ground. Here and there a small cooking fire blazed or glowed with coals. Headquarters upstairs was a bee-hive of activity. A storm was gathering and at noon the rain began. At dusk the Confederate exodus started, the march back to the Cumberland

Valley. After a violent night thunderstorm the last of the Con
federates had left his home.

"Cabbot emerged from hiding, his eighty-five hour rendezvous
with destiny. All available chairs had been grouped in the
livingroom. There were bloodstains on every bed in the house
and a corpse on one. Most of the towels and sheets were gone,
no doubt used for bandages. The boots and shoes of the men
of his family were missing.

"Wellington, freed from his corn-crib prison, shouted canine
cheers and spurred mud high in his relieved gallivanting around
his master but Cabbot's wonderful little mare, West Wind, had
gone with the retreating sea of men and guns and jolting
vehicles.

"By the barn stood a grisly pile of the steers' heads, hides, legs
and entrails. Cleanup and burial would claim the next several
days but first Cabbot would walk to town to learn more of the
extent of the victory and try to find some food.

"In due course," the lawyer went on, "the Federal Captain
was physically fit and back at the head of his company. The
war had taken a very different turn. After Meade's victory at
Gettysburg and Lee's escape across the Potomac, President
Lincoln had matched the conquering Union leaders of the
'West', Grant, Sheridan and Sherman, against the shadow-boxing
Confederates in the wilderness area of Virginia.

"Late in the spring of '64, Cabbot was camped along the
Rappahannock. It wasn't trout country but at the chance to
fish, out came the Phillippe rod, the Hardy reel and the trout
flies and leaders. Maybe he could hook some bass.

"As he rounded a bend, sunshine danced on a flexing rod
upstream. A walk through the woods took him directly to the
other fisherman. A tall fellow, he stood in the shallows, casting
toward a large, submerged rock in midstream. The single fly
dropped in a pocket behind a rock, hung there a moment, and
then came a boil that would fill a washtub. The angler struck
back and the long rod arched. Time after time the hooked fish
jumped completely out of water in a beautiful display but the
fisherman was in command of the situation. Presently he backed
up and skidded the bass out on a sandbar.

"'Nice going!' cried a hearty voice from the bank. The startled
angler faced the intruder.

"For a moment the two stared at each other; then they in
unison each uttered, 'We meet again!'

"'What happened to you, Captain?' asked the Federal soldier

[239]

of the one now in civilian clothes. 'Your arm?'

"'I got it at the Broak Road, May seventh, a .50 caliber Spencer slug. Just before Longstreet was shot through the neck and shoulder by one of our fellows. They took us back together. As we left, Ol' Pete was giving orders, bloody foam spurting from his mouth. Quite a man! He'll fight another day.'

"'Glad to see you came through!' commented the Union Captain heartily. 'How's the bass fishing?'

"'Getting better all the time. Their introduction is interesting, particularly to me, because a friend pioneered the redistribution. Do you know anything about it?'

"The Northerner didn't. 'Tell me; I'm interested.'

"'Well, right after the railroad pushed west to the Ohio River at Wheeling, General Shriver moved some from that watershed, where they were native, to the Potomac. That was in 1854. He made the largest perforated tin container that'd pass through the trapdoor of a locomotive's water tank. As the thirty bass were brought eastward over the line, the water was freshened at the regular stops. From time to time thereafter he transferred more bass.

"'They certainly did well in their new home. Once their offspring spawned, their first big generation spread all over the Potomac, moved out into the Chesapeake Bay and up other rivers. There are a good number now in the Rappahannock and its feeder the Rapidan but there'll be more and bigger ones. It seems safe to predict that after this war there'll be successful plantings in Pennsylvania's big streams and New York lakes and all of New England. Wonderful fish, Captain. You'll appreciate them even as I do your trout.'

"'That's intensely interesting background and I'm glad to have it. Marsh Creek near home flows into the Potomac. Lord willing, I'll try it to see if they're up there, too.'

"'They will be sooner or later, for sure. I don't believe your trout flies are just right for bass. I've had the chance to experiment enough by this time to have a pretty fair idea of what they like.'

"They heard voices back in the woods. 'A patrol of yours, this time, no doubt?' the fisherman asked, smiling.

"The blue-uniformed soldier nodded.

"'Here,' said the other, 'take these flies and a heavy leader—a Lord Baltimore, a Colonel Fuller and a Yellow Sally, my own ties.' Clumsily he fumbled them into the Federal's hand. 'They'll do you some good down this way.'

[240]

"'Where are you from?' Cabbot asked him, as he started to dodge behind the bushes.

"'This side of Warrenton. Good luck, Captain.' And he disappeared."

Curtis Prentice broke the spell he had cast. He filled tall glasses for his friends.

"In destined time peace ruled the land and there were old ties to be taken up again.

"Cabbot told his father that he was going, alone, down to fish the Rappahannock for bass and to look for a certain fly fisherman near Warrenton. His father was disappointed that he didn't feel greater obligation to visit kinfolk down that way but reconciled it with the thought that the strained relations of war did odd things to its victims. 'What must a soldier relive in his cluttered mind?' he wondered.

"Down below Warrenton another restless young man had a haunting desire to make a trip. He told the family that he was going to Chambersburg to fish Falling Springs for trout and look for a stranger near Gettysburg who was a fly fisherman. His chagrined father felt that the primary object should be to spend time with his brother's family but the thought that his soldier son might consider all Yankees damned people helped to explain it all. 'The ravages of war leave their scars on the minds of participants,' he reflected. 'Why, he won't even permit me to accompany him'."

Prentice interrupted his story with a chuckle. "You know what? The Confederate Captain showed up at the Gettysburg homestead at the same time the Federal Captain appeared at a certain farm near Warrenton. Each had a strange suspicion or powerful hunch. Was it common sense or uncommon wisdom? After talking with kinfolk, each proved to his satisfaction that he'd met his fighting cousin out fishin'. Both families learned of those two brief meetings.

"They missed connections that time, just a month after Appomattox, but they got together a lot thereafter.

"And could you guess it? In the bonds of devotion they exchanged fly outfits each time they fished together until finally neither knew which was Federal and which Confederate equipment. They were as close as any two men living apart could be, each frequently visiting the other, and they lived to ripe old ages too.

"One was my great grandfather, the other a great uncle. The friend of Samuel Phillippe who gave his son and also his nephew a fly-fishing outfit is the first of our Prentice family of whom we have knowledge. He set the tradition that the boys attend Lafayette College. It was as a student there in Easton that he became a friend of the pioneer bamboo fly-rod man."

Tenderly Curtis Prentice placed the individual rod sections in their proper places in the shallow glass-topped cabinet, then hung it on the wall like a framed picture.

"You can see why these collector's items are precious, too, as family mementoes of the Civil War. They're passed down to the youngest male when stewardship is relinquished by the passing of a Prentice who holds them. Now that Uncle Foster II is gone, my Junior is their guardian for the rest of his days."

"Interesting, interesting," commented old Adam Beck. "You certainly come honestly by your devotion to fly fishing. Yep, yep, indeed you do. Blood's thicker than water, but fishing waters, they are thick too."

CHAPTER 9

"Wahoo!"

CHESTER LOWER was gay as he talked fishing with Adam Beck at a private-like little table snugged away in a far corner of the latter's small-town restaurant. The steaks had been good and all the trimmings too. Adam felt that his self-invited guest was like a bird dog that had eaten, unnoticed, a "dead bird" and then sneaked away.

Cheppie gulped his last swallow of after-dinner coffee and then baffled his host with the assertion, "My blood's tired. I'm no longer going to run all over the place trying to find rising trout. For the rest of my fishing days it'll be one stream, in fact, one long meadow of one small stream, and bank fishing at that."

Searchingly Old Adam looked into the eyes of his middle-age friend. "Don't cancel yourself out, young fellow; you're the picture of health." Then he caught the twinkle in the other's eyes. "You sure this isn't by choice and not necessity."

Cheppie burst out laughing. "Let's put it another way, Smartie. I just bought old man Buller's meadow and I never felt better in my life."

"So that's why you've been so smug. Now I begin to understand. You're looking forward to discovering every feeding station and hiding place; you figure at least a nodding acquaintance with every trout. You want to be able to fish your newly-acquired water well, maybe sort of show off a little. You don't mean tired blood; you mean fishing cream."

"Top cream," corrected Cheppie, "not just cream. I mean something else, too. It took me 25 years of fishing to learn that the variety of the same locality is amazing. No two evenings are alike. You know that stream well. Now please tell me what flies work best there."

"It's a three-fly stream. Sure, you can take an odd trout with 'most any pattern, but there are three indispensables."

Cheppie leaned closer. "That's the kind of information! The three flies?"

"The hatch of the little yellow drakes, 'the sulphurs,' is wonderful on Little Cedar. From early May to 'hopper time they'll be on the water every calm evening—both duns and spinners. And those well-conditioned wild browns are willing to rise freely. It's important and impressive, this hatch."

"The pattern? How about the pattern?" Cheppie pressed hard.

"Throughout May, a 16 Pale Evening Dun, then as the flies get smaller and the trout more discriminating, 18's and 20's. I like a bastard pattern, though. Either orange gantron body or some orange hackle intermingled with the honey. The addition of orange handles the super-selective individuals but don't ask me why. Learned it by trial and error."

Cheppie was scratching notes in a little address book. "How about pattern number two?"

"LeTort hair and turkey wing 'hoppers. In July, an inch long. About an inch and a half in August and for the tail-end of summer a big one to try to fool a very big brown."

Cheppie rubbed his balding noggin as with ball-point pen he decorated a paper napkin—the notebook was too small and slow—with marks that reminded patient Adam of cuneiform inscriptions. "Fine!" he said, looking up like a mink breaking surface for air. "Go on."

"Number three is a fish-finder when trout aren't surface feeding and that'll happen even on Little Cedar. My favorite's a badger spider with a peacock-herl body."

"I'll get some of each from Spider Webb. Thanks for the information. With your help I'll be traveling a royal road. Next thing is to make two blades of grass grown where now there's only one. Stream improvement and good management. That's where you come in again. Give me a prescription for a trout stream, Doctor. Spare nothing. Name it and it'll be done. Bulldozer, chain saw, logs, rocks by the truckload—anything. Furthermore, when the Paradise is created, I'll establish the killing restrictions you recommend. We'll fish there together."

Adam gave him a hard look. "Showcase fishing. Yep, yep. And it wouldn't be right if the owner wasn't the star performer."

Again Cheppie rubbed his shiny pate as one would scratch a match for light. It came. "Okay, Smartie; so I'm a suffering hero. But let's give it another name. Call it fishing insurance for our old age, a trout endowment, something for me and my friends to enjoy. Now, about the facelifting, Doctor."

Adam pondered for a long moment. The meadow was one of his well known and most loved haunts—Cedar Run, the greatest little trout stream of them all. It was blessed with a boundless supply of the elements leading to production, growth and surface feeding. It lacked neither food supply nor rate of natural reproduction—a perfect blend in natural balance and that two-month-long evening sulphur hatch was elegant. There were many times, as daylight grappled with darkness on a mat of multi-colored clouds, that trout rose with abandon. "The sun and the stars shine bright on Little Cedar," he mused.

"Wattaya mean?" queried Cheppie, as yet incapable of appreciating Adam's emotion.

"I'm thinking this: when you go to a doctor and aren't satisfied with his diagnosis, what do you do?"

"Go to another, naturally."

"Naturally," echoed Adam. "That's what I mean."

"It can't be that expensive?" Cheppie blinked; maybe he even hedged. "Or can it?" As an afterthought he added, "You wouldn't line the streambed with agate marbles and riprap the banks with mahogany?"

Adam shook his head. "It's no deal, Cheppie. No exploratory operation. That's what you expect. You've made up your mind to do a lot."

Cheppie adjusted fast. "You mean I want to do too much, like gilding the lily?"

"I understand the results you're after, only . . ." Adam hesitated.

"Only what?"

"The way to bring them about."

"I'm interested in results, not effects. I believe you when you say you know the type of fishing I want. Do you know how to get it?"

"Believe I do, but it's still no good."

"Adam, I can't understand you. First you're good enough to tell me how to catch these trout; now you hedge when I ask how to increase their size and number. You and your partner'll fish there, too, you understand. You implied that the work wouldn't be extensive. You mean it'd be cheap?"

Adam nodded.

"How long would it take?"

"Not long."

"I'm skeptical."

"Knew you would be."

"Now look here. Spring's going to bust out soon. First thing you know, another trout season will be upon us. Once it opens there'll be no more improvement work, just fishing, and a year'll be lost. I'd like to have the job done by the middle of April, while I'm in Florida. My question is: will you please take over while I'm away? Do whatever you think should be done and when I'm back I'll pay the bills for material and labor? Will you do that, please?"

"I might."

"'Might' nothing! I need your help, for I don't understand this sort of thing and you're the recognized authority. Will you promise to do it?"

"That's quite a challenge."

"Yes or no, Adam?"

"I suppose."

"Okay, it's a promise, but like pulling teeth to get it." Cheppie left and for five minutes Adam sat quietly, a little smile playing under his white mustache. Then he got up to go on with his job.

After the evening rush of the hungry, Adam got hold of his youthful fishing partner, Frank Hunter.

"Good news today, Boy," he told him. "Our favorite sulphur meadow won't be closed, after all. It just changed hands and the new owner's a friend. In fact, he's looking forward to our fishing there with him and he wants us to help him improve it." Frank grinned in his easy way, and Adam went on. "Yep, Chester Lower has saved the day. From here on that's where he'll be doing his trouting. What a relief, eh, Boy?"

In its due but ever-lengthy time, trout season was about to open, and a tanned and somewhat anxious Cheppie was back from Florida. The three met at the Beck eating emporium.

"I was just out to the meadow," said Cheppie. "What happened? Were you sick or something?"

"No, my health's been excellent," Adam replied. "Sure've been busy, though, very busy." Then he explained, "Getting ready for the trout season."

"So that's the trouble?" shot back Cheppie.

"Trouble?" parried Adam.

"You promised to improve the stream. This morning I went out, expecting to see new pools. It's the same old glittering watercourse, as unchanged as the stars above. Now I learn you've been 'busy.' This is a fine kettle of no fish. I'm disappointed." He looked it, and mad, too.

"I was afraid you would be, Cheppie. 'Glittering watercourse.' That's what I tried to tell you three weeks back while you were turning the heat on me."

"Now we've lost a year, unless"—Cheppie almost glared—"unless we cut into the fishing season."

"Dedicated anglers can't afford to sacrifice precious fishing hours. Life's too short. But don't worry; your stream should produce."

"Produce! I'd hoped for production such as we'd never seen. Indeed it'll have the same old unpopulated stretches. More skim milk than cream."

Adam assumed a dead-serious air. "Can't agree with you. I have high hopes, myself. Once the sulphur hatch breaks, you should have surface feeding in abundance, all up and down the line. It should be as interesting too to fish the water as to fish the rise."

Cheppie's reaction was bitter. "Fishing the water, you fish the blank water; I'll stick to the holes. There are only four pools and that's it. All the rest's flat and shallow, as useful as the holes in doughnuts! You try to catch them where they ain't; I'll put my time to better use."

"Trout surface feed best in shallow water," the old pro interjected.

"Only fingerlings use bleak shallow water," Cheppie growled, and stamped away.

Young Frank turned to his idol. "This is rough on Mr. Lower."

"Sometimes," Adam reassured him, "explanation is inadequate. It's better this way."

May second, blue bird weather, found the three together in the meadow. Spring's triumph, her half-stately, half-abandoned grand march, featured foliage, flowers, bird songs, sparkling water—and the first isolated drakes. Adam took charge of the proof fishing.

"How many trout do you figure you have?"

"About a quarter as many as there should be," was the ungracious retort.

"How many's that?" persisted Adam.

Cheppie frowned, took off his appropriately ancient felt hat and rubbed his dome, which glistened with the sweat of irritation. "I figure a dozen or two in each of the four pools. A hundred legal-size in the meadow at most. With four more pools there'd have been twice as many." He sneezed, shook his head, replaced his hat. "Too much sterile water."

"Boy and I'll skip the pools and fish the flat water. Boy, you take 'em west; I'll take 'em east. You go first."

"Double talk," grumped Cheppie, "won't catch fish. It's hopeless unless four inchers will take those big flies."

The three stood at the lower end of the meadow on the left bank as they faced upstream. Attached to the leaders of the

[249]

old man and the youth were identical flies, badger spiders with herl bodies.

Frank eased toward the water's edge and lengthened his line with false casts. The fly delicately fluttered to the surface, some twenty feet upstream. Lightly, right on the tips of its toes, it jauntily rode the bright water, some six inches from his bank. Then, with a swirl, the fly disappeared. When he lifted the tip, the rod became a throbbing arc. The fish, a nice one, was landed.

Nary a word was spoken.

Adam sneaked streamward to a point close to the spot where Frank had released his fish. Expertly he measured the line in the air so the fly would drop diagonally upstream and within several inches of the opposite bank. The first drifts were unproductive but he continued to concentrate his efforts on the same limited area. Suddenly there was a slash but the trout rejected the fly with nice judgment. Obviously it was a fine fish. Adam reeled in and motioned his partner to proceed.

Frank took a new casting position and dropped his fly just off the edge of the grass, straight upstream. This try wasn't as easy as his first. Again and again his fly rode the same line of drift. Then came a slashing rise but he only scratched the fish.

Again it was Adam's turn. On the first cast he drew one out from under the opposite bank. A good fish was played, landed and released.

They bypassed the pool above and put their spiders to work along the edges of flat water, just as before. Receptive fish waited at the casting targets, mute evidence that fish were there.

Cheppie was fit to be tied. "All right, you can talk now. How much farther should this go on?"

The pair looked at each other trying hard to be poker faced. "Tell him, Boy," said Adam.

"It should continue upstream, Mr. Lower, right to the boundary line."

"I don't understand," admitted their host. "I don't understand where these trout come from. You mean there are good fish strung out beside each bank in all this flat shallow water?"

Adam grinned and nodded to Frank as if to say, "Go ahead, Boy."

"We think there are, Mr. Lower. There should be many more in this flat water than there are in the pools."

Off came the shapeless felt and the polishing process was resumed. "I'm more confused than ever. I concede you fellows are master technicians, real artists, in fact; but you seem to be endowed with some special knowledge. Why do trout hug these shallow shorelines?"

"They're in their places, sir."

"Places?"

"Yes, hiding-places."

"No place for them to hide in this thin water."

"The whole thing is Mr. Beck's idea. Brown trout like overhead cover, particularly the better fish; so we gave them what they like."

Adam looked at the powerful frame of his young friend, then into those flashing honest eyes. A realization came to him almost as a shock: his spiritual son was no longer a growing boy. Suddenly, it seemed, he had become as much man as he had been youth. A great personality, a keen mind, what a future is his—if this old world just behaves itself. Adam realized something else too: he had become an old man; he knew it now. Maybe he had been a half-century ahead of his time. Wouldn't it have been wonderful had it fallen his lot for the two of them to grow up together, to fish together for many seasons and together champion the cause of conservation, so dear to each? Their beloved trout fishing is in trouble. It needs protection and fixing. There is unnecessary pollution, unjust exploitation, bad fisheries management. It needs champions. Frank Hunter is a great one—not one in the making but the finished product. Wouldn't it be wonderful to work on and campaign for this with his boy—shoulder to shoulder. His thoughts were interrupted by Cheppie's staccato voice.

"This I must see." He stepped into the stream for a better look at its edges.

"It's like a pool table. I don't see any places," he objected, as he peered at one bank, then the other.

"Maybe that's good," laughed Adam. "Now walk over to the other side and stick your foot under the bank opposite that little bush." He pointed with his rod.

The booted foot disappeared under the sodden bank. He swung it like a pendulum and it bumped a rock upstream, then one down.

"Now lift upwards," advised Adam.

The boot toe thudded against something flat. First Cheppie looked surprised; then he beamed. "A perfect trout haven, an invisible hideout. How's it made?"

"Simplicity itself," explained Adam. "Two chunks of limestone about a foot cube at each end of a four-foot piece of oak board. That's all there is to it. The boards are submerged; so they'll outlast several generations of anglers. We packed sod on top of them so the grass hangs to the water's edge."

"With a tunnel and a trout home back of it," interrupted Cheppie. "Ingenious! How many'd you put in?"

Adam's laugh was hearty. "Twelve this time."

" 'This time!' what do you mean?"

"Cheppie, it's like this. For the last two years, each spring and fall, Boy and I have put in a dozen, twenty-four a year. While you were south we again met our semi-annual quota. That puts it up to sixty now, but there's room for more. Last winter Ned Buller advised us not to bother any more, for he'd decided to make some money out of the place. If he couldn't sell it to some fishermen he'd rent it as club water."

"Well, it's a fisherman," said the rodless angler. "And he has fishing friends and fishing obligations, too." He frowned. "Some drifts of the fly are as hot as a firecracker, some as cold as an iceberg. It's spot fishing, sixty invisible gold mines. You've got to know the exact location of each. I'll mark 'em with stakes."

"Stakes wouldn't be very pretty; besides, Boy and I already have marked the spots."

Cheppie glanced about. "You did? I don't see anything."

"Are you familiar with wahoo?"

Cheppie stared at the two and a blank look it was. "Wahoo? Yeh, I feel like yelling 'Wahoo'!"

"The noun, not the verb," prompted Adam.

"Never heard of it."

"Beauty unsurpassed in its own botanical world; that's native wahoo. It's a large shrub or a small tree, as you please, which the nursery men haven't latched on to—at least so far. Perfect environment here—rich damp soil. It bears a mass of tiny maroon blooms in June. The big leaves turn flaming red in the fall and the winter fruits put bittersweet to shame. Scarlet berry inset in a large purple capsule. Amazing how such a little flower can develop into such a large berry. There's a wahoo planted opposite each trout hide."

"Logical landscaping and novel markers, too." Cheppie looked around. "I see them now. Hadn't noticed them. Yes they show up and they will grow. But where'd you get them?"

"Now and then, bird hunting, Boy and I'd run into a colony, mostly in wooded stream bottoms. These came from along the Conodoguinet. No, we didn't deplete any colonies. This is one

[252]

of those inorganic situations where there are males and females for pollination and fertilization."

"Sixty of them!" Cheppie was thinking out loud. "That represents a lot of digging and lugging. You and Frank have sure been busy."

"It wasn't tough. Frank's the best digger and lugger you could hope to find."

"I just hope," volunteered Frank, "that I'll be as good a man as Mr. Beck when I'm his age. Actually it was easy and fun too. The ground was soft and there weren't any rocks. We balled the roots and carried them to the car."

"Think of it!" said Cheppie, soberly. "You two did all this hard and effective work in my stream and by my stream and I was too dumb and blind to recognize it. And I was mad at you, Adam; I blamed you for letting me down. Forgive me, please."

"Forget it, Cheppie," Adam's smile told his side of the story. "Remember, it's results we're after, not effects. Now tell me, isn't it better to witness good than be told what might happen?"

"Of course. That's the secret of an understanding friend. You know, this is the biggest eyeopener of my fishing life and it's been full of surprises—and," he added, "things to unlearn. I can't tell you fellows how I cherish this meadow. We'll fish here a lot. Know what? We'll call this place 'Wahoo'—the verb, that is. Like this—"

If fish can hear, they'd have fled in panic at his shout. Frank, who was keen of ear, said later that the York Hills echoed it, and they were five miles away.

CHAPTER 10

Ricochet

YOU AND I know that in the nature of things justice seldom takes a nap. If she does, it is but a fitful nap and she comes back on the job energetically.

At all practical ranges Lucius Cribbs—Little Caesar to his fishing acquaintances—could cast a dry fly into a rosette, its hackles landing delicately. Observant and quick to catch on, he could tie the most effective flies. Although there was no snow in his hair, he had so learned the sequence of the hatches that often he found himself at precisely the right place at the proper time.

But L. C. bore a cross. The infernal jealousy of this unhappy little angler made him so boastful of achievement and secretive of method that the truth was not in him. All the crowd knew it—that is, all but one. Therein lies a tale of subterfuge that bounced back.

One soft and gentle spring evening he stood planted waist deep in the clear water facing a wooded arc of the stream. The only interruption of the bird chorus was the periodic plop of some surface-feeding trout as a floating mayfly met its doom in the concentrated line of drift. From one position L. C. could skin the bend of its spreckled brown beauties, working from the lowermost fish right up the line. His time-endeared creel rapidly grew heavier, a completely satisfying feeling to him. Later he'd display his spoils at the fishermen's rendezvous.

This May 26 was the anniversary of another heavy creel for him at this very place and under the same set of circumstances. Just as before, the hatch was so good, the rise so fine and his skill so keen that taking trout became routine. It was as automatic and certain as anything in anglerdom can be—though that's not much!

A dramatic voice with a once-familiar deep ring broke into L. C.'s kingdom of glory. "I've been observing my old student in his favorite pursuit. Your angling technique is superb and your success equally outstanding. You are to be complimented and envied. Could I but land a brace of trout some evening on the dry fly, it would be reward enough. How do you do it, Mr. Cribbs?"

[255]

L. C.'s hard features softened with a smile too condescending, too all-wise, to be pleasant. Yet there was in it a childish pleasure at being asked for the how-to.

"It's all in knowing how, Professor Heart," he puffed, in a slightly effortful, explosive manner. "Just give them what they want. Do everything just right. Make no mistakes. Then it's like taking candy from a baby."

The lecture continued, carefully free of specific advice. "The duffer's holiday is over," it concluded. "All the suicide trout are gone. From now on the men are separated from the boys. This is the most satisfying fishing of the year." And, after a pause, "The bunglers give up and the streams aren't so crowded."

The tall, gaunt old fellow flinched. A classroom problem rose like a ghost. To make the student want to learn is the teacher's hardest task and it had been hopeless against all trying with Cribbs, who had chosen his English 6, the Elizabethan poets, simply to fill his elective schedule with a course that looked like a snap, though it wasn't! But see the fellow now in this element, his province.

"I must be an exceptional duffer," the professor conceded amiably, eager to overlay and to forget L. C.'s discourtesy. "Yet I never give up, even though I admit I cannot capitalize on such a rise as we are witnessing this evening. It appears that the prime problem is the choice of fly. Would you tell an old bungler what pattern it is that works so admirably under these conditions?"

L. C. frowned as if in deep thought and his beady black eyes flashed toward the Number 18 Pale Evening Dun dangling from his long fine leader.

Then in Indian-fakir style he dug down fast and far. "Major-Domo, Professor, a Number 14 Major Domo." That was the bait he'd make his pupil swallow. "It's one of my special pets, absolutely indispensable."

So the quick lie trapped the honest naive professor.

"Thank you so much, Mr. Cribbs, for the valuable information. In due course I shall secure some."

"That's right, Professor. Don't be without them." And L. C. went on about his routine of filling out the limit.

As the old man melted into the deep evening shadows, L. C. sneered under his breath, "Goodbye, empty creel!"

In the more polite jargon of the angler, the swamp gas had taken effect. The sportsman and the sporting man had met and what a difference yawns between them!

Professor Heart well knew how time, effort and mentality underlie mastery. He took the advice graciously, not realizing that its inappropriateness would make a brass monkey or a granite angel weep.

"My flies are valueless," he admitted to himself. "I have nothing to satisfy the fastidious taste of these selective trout this evening. Apparently that Major Domo is mandatory. I'll procure some from Webb."

Appropriately named, "Spider" Webb produced his art on a commercial basis and right properly he prided himself on his beautiful attractors and deceivers and on his encyclopedic knowledge of patterns. Name one and he knew about it; ask him to tie it and he had the material and skill to produce it.

But when the kindly professor asked him, "Please tie for me one-half dozen Number 14 Major Domos, the indispensable pattern of Lucius Cribbs," Spider had to bluff. If he couldn't get the specifications from "The Dictionary of Trout Flies" he could wheedle them from L. C. when their paths crossed again. Let no one suspect that any fly whatsoever was unknown to him.

"All right," he agreed. "I'll be glad to oblige."

In due time Spider had his chance. "How do you like your Major Domo tied, L. C.?"

Already out on the limb, Little Caesar had to move farther along. "Well, let's see," he stalled; then got up steam. "Tail, bronze-blue hackle wisps; body, urine-burned fur from a vixen, with orange gantron ribbing; wings, grizzly hackle points tied spent; hackle, grizzly and ginger intermingled."

And that was that. All three parties, each in his own way, were to be satisfied.

Time's irresistible march went on and at last Spider produced the flies. Patient Professor Heart received them graciously and thankfully, Major Domos straight from the mind that had conceived and the hands that had fashioned them.

The bleak winter rolled along and at last came that glow in the east. Spring was mustering here forces for the grand march. Every trout fisherman eyed the calendar, daily tolling off the numbers until the traditional opening arrived.

Finally the fellows were at it again, satisfying that desire to emulate forebears who had won their food from nature. Little food these moderns won, in poundage, but their other rewards were rich beyond the dim dreams of prehistoric men. A relatively dry, advanced spring had put the streams in great shape. Trout rose to the hatches, which paraded in order. The dry fly reigned supreme. Small wonder that anglers live a hundred per cent alive and keep happy!

Inexorably came the unexpected and the entirely unpredictable.

The soft sun rays of late May left the stream and as the shadows slowly lengthened, the aquatic-insect world came alive. Above, scads of insects milled about the highest foliage. To blend with the sound of rippling water, the bird chorus produced a symphony that would have led an orchestra leader to throw up his hands in despair.

"By shallow rivers," murmured the professor from his form-fitting seat at the base of a streamside elm, "to whose falls melodious birds sing madrigals." He felt the same sort of glow that Izaak Walton must have when he too quoted those lines from "that smooth song which was made by Kit Marlowe." And Kit, too, wondered Heart, might he not have found time from his roystering and from his outpouring of genius to steal a now-and-then day of quiet fishing?

The changing greens along the stream reflected in the clear water and the rich colors in the western sky delighted his eyes. Bird lullabies, directed no doubt to the patient little hens on the nests of eggs, pleased his ears. He was at peace in his world.

Although he didn't realize it, he was not alone. Adjacent to the tail of the downstream flat stood an impatient figure. Keen eyes searched the treetops for the insect specimens. L. C. could hardly contain himself while the hatch developed. Why couldn't they pair up and mate faster? Why couldn't they drop their eggs from above sooner then fall on the water quicker? Surely no insects or any other animal life should question the majesty of man!

The initial rises of trout climaxed the fishing day as the first spent spinners dropped exhausted to the shimmering stream. Above the surface, the great dance was at its zenith. More and more of the delicate little insects performed their chief mission in life, the depositing of the precious egg masses in nature's dictated environment.

Anticipating the rise of trout, Cribbs moved into casting position. From his place in the middle of the tail of the pool he batted to the water with his rod tip one of the dipping insects and the current delivered it to his outstretched palm. Why, he wondered as he gave it close scrutiny, was this particular hatch so hard to imitate?

An angling accomplishment he desired was the development

of an effective fly pattern for this particular situation. It would solidify the one weak link in his almost perfect repertoire.

Sharp inspection assured him that his imitation did resemble the natural but somehow it never had worked. Could the reception of a trout's eye be so limited in scope and so magnified by its narrow compass that an effective artificial simply shouldn't appear to a human to resemble the natural? He might need to multiply his fly-tying effort. Was it really perfect?

But it was time to cast, for a trout had put up within range. Masterfully he worked out the line then lightly dropped the fly five feet above the spot.

The deceiver disappeared in a dimple but when he lifted his rod tip there was only a feeling of emptiness. With a fly which is not just right a trout has a way of effecting a last split-second rejection which causes a surface display. For a split-second, too, it stimulates the angler. Then the letdown comes, as swift a deflation as that of a sharp object piercing an inflated rubber raft, the blow-boat mariner's nightmare.

"All you did was drown it," Cribbs grumbled at the unobliging trout. "Same old story." A glance upstream revealed the professor had tied into a fish. "The accident of the year!" breathed L. C. whose jealously never lacked for tender loving care.

More and more trout refused the Cribbs counterfeit. L. C. cherished problem fishing and he had waxed eloquent on its solutions, but this "blasted hatch" exasperated him. In succession, the butterfly character of his moods changed from expectation to doubt, to hope and finally to despair. Again he noted, a hundred yards upstream, the professor was into another trout.

Little Caesar's attention was now divided between his own fishing and watching the upstream angler. Heart was busy playing, landing and releasing fish. Indeed, he spent more time on these operations than on casting. The two men differed in effectiveness as chalk differs from Cheddar cheese. L. C. was used to such contrasts and had gloried in them. This time fate had pulled the rug from under him and his vanity would limp lame.

Most of us bow to what's inevitable but not L. C. He left the scene of his failure absolutely fished out, like a fished-out stream, to catch that educator before he got away.

His uneasy approach led to the big elm beneath which the professor had day dreamed, not of great fish but of great fishing, more of beauties above than within the shining stream. Cribbs was about to call out his questions when a reel screamed.

[259]

"What's up, Professor?"

Back came the answer out of the failing light: "I am into the biggest trout with which I ever tangled."

"Do you need any help?"

"No! No, thank you. If I cannot land him without assistance I do not want him."

"How big?"

"Tremendous, I am certain."

Some minutes later it was apparent that the great fish was tiring, for the reel sang less stridently, less desperately. Time dragged by in still suspenseful seconds; then a flashlight, out on the stream, played on the water ruffled by the back of a big fish.

"I have him!" cried an excited voice. "He's in the net!" The angler spraddled out with his prize to the nearest land, the opposite bank.

The jubilant professor had outdone himself, had tasted the nectar of the gods. Never before had he taken a trout on his first cast, hooked fish in such rapid succession, or caught a big one on a dry fly. Now he knew the satisfaction that comes from fishing the water well and the pride that a real trophy brings. He admired the great spotted form in the bag of the net, then promptly administered the quietus. Lovingly he removed the bedraggled fly and dropped it into the fly-box.

"Come on over, Professor," half directed and half implored a subdued voice from under the elm.

"Be right there. I'd forgotten all but the fishing."

When Heart had sloshed up the other bank, with some assistance, he was effervescent. "This was the greatest evening of trout fishing I ever experienced! Never did I suspect that a fly pattern could be so efficient. It was plainly evident that the trout could not differentiate between it and the natural."

"But," interrupted L. C., "what d'ya use?"

"Your fly, my boy, your indispensable pattern. I owe you a great debt of gratitude. Had you not conveyed to me your cherished knowledge, last season, I should not have experienced this superlative evening. Several times, to make a comparison, I removed the great Major Domo and substituted another. The trout positively would not touch it but when I reverted to the real pattern it was, as you put it, 'like taking candy from a baby.' It is truly amazing how selective they can be. Their vision at close range must be most acute."

Little Caesar's sneering smile was now a reverse curve of

dejection. He hadn't the grace to bend before he broke. At this particular time of the season his pretty box of flies was so much dross. Too haughty to admit poor judgment, too proud to seek advices, he squirmed on the horns of a dilemma. Defeated, he muttered as he stole away into the night, "Major Domo, what can you be?"

Time was running low on the brief fly-fishing career of the professor, who had not turned to the outdoors for relaxation until past middle age, when his doctor advised him to do so. In spite of his eagerness to learn, the main points of refined angling had escaped his unguided approach until near the end. Since he was a lone wolf, but little helpful advice had flowed his way down the river of angling experience.

Now at last he understood. The idea is to deceive rising trout with a choice counterpart of nature, attached to a cobweb leader which appears to be too fine to hold and let it be carried to the fish ever so daintily and naturally. Then comes sinking the barb and playing the fish; and a bent rod, like an archer's bow, is a wonderful thing to feel.

All such moments of suspense, all the thrills of conflict in flat-flowing water, and the complete satisfaction of victory finally came to Professor Heart. Now he had become an angler in the strict sense of the word. He had, too, built his store of memories, those heart-beats of the past that can enliven any dull present—or even sweeten a sad present.

This tale of subterfuge is also the story of the brilliant span of Major Domo as it was fished by the Professor and never employed by any other.

CHAPTER 11

Well Eeled

THE RICH flat water by the house was a tough taskmaster. Not that the stream didn't harbor fine trout, well-conditioned and stream-bred, but the environment made for most exacting fishing if satisfactory results were to be obtained. Imitations had to be close, leaders fine and presentation perfect.

In spite of the stream's great challenge and the wonderful problem-fishing it presented—or maybe because of them—such water might not be the ideal medium to help breed into a boy a profound love of angling. So Curtis Q. Prentice was concerned.

Curtis Junior was twelve years old and so far he'd shown more interest in baseball and swimming than in fishing. It wasn't because of a lack of ample and fine tackle, either.

One afternoon when the elder Prentice returned from his law office, Junior met him at the home curve of the graveled drive, displaying a large fish. At late last he'd caught his first big brown trout.

Elated, the father admired the "mighty trout" and asked if it had put up a good fight. Deflated, Prentice took in the caveman answer, "Naw, all he did was try to get away. But I yanked him out on the bank, and the gut thing didn't break. He was my meat."

Now, a dry-fly purist is a happy sort of fellow in his sport but he's plagued with the wish to convert—oh, say two or three—good friends to it; and naturally an only son is a top candidate for his plots and plans. Suggest, encourage, aid—why, sure, but there's also planting the seed of wanting to know. Was Junior desert dust for the nurture of this grand lifelong sport, and with it right at his door, too, a part of the patrimony he'd inherit?

Youth calls to youth, they say, and when a new family moved into the modest farm home downstream it wasn't long before Junior and Roosevelt Jones met and took to each other. Eldest of an ever-increasing tribe, "Rosie" was a whizbang in the ageless campaign of boy vs. fish. In his first home country he'd been "learned good," and in the ruthless Rosie, Junior recognized a considerable fellow in his own right.

[262]

Young Jones saw in his new friend one endowed with the greatest array of equipment he'd ever marveled at—and plenty for two. So at first he overlooked the vast age gap of three years and before he knew it both boys were knit together as allies who had in them more than a light salting of the piratical.

The senior Curtis was pleased, even though the thought ate him that too darn many trout were being killed out of the stream. At the Prentice table they had plenty, and the Jones crowd, as he'd glimpsed them from his car, looked better nourished than ever before.

At any rate, Junior was over the hump. His father's delight sparkled as the boy traveled the cherished line and no longer a question mark hung on the horizon. "Good work, Roosevelt!"

All Junior needed now was the channeling into sportsmanship, fly tying and advanced angling technique. On his thirteenth birthday Junior was given a still finer fly rod and line-to-fit, with these words: "This is a *lar*, a household god. The fly rod in America must enjoy a popularity and respect comparable only to those of the long-bow in England and the rifle in Switzerland." (Prentice's legal summings-up had won fame in the county courthouse for their ringing eloquence, though at times they ran long enough to set off a shuffling of feet and a clearing of throats.)

But Junior's casting had become a lovely thing to see. Streamcraft, too, was taking form, and thanks to Rosie he certainly knew where the trout were and how to sneak up on them.

His mother, though, couldn't understand his increasing practice of being late at meals or missing them entirely with the excuse, " 'Don't run away from rising trout;' that's what Pappy says."

An admonishing mother would counter with, first, "Please don't call your father 'Pappy'," and second, "We cannot tolerate tardiness or absenteeism at mealtime." All this ran off Junior like rain from an otter's back. It was discouraging, too, when paternal action failed to back up maternal demands.

In these sword-crossings Father always assumed the mediator's chair and expressed emotions that quelled Priscilla. "Graceful deportment sits well, my dear, but remember, our son must prepare himself for the golden days. He will reach his heart's desire out fishing, rejoice in it and realize that 'The best things in life are free.' This is his critical period of transition. Intent and intelligence, or lack thereof by the user, are the accountable agents. He must be equipped to dig down into the fishing lore stored in his brain and enjoy the solid foundation of angling built on experience. This is not just a pastime but a sport that is an art. A great force urges him. He must pursue the latent desire to follow remote ancestors who by necessity lived mainly on the fruits of fishing and hunting. Then it was all defense or offense—war of chase. In a climate of freedom there always will be room for adventure. Mark you, one of these days he will produce a brisk surprise."

This is a good sample. There were others like it, but even audience boredom can't kill truth, of which these dissertations were samples, too.

That summer Priscilla finally surrendered to her two wonderful anglers. Matters of consternation became the inevitable and so accepted. As for daughter Mary Ann, she kept her convictions locked in a calm silence. With a different father and a different brother she might have learned delight in the song of the stream but she had what she had.

The next father-and-son step came by bribery. Junior must think in terms of quality and conservation, of sport and not of kill. He must return all small trout and for an offsetting reward he'd receive 25 cents a foot for fish over twelve inches long.

This proposition came next morning before father Prentice left for the office. Junior was satisfied and seemed to comprehend the angles.

But the heavenly choir must have wept—or more likely laughed—as campaign strategy took shape that afternoon. When Rosie heard of the new deal he quickly dominated the situation.

"Judas Priest! Will we make a lot of money! We're in business, big business. We'll split fifty-fifty. D'you know what a sittin' duck is?" Junior was pretty sure; so Rosie divulged his plan.

That afternoon money destroyed ethics as gunpowder destroyed the historical epoch of the armored knight on his great charger. Necessity's two children, Ingenuity and Patience, took over.

With this prospect of private enterprise Junior sought from his father, at dinner that night, a reaffirmation of the proposition.

"That's still a deal, is it, Pappy? A quarter a foot?"

"Yes, son, but I'd rather not be called 'Pappy'."

"Okay, No matter how well I do, it still sticks?"

"Certainly. A deal is a deal." And with finality he added. "More power to you!"

Reassured, Junior impatiently awaited permission to leave the table to join his new business associate and "go to work."

[264]

As the screen door slapped behind the departing boy, the summer breeze carried back prophetic words: "Sittin' ducks. I'll hit the jackpot and be well heeled!"

"Young America," sighed Priscilla. "In a way, though, I hate to see the children grow up; they're so innocent. Where do you suppose he got the idea that it's acceptable to call us 'Pappy' and 'Maw'?"

"From the Jones boy, no doubt. But we can't separate those kindred spirits. Then, too, Roosevelt's strong and capable, a good person to have around in case of emergency."

Finally the evening star shone; then an orange moon cast its eerie glow just above the horizon and through the thickly leaved trees. A concerned mother turned to her husband. "I have a feeling that something's not right. Won't you go out and look for Junior?"

"Nonsense," declared Father. "Now is the time the big trout are moving from cover and smaller ones are surface feeding. Little wonder he hasn't come back. Just be patient. He'll barge in safe and happy and possibly successful. Give him another half hour. You must understand how anxious I am to see him develop into a polished angler with a deep passion for rising trout."

That had to do and in time Junior made his return. It was noisy and triumphant. "You owe me at least four bucks, Pappy. Look it!" With difficulty he swung a reeking burlap bag from his back to the porch floor. His mother was aghast at his disorder and wetness.

"What is it, Junior?" Curtis Prentice let his guard down. Anxiously he spread wide the mouth of the sack and peered into the dark recess.

"Junior," challenged Priscilla, "you're a mess! It's late, and we were worried."

"Aw, shucks, Maw."

"'Mother,' not 'Maw'," corrected Mary Ann, the unbreakable.

Prim and proper Priscilla Prentice cautiously approached the dirty bag to peer into it, believing—bless her!—that that was the thing to do. Her soul was attuned to less grotesque things than the sight which met her eyes. She recoiled.

Mary Ann's courage and curiosity held, though she moved up with caution. Unlike her mother, Mary Ann made no attempt at control. A raucous- and venom-laden-voice exclaimed, "Horrors! Snakes!"

Viewed against its gracious background, Junior's loot of eels lost much of its glamor. No one answered his question: "Aren't they beauts? There's about eighteen feet of 'em, don't you figger?"

"Say 'Good night,' Junior, and go to bed." Father saw the need of taking over, and reluctantly Junior followed the directive.

"This is amazing," Curtis Prentice said a moment later. "Stretched out, they're as long as a polygamist's clothesline. Predatory creatures! They have no place in a trout stream. It's good riddance. Possibly he can eliminate some more and we must encourage him. We'll have one for dinner tomorrow. I'll clean it tonight."

"Horrors!" reiterated Mary Ann. "Eat snakes?"

"Please don't wear thin my patience," remonstrated her father. "Eels are fish, not reptiles. Those that come from clean places are of fine sweet flesh. As unidentified seafood you'd relish them. The boy shan't be discouraged. I want both you and Mother to eat some. And," he added, "a compliment or two would be appropriate. Look on it as scientific exercise."

"What will we do with so many eels?" quavered Mrs. Prentice.

"I'll clean one and dispose of the others. No doubt they'll be most welcome in the Jones household."

Well after midnight the struggle to separate hide from flesh ended.

"Like trying to turn a garden hose inside-out," Curtis had to admit to himself. "Hereafter I'll employ Roosevelt Jones' services for anything like this. It will look better," he reassured himself, "after being cut into sections and fried to a golden brown."

The next day's dinner proved to be an occasion. First came the payoff with fanfare, Junior separating his father from five dollars. He was duly complimented on being a provider of family sustenance. Mother actually disposed of a serving of eel, and Father played the role of a gourmand. Mary Ann, though she had nothing to say, nibbled a little and managed to get some down. As for Junior, he proclaimed it "the best-tasting meat ever brought to the house." It made a happy family scene.

Wiping a greasy mouth, Junior announced, "I'm full. Will you excuse me so I can catch some more while the gettin' is good?"

"Remember our house rule, Junior," restrained Mother. "We understand your eagerness. After we've all finished dessert you will be excused."

[266]

The head of the house bridged the gap. "Your feat yesterday was remarkable. What did you use for bait? When I was a boy my favorite was a piece of tied meat."

"You said it," answered young Nimrod.

"Tell us, Junior, did they put up a good fight on your new rod?"

There's no special warmth in being perceived. "Well," the boy stalled, "I didn't exactly play 'em."

The father looked at his son with cross-examining eyes, "What did you do?"

"Oh, they were trapped."

"You mean you used your wits to bring about their capture?"

"Yeh, that's it. When they ran inside an old milk can we lifted the can and dragged it out on the bank."

"Did you trap them all at once?" Suspicion entered Father's mind.

"Nope. It wasn't that easy. Just one at a time. But I know we can get some more."

"You mean from the same hiding place?"

"Yeh, Pappy."

" 'Father'," sighed Mary Ann.

"There's more there, mebbe a lot more. Once one's chased out, we block the hole so he can't get back in. Sometimes he hides in the can."

Father looked at him dubiously. "You mean they stay in a place with but one opening, which can be closed?"

"Yep. When one comes out we block it fast with a piece of board before he can turn 'round and go back in."

"Why, how clever, Junior!" exulted Mother.

"What do you mean by 'we'?" demanded Father.

"Me and Rosie."

" 'Rosie and I'," enunciated Sister, distinctly.

"How do you chase them out?" Father was puzzled.

"That's easy, Pap—Father." The female chorus died aborning. Junior went blithely on. "I pound hard with a club."

"Just where is this stronghold of eels in our trout stream?" In the practice of law you learn infinite patience.

"Down in the next meadow. 'Bout halfway down, above the big bend."

Wrinkles furrowed the attorney's brow. "I can't understand why eels would congregate there. It's shallow water and not much cover. What is this hiding place?"

"Well, you see, Father, Horst's old mare passed out there."

[267]

"You mean she's dead?" asked Sister.

"Yep, she died right at the bank and fell into the water. All you got to do is beat her hard on the belly and an eel comes out."

Mary Ann retreated violently to the porch railing and unswallowed. Mother turned green and bolted. They'd heard enough, though not all.

"Just one question," Father managed. "Where is the head of the horse?"

"Oh, that's on the bank; she didn't drown. They come out the other end."

Suddenly Junior found himself alone at the table, the crisp five-dollar bill in his hand, and in his ear the ringing words, "Just trout from now on." It was the pronouncement of the law, the judge and the jury.

Fourteen hours later, Curtis said to his much deflated son, "You've reached the depths . . . but I know it was fun. How about some real fishing now and we'll take in Rosie, too?"

"They're moving away this Saturday."

"That being the case, I'm sorry for you'll certainly miss Rosie, but I'll try to make it up to you."

That made the biggest lie Curtis Prentice had ever told, a fair prophecy and a promise kept, all in one straight-out sentence.

CHAPTER 12

Whirl Away, McSneek

THE HISTORY of fishing for sport is a story of refinement.
Sharp competition develops advanced operators and operations.
Resourceful anglers use their heads—or more formally, "improve
their technique"—to beat the game.

But there's nothing final about this and fish wise up too.
Although trout rise and strike when hunger overcomes shyness,
they do become more alert and shy under pressure. Smarter
fish, the surviving fittest, are pitted against improved technique.

Tall, firmly-knit, serious-looking Curtis Prentice believed this.
His lawyer's mind told him it was so and for precedent he
quoted his old wrestling coach: "There's a break for every hold,"
and "Always change a losing game." Sooner or later man or
fish must win; there could be no lasting stalemate.

But the gently fanning fins of a great old brown trout in the
stream that wound through his country-home property waved
his argument away. All Curtis knew—and that was plenty—he
couldn't take the old fellow. Ever resourceful, the lawyer surrendered gracefully and used the situation as a show-piece of
evidence to prove how wise a trout can be.

Mid summer it was, with Japanese beetles in full bloom and
the water low and clear. Majestically the big trout would rock
up in his unique line of drift and with complete confidence
take one of those irridescent foreign importations. This delighted
all observers. "Look at that big surface feeder!" Curtis would
gloat. "See that line of drift he's chosen."

This particular evening veteran dry-fly fisherman Adam Beck
and young Frank Hunter were his audience and there couldn't
have been a wiser or more appreciative one. "Now you see,"
said Prentice, "the willingness of a well-conditioned big trout
to rise freely. You two engineer fly designs and style of delivery
but I'd like to see you contend with this situation."

The trout had taken his station under the drooping boughs
of a weeping willow which a violent wind had uprooted some
years ago and laid across the stream. The foot-thick butt had
lodged atop a rock that broke the complete fall so that two main
sectors angled over the stream like the ears of a running rabbit.

New branches, green wood, rose heavenward from the trunk, in effect a line of young trees, each arching its limbs so that the water's surface was a perfect haven of the limp snags of trailing leaves and tough slender stems. Into this verdant mass the line of drift funneled into a "V." Deep in this conical opening, where few sunrays filtered through, lay the trout's fortress. Confidently he surface fed at every provocation.

A nearby rose bush provided plenty of ammunition, and as fast as Curtis tossed beetles gathered therefrom into the current they were carried to the feeding station and engulfed in blood-stirring rises. "He won't let a one go by!" cried Adam. "He takes them with reckless abandon."

The old chap studied the lush vegetation and the adjacent cash crops. He recognized a still more valuable crop, trout. "You have a problem here," he remarked, "and it's tough enough to rate special attention. Interesting," he mused, "interesting."

"What do you think of him, Adam? Isn't he superb?"

"He sure is! He's asking for trouble, though, with that brazen display. Yep. Yep, he is."

"Trouble?" Curtis was rocked. "Why, the Devil himself couldn't cope with such a preposterous proposition. See all those trailing leaves!"

"I don't know about Old Scratch, even if he used his pitchfork, but I know who might hook and play him and do it cleanly too."

"How?" exploded Curtis. "I'd have to see that. It just can't be."

"As the songs says, 'With a little bit of luck'." Adam looked at Frank. "Curtis can bet on the trout; I'll bet on you, Boy." Then in all seriousness he spoke the cryptic words, "Whirl away, McSneek!"

Apparently Frank understood, for he nodded.

"Go to it, Boy," urged curious Curtis. "It'll take a brilliant exhibition of hooking and playing and I want to see it. I won't laugh when you lose. In spite of Adam's confidence I think it's impossible."

Adam turned to Frank, too, his blue eyes twinkling. "You're dying for an evening's fishing. Haven't had it for a full twenty hours!"

Head and broad shoulders bent in sharp attention, Frank inspected his leader, then tied to the end tippet the fly of his choice. Observant Curtis noted from a distant that it was big and wild and looked nothing like the natural upon which the trout was feeding.

[270]

Frank took a casting position some sixty feet upstream from the feeding station and in as direct a line with the churning V as the bank let him. The young man's false casts were positive and Curtis thought that they drove the fly through the air harder than necessary. It seemed there was a strange noise as it swished back and forth.

Curtis cocked an ear and turned to Adam. "What's that buzzing?"

"That's McSneek winding up."

"I don't get it."

"Watch."

Frank cut loose. The cast looked bad to Curtis—very sloppy. It rose high as though the line had inadvertently slipped from Frank's fingers, then the fly fluttered to the surface on a sort of pile of loose leader at least ten feet above the logical destination. Much to Curtis's surprise, Adam exclaimed, "Just right!"

Lazily steadily the big fly rode on the limpid water into the gaping whirl of the entanglement. All this time, the leader slowly straightened. There was something fateful in the progress.

Adam could stand it no longer. "Whirl away!" he cried.

Frank lifted the rod tip, tautening line and leader. The fly responded, flipping and flopping on the water, dizzily moving deep in the V. A slight lift of the tip set it wobbling upstream, jitterbug fashion.

Quietly, as though exhausted, it drifted back into the V. Before the wig of leaves could entangle it, the rod checked it. Again twisting and flipping on the surface, it seemed to dance to the angler's rhythm like a live insect desperately giving its all to become airborne.

There came a surge and a most impressive boil.

"He's on!" cried Adam. "Good boy!"

"But not for long," thought Curtis, smiling secretly.

The trout settled back, deep under the willow sanctuary, without panic, confusion or bolting. There was only smug complacency.

"Good," said Adam. "That's the 'little bit of luck' we needed. Now here goes!"

Frank did what the lawyer considered a strange thing. He pointed the rod tip directly at the fish and transferred the cork grip to his left hand. His right clamped down and froze the reel. Deliberately, cautiously he backed up, the fish making no apparent resistance. Amazed, Curtis watched him walk that big, strong, fresh trout right out of its impregnable hiding place.

One jump or one roll, which Curtis fully expected, and the leader would have been hopelessly fouled in the draping foliage, but the fish resisted not one bit. Slowly Frank walked backwards ten, forty, eighty feet, the fish merely hanging on and letting itself be towed away from security.

Frank eased forward a couple of steps. Up came the rod.

Adam turned to an open-mouthed Curtis. "Boy can press his advantage now."

Suddenly the fish wakened into action, turned tail and bolted downstream; but, as though it were winded, the run didn't carry to the willow. Frank worked it back, reeling with the rod tip high. Subsequent runs were weaker. If the hook held it would be only a question of time and unrelenting skill. The hook held.

Expertly the angler netted the great prize for them all to admire. Big and blocky, beautifully proportioned, with spots standing out like dark polkadots on a light tie; it was a very special specimen of a female brown. Frank slipped the hook from her jaw and gently eased her from the net and back to freedom. "Can't liquidate a creature like you, the top performer in the meadow. In a day or two you'll be operating as before. Be more careful. Good luck!"

Adam winked at Curtis, enormously proud of his protege. Full satisfaction is a quiet thing.

Their host was silent as he watched the great form regain equilibrium and slide from sight into the channel. Then, as though recovering sociability, he smiled at them. "I've witnessed the incredible—no, the impossible. Never saw or heard of anything like it."

He shook the bewilderment from his brain as a dog sheds water from his coat. "We must conduct a post-mortem. Obviously Frank and the trout did exactly as you expected, but . . ."

Adam's happy laugh interrupted him. "Everything was just right. Did you pick a loser?"

"I'm learning a lesson. Please talk."

"We call it 'whirl away, McSneek.' It's our standard procedure with a downstream cast into an obstruction. Where a natural drift is too complicated we make McSneek dance in the trout's window."

"McSneek, then, is the fly?"

"Yes, and best of all for the purpose, but our McSneek is different. First let me tell you about the origin of the pattern, then what we do to it.

[272]

"Four members of the Anglers' Club of New York decided to tie, at the vise in the club-room, a fly that would embody favorite features of each of them. Step by step a pattern developed with a black hackle wisp tail, black ostrich herl body with a wide silver band à la Royal Coachman, white fan wings and black hackle. These men were MacGregor, Smith, Neefus and Knight. Mostly from initials, they created the name Mc-Sneek. Soon after, Jack Knight told us of the pattern.

"Then along comes Fred Everett to fish with us for his first time in limestone water. He was a gay spirit. Those who got to know him well, on his many trips into these parts, miss him . . . When he first showed up he wasn't prepared for our water—flies too large, leaders too heavy. His first day was rough. Little Caesar, the gadgeteer, was brazen enough to tell him that evening he'd better read the Winchester chapter in Lord Grey's classic, *Fly Fishing*, so he'd understand that dry fly fishing is an exacting science. Fred laughed it off but at his first opportunity he read the book.

"He was a good performer; make no mistake about that. The second day he taught us something, even though he had to struggle with what L. C. called 'bull-rope and balloons.' In his box were some Fan Wing Royal Coachmen he'd tied with double wings—two thicknesses. The idea was a fly with air resistance enough to twist the leader. Sound queer? Once on the water, the leader'd unwind and twirl the fly. Fred called it jitter-bugging, and he jitterbugged with success. He'd cast it downstream on a 7½ foot, 2X tapered leader.

"Fred never carried a net and he took delight that day in calling in that pot-bellied little dictator. 'Help, L. C.!' he'd holler. 'I've got another good one at my feet. Do you want to scoop him'?"

"Good for Everett!" broke in Curtis.

"Frank and I," Adam continued, "adapted Fred's principle to various fan wing patterns. Finally we settled on McSneek. We use it only in special situations."

"Like under weeping willows," interrupted the good loser.

"And in front of brush piles and beds of cress," added Frank.

"A light dawns," smiled the host. "Now I understand your 'Whirl away, McSneek,' a double fan wing on a stout leader cast downstream. But how about that strange business of leading the trout away from the willow?"

Adam turned to Frank. "Explain this to Curtis," he laughed, "if you can."

"I can't explain why, for I don't know; but I can say that Mr. Beck discovered how to tow a hooked fish that hasn't gone into action, if you do it slowly and carefully. You can't do it, though, by reeling. Fish resist the sound or feel of the metallic click telegraphed along the line. Maybe a throbbing rod enters the picture, too. A low rod, frozen reel and careful walking are something else again. For some reason they rarely resist them. The trick's to move them far enough from the hideout so that when they get scared and bolt for home they're too far from base to make it safely. The long power run eats up strength— makes them somewhat like a punched-out boxer."

"Suppose," ventured Curtis, "that fish hadn't taken McSneek on the first try, what then?"

"Give him time to forget," Adam replied promptly. "Maybe he saw the heavy leader. Go away, come back later, try again. Sooner or later—and often sooner—he decides to take a pass at that animated fraud. As you know, trout feed more confidently close to cover than in the open."

Curtis, ever appreciating craftsmanship and trying to learn, caught on fast. "I see," he said. "You two had a plan, really a system. You could easily have weegled me into a bet on long odds, for I'd have considered I had a sure thing. Know something? I thought I knew all the tricks of you experts but evidently some don't get into print. This was the most unique exhibition I ever saw, and I'm the richer for it. Could be there's no such thing as an impossible angling situation."

"There isn't." Adam was positive, and neither of them doubted him.

CHAPTER 13

Enchanted Meadow

SOME CALLED him Mr. Angler—and he loved it. When in action, the fly rod appeared to be a part of him and flies as they came from his vise were masterpieces of the craft; he was keen, observant, resourceful, and experienced, a highly efficient operator. His conceit would have been complete except for one thing. He never received an invitation from old Obie to fish the famous Enchanted Meadow, a rendezvous of the most ardent anglers and some of the greatest. A thick hide covered his stubby little frame, which shrugged off his initialed nickname, L. C., which stood for Little Caesar.

The life of the elderly Oberdick over the years was centered around trout. When Obie was not fishing his beloved Enchanted, he was conducting related experiments: redistribution of insects, stream improvement, development of finer strain, in fact anything which might have a bearing on the fishing in the meadow. To all his angling friends, he was Mr. Trout.

L. C. knew a great deal about the Oberdick setup, in spite of the fact that it was not his privilege to fish there. It irked him all the more because the old man loved to show it off to his fishing guests and anglers talked about it a great deal. It was particularly obnoxious to him when someone, upon learning that he did not fish the famous meadow, registered surprise. He passed it off by implying that he did not care to go there—too easy, too many trout. Even this explanation got him into trouble, for some claimed that it was fishing of the most exacting type: smooth, slow flowing, clear water, an abundant food supply and shy fish because they were fished over every day of the season, many being hooked and released.

Problem fishing was what L. C. loved above all else and he had made his reputation by taking fish under exacting conditions. Dainty surface feeders were his favorite target, selective rises a prime challenge. He had no peer at picking them out of lines of drift situated deep under overhanging foliage. The man was an artist.

Reconciled to the fact that requests or connections would not bring about the desired invitation, he vented his wrath on the old man, belittling his efforts as a technician and has capabilities as an angler.

It was the season of the year for the great Mayfly hatch on Little River and a dozen club members were on hand in the hope of experiencing the best fishing of the year. Grouped around the club's great fireplace, they were discussing the evening of fishing just completed and appraising the possibilities of the hatch and rise during the course of the next few days.

L. C. was in his element and he was gloating; he had caught a 20-inch brown trout that evening.

"I knew his hideout and I knew the feeding place he would move into at dusk. It was simply a matter of outwaiting him. He tops last year's record fish for the club. However, I might do better yet, for I know where there is another every bit as good which I'll work on tomorrow evening."

"You caught a fine fish," said the lawyer, "something to be proud of. I congratulate you. It is very much like the one I saw Obie land last Tuesday evening when the hatch broke in his meadow."

L. C. flushed. Like a fencer, he struck at the opening.

"The old man, of course, catches a lot of fish; but he's not really great at the tough situations. He'll get by on the routine fishing but he lacks resourcefulness and real casting ability. I'd like to take him on in his own back yard and show him how to pick off those pets of his."

"He knows every hiding place, every feeding station, yes, every fish in that water," interjected the doctor. "He would look good anywhere else, too. As far as I am concerned, he is the old master."

"Correct," added the proprietor of the restaurant. "And the man never drew breath who could outfish him in that water."

"That's a lot of bunk," countered L. C. "How can he be that good? He's too feeble to reach out accurately for the tough ones and his eyesight is not keen enough to catch everything that goes on. I have seen some of his flies, too, and I don't think they are so wonderful. If he became involved in a contest with a real fisherman, he'd take a beating."

As he spoke with finality, his keen eyes, like those of a hawk, went from one to the other in the group. "If you fellows are afraid to arrange such a meeting, I regard it as an admission on your part that you realize it would be no contest. If the old man says 'no,' we'll all know that he is afraid of taking a beating on his own place."

Having announced his ultimatum, he picked up his empty glass, rose to his feet, and started across the room. Looking over his shoulder, he added, "I'll be back directly; then you let me know whether you are all talk or whether you're game."

In another minute he returned, glass refilled. "Well, are you afraid, or is it a deal?"

The powerful lawyer could take it no longer. "If we arrange such a contest, will you be quiet?"

"Yes, I'll even go somewhere else and celebrate."

"All right. I'll tell Obie exactly what you have said and ask him if he'll go through with it. Now, are you satisfied?"

"Partly. What are the bets?"

"My rod against yours."

"Fine."

"My reel and line against yours." Adam backed up Curtis.

"Right."

"My box of flies against yours," volunteered Doctor Hoffman.

"Splendid!" And L. C. deserted the group.

When Curtis Prentice explained the situation to Obie, the old fellow was agreeable. "I would like to see for myself just how good he actually is. Friends tell me he is fantastic. This places me in the position of a competitor, not a host. There is a special reason why he is never an invited guest. Let's make it next Saturday, an all-day affair with an hour out for lunch, which will be ready for us at the house.

"There is only one thing though." The old man registered uncertainty. "We may lose. The best line of drift in the entire area is at the far side of the wide water by the cliff. The finest concentration of trout in the meadow is located there and there always exists some surface feeding activity. No longer am I able to reach it with a long cast. Maybe he can and maybe he will recognize its potential. That could beat us."

The Enchanted Meadow was an interesting phenomenon. Obie's father had operated a quarry and a limekiln near his house. One day a blast opened a fissure in the great ledge and a tremendous channel of ground water belched forth. In short order it filled the little basin from which stone had been removed and swamped the limekiln. The stream of water worked its way across a flat field and entered the big creek at the extremity of the Oberdick property. Sometimes when ground water is tapped at a quarry, pumping makes it possible to continue operations but in this instance the volume was too great. Mr. Oberdick simply transferred his activity to another side of the hill, where he constructed a new limekiln. Ultimately the stream became the pride and joy of his son, who possessed a passionate interest in angling and had a natural inclination toward scientific research.

Over the years, Obie developed it into the most extraordinary trout fishing. The course of the stream was altered so that it meandered through the field, actually tripling the distance of its original course. Just before it spilled into the creek, it cut against a ledgy wooded hill, half a mile by stream from the spring but only two hundred yards in a straight line. The old quarry bed was now a spectacular quarter-acre pond and trout actually swam in and out of the kiln.

The outside of the undercut banks at the bends had been planted in red osier dogwood and black alder. Here and there were clumps of the hemlocks into which the aquatic duns flew for their molt. There was no necessity to step into the water; it was like fishing from a lawn. The greatest width was 100 feet; but, for the most part, it was 50 to 60 feet wide. The depth, to a large degree, was uniform, three to four feet.

Obie saw to it that it contained a fine head of trout of a specially selected strain. Angling was kept on a high sporting plane with a minimum of killing.

The short stream contained stream-bred fish, for Obie was able to develop successful spawning conditions by dumping many tons of river gravel in the section with the fastest flow, that area between the little pond and the flat meadow. The stream which the short Enchanted fed was a warm-water creek, hence there was no possibility of a supplementary supply of migrating trout.

The group which gathered there that fair June Saturday was most certainly prejudiced. Obie had a rooting section but it was a polite and reserved one. Everyone who was going to be there arrived well before the starting time, 10 o'clock.

There was nothing new to L. C. about this sort of water. He knew that it was a matter of fine leaders and special flies and he had come prepared. Low-riding imitations of the black ant, the little cinnamon ant, and the leaf hoppers were vital. In the evening, there might be a need for the high-riding sulphur fly to imitate the yellow drake. In his fly box was a full compartment of each one of these four patterns, in addition to various and sundry standard dry flies, which he knew would be of little or no use in this water.

Since there was still an hour before the contest would get

underway, L. C. made a tour of inspection but in order that no trout would be frightened or made suspicious, he kept well back from the water's edge. He walked all the way down to the end, then loitered opposite the wide water at the cliff.

"No matter what happens, there will be no welshing," he announced, as he joined the group. "Is that clear?"

"Agreed," consented Obie, and the rest nodded.

Registering relief, L. C. continued, "I saw enough coming up to keep me very busy for a while. This is going to be a day packed with action." But he wasn't taking any chances; he was going to learn everything he could so the situation would be under perfect control.

Next he directed his attention to the source. A footbridge, with a railing on the lower side, crossed the stream at the tail of the pond. It served a triple purpose: casts could be made from it into the little pond nestled in an amphitheater of honey-suckle-draped ledges; it could be used as a catwalk to get to a strategic position on the other side of the stream to fish the dropoff of the gravel bed; and it was utilized by Obie for the distribution of additional, clean, loose gravel.

As L. C. carefully and slowly made his way on the walk, Obie turned to the doctor. "He has already located the con-centration downstream at the foot of the cliff. Look at him now, spotting them in the pond with the aid of those special sun glasses. He has things pretty well lined up—he's smart."

It was apparent that L. C. was satisfied with what he found above the bridge. He turned around and directed his attention to the rippled gravel area below. Long and hard those searching eyes covered the water.

Turning to his friends, Obie advised, "there are a lot of little trout over the shallow gravel, but right where it drops off into the deeper, slower water, there are quite a few good fish. It is the only place in the whole meadow where they take well when you fish the water. When there is not much coming up, I always try it here, but it is more interesting to be able to fish the rise."

Now L. C. investigated possibilities under the bridge. He leaned over the high rail and bent his neck like a goose.

"There are big fish under that overhead cover," Obie com-mented to the group around him.

L. C. must have spotted something of special interest, for he peered intently at one spot. Cautiously he changed his position to get a better angle. He stretched further—the gooseneck arched even more. Suddenly the fly box slipped out of the front pocket of his wading vest. It bounced off a protruding crossbar which supported the boardwalk. The lid flew open and dry flies jumped in all directions. Some dived directly to the surface and others fluttered off on tangents.

The water was diverted in two general directions at this point by a heavy post which was a bridge support. It divided into two main funnels. From this, sinuous currents rippled away like the muscular structure of a boxer's back. A gross of dry flies jauntily rode on the surface, like a raft of ducks. The coverage and distribution was amazing.

Suddenly L. C. snapped out of it. His mouth closed and he was transformed into a bundle of energy. Quickly he covered the 50 feet of catwalk to the bank, made a swivel-hip turn like a shifty halfback, sprinted 100 feet down the meadow, jumped into the stream, and plowed toward the center as water flew.

He shook his head and seemed to fumble in various directions at one time.

"Take off your glasses, L. C.," shouted Adam. "You can't see through them now."

Little rings on the surface of the water made their appearance. They were made by feeding fish. Trout were deliberately picking out the artificials which looked good. The flotilla was diminishing in number. The trout in the gravel area were particularly busy little fellows.

The advanced guard of the flies arrived at the dropoff. Dimples in the surface were now deeper and the widening rings heavier. Fly after fly disappeared.

L. C. started to snatch but all he did was submerge the first several flies. He changed tactics permitting one to drift into a half-submerged palm. It hesitated for an instant in the backwater and, as he raised a closing hand, it sailed around the side. It was a confounding proposition. Finally he made an accurate grab and he had recovered his first. Then he retrieved the fly box.

Now L. C. was getting the knack of it. He came in on the fly from the back with a quick motion. Most of them he went after in this way were recovered. He would make a successful grab, slap the fly in the box and grab again. Before his artificial hatch spent its course, he had reduced to possession only two dozen.

"Remember, L. C.," reminded the doctor, "no matter what happens, no welshing."

The bedraggled contestant emerged from the stream. His face was purple with frustration.

"It's time to start," announced Curtis.

L. C. collected his tackle and made a bee-line for the end of the meadow.

He attached a sodden fly to his leader, dried it by blowing on it violently, then started his casting. Seventy, eighty, ninety feet, finally the fly was drifting over the incessant feeders at the base of the ledge. One by one and cast after cast deliberate forms moved under the fly, their noses about three inches from it; and one by one, they sank out of sight, the fly untouched. It looked interesting to them but not good enough. After a few more floats, they did not even move up to take a look, the pattern was not right.

Everywhere it was the same situation, rejection of the fly. There were plenty of willing takers, some of which were very fine fish, but every last one seemed to be immune to the remnants of the wares of L. C.'s box. Their relatives up stream had taken care of that by gobbling up all the good ones. Like the weary boxer who can no longer raise his hands, Little Caesar was through.

Meanwhile, further up the meadow, Obie, fishing carefully, was landing one about every ten minutes.

By intermission time, he had released an even dozen and kept one big fish. One would be enough; he knew that. The score was 13 to 0.

"This is no contest," L. C. admitted, from the depths of a tortured soul.

"In all rivalries," admonished Adam, "the contestants must be in fine shape and well prepared. Furthermore, one bad mistake is frequently fatal to success. Do you admit defeat? If you capitulate, the contest is terminated."

L. C. nodded.

"All right," added the doctor, "then you have no one to blame but yourself. Now take your choice! You can honor your debt by surrendering your equipment, or you can keep your equipment and henceforth sever all connections and associations with each one in this group."

L. C.'s eyes fell, as he considered the proposition.

"Here," he bluntly stated, as he pushed the equipment into the doctor's hands. "Give the other two what is theirs." With that, he beat a hasty retreat. There would be no more fishing of the Enchanted for him.

CHAPTER 14

Oblivion and Resurrection

"LIKE OSCAR Wilde's dead mackerel in the moonlight," remarked maturing Frank Ward Hunter to his aging friend, Adam Beck, "it glitters, but man, does it stink! The defeat of justice is tragic and when it has to do with nature there's always a penalty. Right now I feel like the over-zealous hen on sterile eggs. I need your help and all the other help I can get. We've got to start the ball rolling and all the bells ringing."

No wonder Frank was concerned. Things had headed up to a planned meeting at which Judge Francis Funk would preside and—he hoped but couldn't believe—be on his side, a side on which he stood by conscience, by reason, by rooted conviction.

But there was an old feud between the Hunter-Ward family and Judge Miles Funk. The warring Hunters and Wards had joined the passing years and only Frank's mother and Judge Francis Funk, her contemporary and a bachelor, remembered clearly what the quarrel had been about. To the rest of the town it had presented a mystery, spicy, guessed at tirelessly, but not understood.

Frank's father and grandfather had been rabid—"good haters," as eighteenth century Dr. Samuel Johnson would have put it. Periodically they had reminded young Frank to "never have anything to do with Funk." The only reason given was, "He talked too much and we didn't like what he said."

Frank had never heard his widowed mother speak on the subject or even mention Judge Francis Funk's name. Whenever Frank broached the matter she terminated it with a finality that suggested a wish to forget. "My boy, we won't talk about that."

The old ill feeling had affected Frank little, for up to now he and the judge had not been thrown together. They belonged to different churches and civic groups. Mutual friends had been the only possible link, for the judge had no living relatives, and the townspeople knew enough never to invite Frank and Judge Funk to the same functions. This tale of a decade past, chewed to the bone, had been all but lost in the next generation. Other feuds and alliances had taken its juicy place.

But a face-to-face meeting was inevitable and now it was imminent. It would be at the Funk home, with the judge as host.

Jackson Hunter and Alexander Ward, Frank's grandparents, had conceived and developed the small-town interests over which Frank presided for his mother. Frank half-suspected, as a grown man, that a clash between these interests and those of old Judge Miles Funk had seeded the present pointless but enduring situation.

"No doubt," thought Frank, "the judge will recognize me when I go to his house, for he's an avid baseball fan and has seen me play with the high school and college teams.' But did this old Nemesis of his ancestors even know he'd be at the meeting? Quite a complication!

So Frank purposely arrived late, fully expecting to be ignored but as he approached the yard he saw that the meeting had not started. But he didn't turn back, stoop to tie his shoe-strings or even slow his usual gait.

When he entered the modest but attractive livingroom, the judge came toward him, hand extended. "Greetings, Frank! Dr. Hoffman just phoned and said that he and Curtis Prentice, our legal friend, will be here in about five minutes. Shall we put the clock on them?"

The meeting, Frank of course knew, was to spark a drive for a new wing on the County hospital.

As presiding officer Judge Funk was both capable and pleasing. "Why," Frank wondered, "did my father and grand-father detest him? Why is Mother so secretive? Obviously he has many friends and admirers. Re-election was proof enough." Ward-Hunter influence never had availed, for every ten years the judge had been voted back in.

In a reasonable time this huddle of high brass ended with everything in order. The volunteer workers' kick-off meeting would be a Monday luncheon in the hotel ball room, and so on. Frank knew that everyone expected a substantial contribution from him or his family interests. They wouldn't be disappointed.

As the little group broke up, the judge was congratulating Dr. Hoffman on a big trout he'd taken, reported briefly in the evening paper. "I think we'd all enjoy a blow-by-blow description. The night is young. Let us repair to the study. Wouldn't it be pleasant to be trapped again in that mold that forms all anglers into a clan?" With that the wise and kindly old man grasped Prentice's arm with one hand and laid his other arm across Frank's broad back. The doctor, who had been motioned ahead with a courtly gesture, preceded them to a comfortable, sunset-facing room that was obviously the workshop, the law library.

Doctor Hoffman told his story modestly, accenting briefly the points of nature's beauty, trout lore and angling technique that he knew would interest them.

"The Doctor's an efficient operator," commented the lawyer. "It's well for the rest of us that he releases almost everything he hooks, even as he once released a No. 16 Pale Evening Dun from my ear."

A serious uneasy Frank turned toward the judge. "Sir, do you fish? I've never seen you on a stream."

Only the judge knew it, but that was the hoped-for lead. "My fishing days are over," he answered. "I'm just an armchair angler now. The other night, though, I had the most astounding dream in all my sub-conscious life—truly amazing. I was back at my old stamping ground, fishing where I loved it the most. The biggest trout I ever saw moved from under the watercress to take a feeding position in the tail of the pool. It was late May, a mild calm evening. The yellow drakes were dancing over the water.

"Amid a spot of silver as slick as glass the trout made a deep rise. The widening rings were lost as the water piled out of that pool of classic stamp. His feast had started.

"I permitted him to consume a few more of the floating flies before I presented the imitation. My fly lit right; there was a slurp. I had him.

"First he settled back; then quick as a flash he bolted and somersaulted in the middle of the pool. Quite a sight! Following this, he circled 'round in his pool, becoming slower and less powerful all the time. Finally the net nestled around his exhausted form.

"It was the pool at the bend of the stream by the house and my dad had come down to witness the final act. We admired that great fish; then I rolled the hook out of his jaw and slipped him back into the pool."

"That was quite a dream," remarked the doctor. "Only in reality you might have kept the trophy."

"It was reality," the judge shot back. "That's the remarkable part of the dream. I had recaptured that evening and I'll never let it go. I'd relived my last cast."

"Your last cast!" Dr. Hoffman showed surprise.

The elderly man was visibly moved. "The last cast," he repeated. "Friday, May 28, 1912."

"Nineteen-twelve," echoed Curtis, softly.

Judge Funk drew a deep breath. "The next day I picked up my rod and walked by Mother's great bed of peonies to cross the lush-green meadow. As I studied the stream from a distance, things didn't look right. There were patches of suds, something foreign to this water. As my step quickened I saw floating forms, trim white objects." The judge half-choked, half-sighed. "The whole horrible truth smote me. The water was a toxic mess. First I saw struggling trout by the dozens, then by the hundreds—all sizes. One after another surfaced, rolled over and sank. It was heartrending distraction. The water's edge was lined with dead sow bugs, scuds, crayfish, nymphs and minnows.

"I walked to the pool where I'd returned the big trout the evening before. He was there. He was lodged against the cress at the tail of the pool—stiff, faded, mouth gaping, gills spread wide, a ghastly sight.

"I was sick, sick at heart, sicker than I ever could be again, or so I thought then." The judge was tense.

"What," inquired the doctor, "had happened?"

"Was it only partly affected, and did it come back?" Frank asked.

"No," came the answer in a quiet steady tone. "Things went from bad to worse. Industrial activity intensified. Soon afterwards the town converted from cesspools to a crude sewage system, which permitted raw waste to be discharged into the stream."

"A running sore," commented Dr. Hoffman.

The massive frame of the judge settled in the chair and all tenseness left his face. "It was here I met Joe Jefferson, who figured in Henry Van Dyke's Fisherman's Luck; and it was he who introduced me to the dry fly. Joe loved to play Harrisburg during the trout season, for when he wasn't needed at the theater he fished the streams of our county. Cedar Run and Silver Spring were his special pets; convenient, too. Once he told me he was trying to induce his old fishing partner, Grover Cleveland, to join him on these waters."

"Cedar Run is a closed book," reflected Curtis. "The greatest little stream of them all. But we're fortunate to still have some rich, limestone, spring streams to fish." The judge's brow clouded, and the lawyer wished he could recall his words.

"President Eisenhower will come to love them," volunteered

the doctor, helpfully. "His Gettysburg home is just on the acid side of the South Mountain, a skip and a jump from our alkaline valley. Falling Springs, Dickie's Run and the Antietam no doubt will be his stamping grounds."

"Mr. Beck tells me that Theodore Gordon fished Big Spring," added Frank.

"That is correct," confirmed the judge.

"It was in my old homestead," he continued, "where I tied a sulphur-colored pattern to imitate our predominant hatch."

"You mean," interrupted Dr. Hoffman, "that the sulphur fly is your original pattern?"

Judge Funk nodded.

"But, Judge," inquired Frank, "where was this stream and where was your home?"

"The stream," came the slow answer, "is the one that flows through this town, stemming from the big springs up yonder," and he pointed over his shoulder to the commercial cress beds to the south. "Our home was a beautiful limestone house two miles below town."

"You mean the abandoned ruins near the stream?" Frank asked.

The judge nodded briefly and went on. "My parents passed away within a month of each other, the summer after the pollution."

Doctor Hoffman shot a quick glance at Frank, and Curtis Prentice, embarrassed, fumbled for a cigarette.

"The house was on the east side of the stream and the prevailing westerly wind made it untenable. When the well became contaminated, I moved to town."

"So your home was ruined," reflected Frank. "The new Hunter-Ward plant killed your stream. Judge, what did you do after you first saw the mess?"

The strong features of the jurist were placid but his mane-like silver thatch shook. "At first I talked about it—too much, I suppose. Then I literally won a fight but lost everything else. That was fifty years ago. What I said and what I did broke up my anticipated marriage to Mary Ward and rent asunder two families that had been very close for two generations. Until my dying day I shall deeply regret the whole affair. Our conduct was not according to due process. But now all is forgiven."

There was a pause that seemed like a thousand moments; then it was Frank who broke the silence. "About that last cast, Judge —we understand."

They took leave of their host, three humble men, to go silently to their homes.

Never before had Frank Ward Hunter been so moved, so sunk in thought. So that was it. The complete story was an ugly one. He thought of his deseased father and the two grandfathers ahead of him, in whose so well-paved road he walked his life's course. Then there were the aging mother and her old beau, still a bachelor. Had he been given a message to take to her?

He plumbed remorse. The highly respected, highly regarded old judge had borne a cross and his death would end the trail of a pioneer family. What about the putrefied valley and the worthless homestead, once so deeply cherished? In his conscientious way Frank had worked to effect the passage of the Pennsylvania Pure Stream Act, and now there was the reaches of the home stream, the judge's section, still a ruin. It might be too late to reclaim that little river for the old gentleman but there were other generations to come. And there was new law with teeth, his law.

In his lonely silence Frank pledged himself to use his influence and his resources to restore the area. Once again those downstream places would be brightened by clean water and the verdant valley would be inviting to live, work and play in.

Later, he dropped in at Adam Beck's. Friendly, public-spirited Frank Hunter, the small industrialist, "Boy" Hunter, accomplished angler schooled so well by Adam, unburdened himself.

"Your simile is perfect, Boy," said his old friend. "Like a dead mackerel in the moonlight, it glitters, but man, does it stink!"

"A spring," Frank footnoted the story of the feud, "and its resultant stream are the world's greatest natural phenomena. Why, Mr. Beck, people once breathed and bred down there below town. Now cattle must be fenced off from the poison and even muskrats can't use the stream. Typhoid came from contaminated wells and other homes, too, had to be deserted.

"Man, like all creatures, struggles for his existence, but he struggles within his own species. He'll desecrate his environment and ruin his key commodity, water.

"Instead of saying, 'What hath God wrought?' he should say, 'My God, what have I wrought?'" Sarcastically he added, "Man the thinker, *homo sapiens*. This thing must be brought into the honest light of general view. This stream, and all the other exploited ones too, must be reclaimed. The day of reckoning is here—just about noon, in fact!"

[290]

"The creature you talk about, Boy," Adam reassured his embittered friend, "the thinker—he does learn by experience and by his mistakes. But to a large extent he learns by hindsight. Don't blame your ancestors, Boy. They operated within their laws and couldn't anticipate disaster. Furthermore, the town had a problem, a bad one. Progress is seldom smooth sailing under fair skies. Was the sea charted without the grinding of a keel on rocks? Even they had a population explosion; things changed; there had to be more jobs. New inventions came and new processes too. From now on, water is the most valuable resource—clean water, water for homes, recreation, industry, irrigation. People are finally hearing the "voice crying in the wilderness" because they've got to replace and conserve what the wilderness gave, including water. Private enterprise, commercial interests, great though they are, have got to be weighed against the common good. The old sacred cows must go, for survival comes first."

Adam laughed. "Quite a speech I made, and you ought to take me over to Harrisburg House Chamber with you to repeat it—not of course on a precious day in trout season! But, Boy, the reclamation of this stream, and the others, is inevitable. It's simply a question of when and who. Now's the time; you're the man. Go to it!"

"Why sure," said Frank quietly. "Of course I will."

A long wordless look at Frank told Adam that his "Boy" was now a man, a man to be reckoned with.

CHAPTER 15

Ad Infinitum

THERE HAD BEEN, with the passage of the years, a succession of new faces on the beautiful limestone streams, the country of the big springs; and one by one old familiar figures disappeared from the landscape as activities were transferred to Anglers' Valhalla. Time had no ill effect, though, on the limpid streams, the shy trout and the dainty insects, all of which spawned a cult of patrons who were dedicated and skilled practitioners.

There were but few left in the path of the Grim Reaper who remembered the patron saint who bided his time between the green meadows he loved and his restaurant, the meeting place of the local outdoor men. Spider Webb, the fly tyer; the patient college professor; Obie, the creator of Enchanted Meadow; Cheppie Lower, the proud possessor of "Wahoo!"; the surgeon, Dr. Hoffman, a fishing duelist, and his energetic stream partner, the dentist, had crossed the Great Divide. In the footsteps of the lawyer there trod an eminent conservationist, his Junior, Curtis Prentice.

Only two of the old contingent remained. Frank Hunter, long since established as the master angler, had taken his place with the all-time great American authorities and writers. The town had never produced a more respected and successful citizen. The great masterpiece of rod building, Excelsior, had been placed in the capable hands of Sonny Hunter, a chip off the old block. And still in the shadow of the great Frank Hunter stood Little Caesar. The mellowing years had taken from him much of the old fire but there still smouldered that Nemesis, Jealousy.

L. C. had a premonition: it was his lot to soon go the way of all flesh. In a speculative cast into the hereafter he hoped he would be presented with angling over rising trout; that would be the perfect life after death.

The day came when they laid him to rest in the beautiful Cumberland Valley near the remains of those he so frequently encountered on the limestone spring streams—the fellows he so much delighted in heckling and out-fishing.

He was met at the great entrance by an imposing figure, a fat man, who said, "You are L. C.—Little Caesar." As he pointed toward the south, he directed his charge, "Follow me."

As they walked across a lush meadow, there was the assuring sound of rippling water. L. C. quickened his pace. Then he saw the bend of the stream, the far bank lined with trees, grass knee high on the near side. His heart beat faster; it was his favorite place. Day was dying in the West. With eyesight restored he scanned the tree tops. Sulphur spinners were milling about, soon they would be on the water. There, propped against the thorn apple tree, was his beloved two-piece eight-footer with a sulphur fly dangling from a fine leader. What appeared to be a good fish rose against the far bank. He searchingly looked at the stern figure who had guided him to the spot.

"This is wonderful," said L. C.

"Go ahead," assured his attendant. "Catch 'em. You'll have this all the time."

In his old-time skillful manner, which had disappeared in recent years, he worked into casting position, false casting as he sneaked along. The fly gracefully snaked over the water, stopped a yard above the surface and bounced back a bit toward a slack leader. After a short fluttering flight it gently kissed the water and cocked there on its toes in exactly the right line of drift. When it floated into the window, deliberately, majestically the trout moved under it. L. C. saw the mouth open and the sulphur disappear. When he gently tightened his connection by raising the rod tip, he felt the resistance of a good fish. Carefully and surely he brought it toward its doom just as he had done thousands of times on earth. Head first it was encircled by the net. While one hand clutched the fish entrapped in the mesh, the other administered the *coup de grace*. As life was deserting a noble body, the top of the creel dropped. An old story with L. C. Automatically he washed and dried the fly. A rejuvenated pair of eyes searched for the next victim.

Another trout rose fifteen feet upstream. L. C. stalked into position preparatory to fishing the familiar line of drift. A perfect cast, a perfect float, a successful catch. Now he had a brace in the creel. Maximum efficiency had been regained.

"This is the life-after-death," he remarked.

His companion yawned. "It will be like this always."

There was a slurp below him and out of the corner of his eye he saw a fish rise exactly where he caught his first. A cautious detour and he was in casting position, the picture of concentration.

Everything worked perfectly again. He had his third trout and, like the others, it was a one-pounder, 13½ inches.

A strange thing transpired. A trout rose where he had killed number 2, the upper spot.

"Heavens!" he exclaimed, "Most anything can happen out fishing."

His companion did not seem to understand the situation or appreciate its significance.

It was a routine matter to capture number 4. The creel was not assuming a satisfying weight.

"What is the limit here?" he inquired.

"There is no limit."

L. C. liked that.

Again there was the sound of a feeding fish downstream.

"I'll be damned," he muttered, "still another one in there."

It proved to be a good trout, 13½ inches.

No sooner was number 5 slipped into the creel than there was a rise above him at the upper position.

"What goes on here," he questioned, but his companion simply shrugged his shoulders.

A change of scenery might prove interesting; so he walked around the bend. There was another beautiful pool, but it was an exact duplicate of the first, and there was a trout coming up at each of the two feeding stations.

It was still light. He looked into the West. The sun hung there suspended half in sight, half hidden by the hill—just as it was on their arrival.

He would walk back and point this out to his companion. As he turned to retrace his steps, he saw the lazy fat fellow behind him, but he was still in the same place.

"What's the stream like in the next meadow?" he asked.

"A beautiful pool, just as beautiful as this."

"You mean exactly the same?"

The fat one nodded.

"How about below?"

"All the same."

"Where are the big trout located?"

"They're all the same size."

"Will the green drake hatch come on?"

"Only what you see out there now, always the same."

"Maybe then tomorrow morning will bring something different.

[295]

By the way, what time is it now?"

"Time? There is no such thing around here. There will be no tomorrow morning."

"Well, I'm tired of this. Let's go and have dinner."

"There's no place to go; there is no dinner."

L. C. was indignant. "This is not real angling. Somebody has made a mistake. There should be variety and problems. This stream should be re-designed. Take me to the keeper in charge."

"I'm the man in charge around here," replied his guide.

"Well good!" countered L. C. "I'll tell you what to do and we'll have a real Heaven here."

His guide laughed, "Who do you think you are?" he said. "What makes you think we'll change this water?"

L. C. flushed angrily. "I'll go over your head, if I have to to correct this mistake," he shouted, "and you will be in plenty of trouble when that happens!"

"You can go to the Devil," was the ice-cold answer.

L. C. was furious now. "Who do you think you are," he screamed, "talking like that up here?"

"Nero," was the answer, "Satan's first sergeant."

ANGLER'S PRAYER

God grant that I may fish until my dying day,
And when at last I've come to rest,
I'll then most humbly pray;
When in His landing net I'm safely asleep,
That in His mercy I'll be judged
As good enough to keep.

Outdoor America

Izaak Walton League of America